the perfect store

the perfect store

INSIDE EBAY

ADAM COHEN

LITTLE, BROWN AND COMPANY
Boston   New York   London

First Edition

ISBN 0-316-15048-7
LCCN 2002102889

10   9   8   7   6   5   4   3   2   1

Q-MART

Text design by Meryl Sussman Levavi/Digitext

Printed in the United States of America

the perfect store

introduction

Pierre Omidyar can still remember the exact moment when he realized that eBay, the clunky auction website he was running out of a spare bedroom in his Silicon Valley town house, just might change the world. It was when he tried to sell his laser pointer.

EBay was called AuctionWeb back then, and it was a mess. It had just seven categories, written in cramped blue-black type against a dull, gray background. The item listings, and there were not many, were mainly for old memory cards, secondhand modems, and other computer geekery. To economize, Omidyar was hosting AuctionWeb on his cluttered personal web page, giving the whole project a distinctly amateur feel.

Omidyar had tried to build momentum for the site by talking it up to his friends and colleagues, but their reaction was cool. Cyberspace was still intimidating enough that even big-name corporations were having trouble getting consumers to spend money online. Yet here was a ponytailed computer programmer who looked about eighteen, with an odd little site no one had heard of, insisting

3

that strangers would be willing to trade with strangers in online auctions. Even Omidyar's friends did not mind telling him it all sounded a little crackpot.

So far, the skeptics had been right. Along with his informal attempts at word-of-mouth promotion, Omidyar had been announcing the launch on Internet directories that listed new websites. "The most fun buying and selling on the web!" he gushed in one post, though AuctionWeb had thus far been the site of few sales and not much fun. Back then, everyone with a domain name and a server to host it was trying to get a website off the ground. It looked like AuctionWeb would be just another one of the horde that faded away for lack of interest.

The truth was, that was just fine with Omidyar. When he had banged out the computer code for AuctionWeb over Labor Day weekend, he thought of it as a hobby, and a chance to practice programming for the Internet. He certainly never considered quitting his day job. Just keeping the site running and pulling it back up from its constant crashes was taking up most of his time, and Omidyar was not the workaholic type. Failure was definitely an option.

It was during these lumbering early days that Omidyar decided to sell his laser pointer. Like the site itself, the laser pointer had been a whim — a cheap junior-executive tool he had picked up in a moment of mild ambition. He had bought it with visions of making impressive presentations at work, but all he had used it for so far was pet abuse, shining a red dot on the carpet and watching as his cat chased it around for hours. Two weeks after he bought it, the laser pointer stopped pointing. Omidyar replaced the batteries, but it still would not work. He was going to throw it out.

Instead, he decided to auction it off. It would be a good way to test out AuctionWeb, he figured, and it would cost him nothing. "Broken Laser Pointer," Omidyar typed into the heading. He gave the model number and said he had paid thirty dollars for it new. He was careful to explain that it did not work, even with fresh batteries. After starting the bidding off at one dollar, he promptly forgot about it.

The first week, there were no bidders. Omidyar checked the sec-

or.d week and noticed someone had actually bid three dollars. Then someone else bid four dollars. Bizarre, he thought to himself. By the end of the two-week auction, the bidding had reached fourteen dollars for something he guessed was worth—well, just about nothing. As he packed the broken laser pointer up in its case and sent it off to the high bidder, it occurred to him that AuctionWeb had a bright future ahead of it.

◆

Omidyar was telling the laser pointer story one cool October morning in Paris at an outdoor table at Fouquet's, the landmark art deco café at the corner of the Champs-Elysées and Avenue George V. Thinking back on those early days by now required a considerable mental leap. Only four years had passed since he launched AuctionWeb on Labor Day of 1995, but what a four years they had been. AuctionWeb was now eBay, and eBay was an Internet legend, an online retailer valued at more than Sears, or Kmart and J.C. Penney combined. Omidyar himself was now worth more than $4 billion, making him the richest thirty-two-year-old on the planet.

Omidyar had moved to France earlier in the year to work on eBay's international expansion. At least that was the official story. He would make the rounds of eBay's new European offices, where young people were starting up country-specific sites, and share what he had learned in eBay's early days. But the reality was that Omidyar was in the process of putting his past behind him. He had lived in Paris as a child before emigrating to the United States with his parents, and he had talked for years of coming back. Omidyar's friends always knew the day would eventually come. But when he made the move, they were convinced it had been hastened by a desire to regain a measure of anonymity after the wild ride of the last few years.

If Omidyar wanted to lose himself in Paris, his new look was a good start. The old Pierre—the programmer from central casting, who wandered the halls with a beard, ponytail, glasses, and shorts with black socks—had not survived the Atlantic crossing. The Pierre holding forth at Fouquet's had hair that was cut job-interview short; his boyish, olive-skinned face was now clean-shaven; and he was dressed in a smart-looking sweater with a red-and-black geometric pattern, and neatly pressed dark pants. When he had dropped in on eBay's Silicon Valley offices recently his new look had been, he said with a chuckle, "a great shock for the office."

Omidyar's transformation was, however, reassuringly superficial. Beneath the Paris flaneur getup, he was the same iconoclastic, self-effacing code writer he had always been. He had come to Fouquet's alone and on foot. There was no limousine, no entourage, and no public relations executive to filter questions, and the maître d' had no idea who he was. When we talked about eBay's rise, he was unfailingly modest, even a little bewildered, by what he had achieved. Omidyar squirmed when I asked him about his wealth— he was, it turned out, still driving his beat-up VW—and launched into an embarrassed monologue about the steps he was taking to give away his billions. And he still had the distinctive aura about him that his friends recalled from the old days. Call it a profound, existential calm.

Most of all, Omidyar still had the pure, democratic vision that had started it all. In Silicon Valley in the mid-1990s, he recalled as he ordered a pot of dark French tea for himself, and a café au lait for me, high-flying IPOs were spinning off enough money to make millionaires of many of his fellow techies. Omidyar believed in market capitalism, but he was troubled by the gap between theory and practice. Financial markets were supposed to be free and open, but everywhere he looked he saw well-connected insiders profiting from information and access that were denied to ordinary people.

It occurred to him that the Internet could solve this problem by creating something that had never existed outside of the realm of economics textbooks: a perfect market. EBay, Omidyar explained, was designed to be just that. Instead of selling products from a centralized source, it connected individuals to other individuals, so that anyone on the network could buy from or sell to anyone else. In the market he conceived of, the playing field would be level. Buyers would all have the same information about products and prices, and sellers would all have the same opportunity to market their wares. The auction format would, as classic economic theory taught, yield the perfect price, because items would sell at the exact point where supply met demand.

Omidyar paused to look out at the slow parade of stylish Parisians and bedraggled tourists passing by; his eyes widened, as if the sight had reminded him of something. The Internet was originally about people, he said simply. It had been started, and nurtured early on, by academics and government scientists who wanted it to promote the public good. But by 1995, cyberspace was being taken over by big business, which saw the Internet as little more than a hyperefficient way of selling things. "If you come from a democratic, libertarian point of view, having a corporation just cram more and more products down your throat doesn't seem like a lot of fun," he said. "I wanted to do something different, to give the individual the power to be a producer as well as a consumer."

That was not the only way people were being left out, Omidyar explained. As corporations moved in, cyberspace was becoming colder and more impersonal. The Usenet newsgroups he had spent countless hours on as an undergraduate had been lively, social places, where users posted quirky and irreverent messages and engaged in long, rambling discussions. But the e-commerce websites that were emerging treated people as just "wallets and eyeballs," Omidyar said with a frown, limiting their self-expression to clicking on items to buy and typing in credit card numbers.

Omidyar had built eBay to be not just a shopping site, but a community. He had, he admitted, encouraged community on the site in part for purely practical reasons. As eBay gained popularity, so many buyers and sellers came that he could not possibly answer all of their questions about how to use the site. By including their e-mail addresses, Omidyar allowed users to communicate directly among themselves to solve each others' problems. And Omidyar created a message board that allowed users to share information with the entire community without routing it through him. The more self-sufficient the users became, the fewer demands they put on his limited time.

But his interest in community was more than just pragmatic. At a time when the Internet was endlessly compared to the Wild West, Omidyar wanted his corner of cyberspace to be a place where people made real connections with each other, and where a social contract prevailed. He wanted it to operate according to the moral values he subscribed to in his own life: that people are basically good, and given the chance to do right, they generally will. In the first year of AuctionWeb's operation, Omidyar introduced innovations that would make his site in many ways the most genuine community in cyberspace.

Looking back on it now, in his new guise of *philosophe de café*, Omidyar could see that it all made perfect sense. Throughout history, he explained, gesturing to the waiter for another pot of tea, commerce and civilization had always developed alongside each other. The first markets arose at crossroads, where traders came to reach the largest number of potential customers. If sales at the crossroads were good, the merchants stored their wares there permanently. If they were the best in the whole region, traders brought their families and settled there. In time, they put up walls and built an infrastructure, and commerce transformed the lowly crossroads into a city. EBay had thrived because it fit this classic model: Omidyar had built both the commercial crossroads and the larger community that always came with it.

Omidyar's idealism is the paradox at the heart of eBay. The very things he did to make his site less corporate were, in the end, what made it the most successful business on the Internet. His belief in empowering individuals led him to create a site that linked people in a network. It is widely recognized today that, in purely business terms, such "many-to-many" sites are far more powerful than traditional "one-to-many" sites, in which a company like Amazon sells directly to consumers. By leaving the selling up to individuals, Omidyar was able to keep eBay completely "virtual": it does not own inventory or warehouses; it does not ship items or take returns. It is an amazingly efficient model that has allowed eBay, which began to charge fees six months after Omidyar founded it, to achieve gross profit margins of more than 80 percent.

Building community, and caring that people connected with each other, proved equally farsighted. The consensus among Internet strategists today is that the best way to make a site "sticky"—to attract visitors and hold them—is to give them just this sort of social component. On the advice of high-priced consultants, many websites now incorporate features like message boards and feedback forums. But in the fall of 1995 there was no Internet conventional wisdom. Alone in his spare bedroom writing computer code late into the night, Omidyar had to make it up as he went along.

◆

When I completed the magazine article that brought me to that Paris café for tea with Pierre Omidyar, I approached eBay about cooperating on this book. I had written hundreds of stories as a journalist, and I had never made such a request before. But it was clear to me then, as it is even clearer to me now, that eBay was easily the most interesting story of the early Internet age, and one of the most important business stories of our time.

EBay is the great winner in the dot-com sector. After the Internet bubble burst in the spring of 2000, eBay was worth more than onetime powerhouses Yahoo! and Amazon combined. In the fall of 2000, when most Internet companies were struggling just to avoid bankruptcy, Meg Whitman, Omidyar's successor as CEO, announced that eBay intended to grow revenue at 50 percent a year for the next five years. Despite the collapse of the sector and a bruising recession, eBay has exceeded those projections. It was no surprise when the *Industry Standard*, the now defunct magazine of record of the Internet economy, put eBay on the cover of its penultimate issue and declared that out of the ruins of the dot-com world, eBay had emerged "unstoppable."

But eBay's real significance isn't its own financial success. EBay has, more than any other company, fully harnessed the potential of the Internet. By connecting more than 30 million buyers and sellers around the world, eBay has permanently changed commerce. Things a buyer once would have spent days, weeks, or a lifetime tracking down—the rocking horse he played on as a child, the exact buffalo nickel he needs to complete a collection—are suddenly available at any hour of the day or night, from a PC in the buyer's home. By efficiently moving goods from people who value them less to people who value them more, eBay increases "social utility," as the economists put it, making people, as a whole, happier than they would be without those goods. For sellers, eBay's impact has been just as profound. It has helped them circumvent the old order of high-priced retailing space, exclusive distribution channels, and costly advertising, and market directly to millions of buyers. In eBay's democratic marketplace, an individual seller with few resources can compete on an equal footing with the largest corporation.

The implications of the eBay model—of Omidyar's original conception of a perfect, global marketplace that everyone comes to on an equal basis—are revolutionary. EBay gives individuals a degree of economic independence that was impossible before the Internet. As many as 100,000 people are already making their living selling on eBay. In time, eBay can be a mechanism for bringing people on the margins of the world economy into the economic mainstream. Many CEOs traveled overseas last year, looking to open up new markets. But Whitman is no doubt the only one who spent five days in a rural Mayan village in Guatemala investigating how local craftswomen can pull themselves out of poverty by selling their handiwork on eBay to buyers in the developed world. This transformative power is the most remarkable aspect of the eBay story. EBay is a company that, more than perhaps any other, does what Omidyar had hoped it would: empower people to change their lives.

EBay agreed to cooperate on this book, and gave me greater access than it had ever given to a reporter. In fact, eBay printed up an employee ID for me and invited me to move into its Campbell, California, headquarters. I attended department meetings and presentations to Wall Street analysts. I sat in while eBay's marketing team plotted the launch of new features. I spent time with eBay's customer-service representatives in Draper, Utah, and in its overseas offices in Berlin and London.

I spoke with employees at every level—from Omidyar and Whitman on down to new recruits—about the company's brief but remarkable history. EBay's venture capitalists, its business partners, even the branding company that developed its famous multicolored logo all shared their recollections. Some of the discussions covered well-worn ground, like eBay's wildly successful IPO. In other instances, we talked about parts of eBay's history that had not come to light before, like how off-base eBay's first business plan was about which part of the company would be profitable; how close Omidyar and his cofounder, Jeff Skoll, came to selling the company early on; and just who thought up the famous, but apocryphal, tale that Omidyar created eBay to help his fiancée trade PEZ dispensers.

My goal of getting "inside" eBay posed a metaphysical question: Where exactly is eBay? It is not a bricks-and-mortar institution like IBM or Harvard University, with a front door or a campus gate. Part of eBay is in its California headquarters, but much more of it is not. EBay exists, like a religion or a social movement, wherever its adherents happen to be. To get inside eBay, I had to travel to the places where it manifests itself—the office of a rare-autograph dealer who is gradually moving his business onto eBay; a convention of clothing-iron collectors in Kansas City, whose world has been transformed by eBay; and the London offices of eBay-U.K., where a webmaster labors to keep Americanisms off the site.

I also strolled a bit, figuratively speaking, down the dark alleys near eBay's docks. I paid a visit to the inventor of "sniping" software—highly controversial in the eBay community—which enables bidders to jump in at the last minute to win an auction. I talked shop with investigators who track down fraud on eBay. And I had a long, rambling lunch in Times Square with a young woman who does a brisk business selling child pornography on eBay.

EBay has its detractors, and I spoke with more than a few of them. I sat down with a hard-driving anti-eBay activist, who publishes a near-daily newsletter that rails against eBay for being excessively greedy and corporate. I talked with a Texas toy dealer who organized the Million Auction March, an attempt to move one million auctions off eBay to protest high fees and perceived insensitivity to small sellers. And I traveled to Pittsburgh to see one of the nation's leading thrift store aficionados, who worries that eBay is ruining shopping.

I also took a leap into eBay's future. I traveled to Central America, to the same rural Mayan village Whitman visited, and met the craftswomen who make the fabrics and belts that they sell for a pittance to middlemen, known as coyotes, who then resell them for up to four times as much in Guatemala City. I went down there with the eBay Foundation and observed as that nonprofit organization worked to use eBay to bring the village into the global economy.

And I hung out on the eBay website. I lurked on the message boards and did countless searches just to see what was for sale. I even bought a few things. Some were practical—the eyeglass frames I wear, a Swiss Army watch. Others were offbeat, like a cotton shirt decorated with tropical fish, sold by a fine arts graduate student in Iowa who put all of his possessions up for sale on eBay. No one can truly experience eBay, of course, without acquiring at least one "only on eBay" item. I now own a small Turkish carpet, handwoven in Iran in the 1960s, featuring a likeness of President John F. Kennedy with slightly Middle Eastern features.

◆

In the movies, it is a screenwriting cliché to have an old man talking into a tape recorder, looking back on his life and career. As I flew home from Paris, it occurred to me that my conversation with Omidyar had been a bizarre new-economy twist on that shopworn device. Hard as it was to believe, his whirlwind Internet career, from starting AuctionWeb as a hobby to retiring with his billions, had unfolded in just four years. At thirty-two, he was far too young to be the wizened patriarch speaking for posterity, and the milestones he had described were almost laughably recent. But we are living in the Internet age now, in which even history must be told on Internet time. And Omidyar—with his little auction website—had managed to turn a few short years into the Internet version of a lifetime.

chapter one

Pierre Omidyar was born in Paris in 1967 to a French-Iranian family that placed a premium on intellectual pursuits. Omidyar's parents had been sent to France by their families as young adults to get a better education than was available in Iran in the early 1960s. Omidyar's father attended medical school; his mother studied linguistics at the Sorbonne. They met for the first time in their adopted land—an encounter that was all but inevitable, given the size of the city's Iranian community—and eventually married. When Pierre, their only child, was six, they emigrated to the United States so that his father could begin a urology residency at Johns Hopkins University in Baltimore.

Growing up in and around Washington, D.C., Omidyar was a typical American child, except for his early fascination with computers. In seventh grade, Omidyar used to sneak out of gym class and make his way to the unlocked closet where his science teacher stored a cheap Radio Shack TRS-80. While his classmates played dodgeball and practiced layups, he used the "trash 80," as it was known, to teach himself to program in BASIC. Omidyar lived in Hawaii during eighth and ninth grades, while his mother did linguistics fieldwork. When he returned to Washington, he graduated to an Apple II, and he was programming in PASCAL, a step up from BASIC. Omidyar used his skills to get his first paying job, computerizing his school library's card catalog for six dollars an hour. "I was your typical nerd or geek in high school," he says. "I forget which is the good one now."

Omidyar arrived at Tufts University, a few miles from Boston, in the mid-1980s, just as the tech world was about to explode. His major was computer science, and his passion was Apple programming. At the time, identifying with Apple was a statement of personal values as much as a choice of technology—the computer-lab version of participating in a 1960s march on Washington. Under the charismatic leadership of Steve Jobs, Apple had styled itself as a hip, iconoclastic alternative to IBM and the other computer behemoths. Apple's view of itself was captured in a now-legendary 1984 Super Bowl commercial in which a lone woman, pursued by storm troopers, hurled a hammer at a Big Brother figure on an enormous television, shattering the screen. Omidyar did his own small part to rebel against mainstream computing by staying out of the Tufts computer lab, which was stocked with PCs, and working from his dorm room on a Macintosh. He eventually wrote his first Mac programmer's utility, a tool for use by other programmers.

In his junior year, Omidyar decided he wanted to spend the summer as a Macintosh programmer. He searched ads in *Macworld* and sent out letters to companies that used the Mac platform, enclosing a copy of his programmer's utility as a work sample. Omidyar got an interview, and a summer internship in Silicon Valley with Innovative Data Design, one of the first companies to write programs that allowed Mac users to draw images with their computer. The internship led to a full-time job, and he took off the fall semester to keep at it. Omidyar fit in easily in Silicon Valley's programmer subculture. With his ponytail, beard, and aviator-style glasses, he had the look. He also had the worldview. Omidyar was politically libertarian, and he liked talking about philosophy, UFOs, and space aliens. After one more semester at Tufts, Omidyar moved out West for good, finishing up his undergraduate degree at the University of California—Berkeley.

After he left Innovative Data Design, Omidyar took a job at Claris, an Apple subsidiary that developed consumer-applications software. Claris was supposed to be headed to an IPO, but while Omidyar was there it ended up being reabsorbed by Apple. The change in plans led to a mass exodus of talent, and Omidyar was among those who headed out the door. For his next venture, Omidyar teamed up with friends, including a former Claris colleague, in 1991 to found a start-up called Ink Development Corporation. Ink Development was producing software for what looked like the next big thing in technology: pen-based computers. The thinking was that users would abandon their keyboards and use a stylus for writing, an approach Palm would popularize years later. "It was going to be great; it was going to bring computers down to the rest of us," says Omidyar. "Of course, the market didn't think so."

A year and a half into their great experiment, Omidyar and his partners realized that pen-based computing was not about to take off anytime soon. As it happened, Ink Development had also put together some software tools for online commerce, and this marginal project now seemed to be the most promising part of the business. The company relaunched as eShop, an electronic retailing company. EShop was moving in the general direction of the Internet, but not fast enough for Omidyar. It was still stuck on the idea of conducting e-commerce on proprietary networks—close to, but still distinct from, the actual Internet. In 1994, Omidyar left eShop. He wanted a job that would let him "do Internet things," he says, as well as put him in more direct contact with people than he had been in his string of programming jobs. Omidyar retained a sizable equity stake in the company he helped found. Two years later, Microsoft bought out eShop, and the stock Omidyar received from the software giant made him a millionaire before he turned thirty.

Omidyar's next job gave him the greater exposure to the Internet that he had been seeking. He joined the developer-relations department at General Magic, a hot mobile-communications start-up.

General Magic, which had been started in 1990 by a group of Apple veterans, was trying to take Apple in a post-Macintosh direction by building a new generation of small, communication-oriented Apple computers that would work with telephones and fax machines. In his new position, Omidyar also had contact with people: his job was to help third-party software developers—programmers outside the company—write software that worked with General Magic's Magic Cap platform. It was while Omidyar was at General Magic, working with both the Internet and with people, that he created AuctionWeb.

◆

It started, legend has it, with PEZ.

In the summer of 1995, Pierre Omidyar was having dinner at home in Campbell with his fiancée, Pam Wesley. Wesley collected PEZ dispensers, and she mentioned that since they had moved from Boston to Silicon Valley, she was having trouble finding fellow collectors to trade with. It occurred to Omidyar that the still-fledgling Internet could provide the answer. He came to Wesley's rescue by writing the code for what would one day become eBay.

The PEZ dispenser story has been told and retold in countless popular accounts of eBay's history. But it is, Omidyar concedes, the "romantic" version of eBay's founding. The truth is, in the summer of 1995 Omidyar was doing what every other smart tech person within a hundred-mile radius of San Jose was doing: obsessing about the Internet and the uses to which it could be put.

Omidyar had not come west with Internet dreams. He had intended to program for the Macintosh, the computer platform he had fallen in love with in high school. But Silicon Valley in 1995 was, like Boston in 1775 or Sutter's Mill in 1849, a place caught up in an intoxicating shared vision of what the future would look like. The Internet was fast gaining critical mass. Dial-up service providers like AOL, CompuServe, and Prodigy were bringing millions of Americans online. Stanford engineering graduate students Jerry Yang and David Filo were attracting more than one million page views a day with a search engine they had named Yet Another Hierarchical

Officious Oracle, abbreviated as Yahoo! If there had been any doubt about the commercial viability of the new medium, it was dispelled—for several years, anyway—when Netscape went public in August with a red-hot IPO that was widely regarded as the opening salvo of the Internet revolution.

Omidyar was ready to enlist. He was no stranger to cyberspace: he had been online for years, going back to his undergraduate days at Tufts. Back then, the Internet was a geeky backwater, the online equivalent of a high school audiovisual lab, where engineering students hung out in Usenet newsgroups trading jokes with punch lines like "3.14159," and *Star Trek* aficionados whiled away the early morning hours debating Klingon history. In college, Omidyar himself had been a regular in one of the geekiest newsgroups of all, a Usenet newsgroup for Macintosh programmers.

By the mid-1990s, however, a new Internet was emerging. Low-key newsgroups were being pushed aside by something far glitzier—the World Wide Web, which suddenly gave anyone with a PC and a modem the power to call up documents stored on computers anywhere in the world. This new Internet, which was making the letters *www* a fixture of everyday conversation, had the power to connect everyone on earth—not through static postings left on a message board, but interactively and in real time. It was clear to anyone who was paying attention that this new Internet was about to change the world.

And all of Silicon Valley was paying attention. It seemed, that summer, as if people talked of nothing else. Programmers and entrepreneurs brainstormed about what the killer application was for this new technology, and plotted how to get in first with a business plan. Selling books or drugs or furniture. Delivering news or groceries or pet supplies. Mixing in celebrities or gambling or pornography. The millions—the billions—would pour in. Compared to the hot ideas bouncing around the Valley that summer, the application Omidyar was wrestling with had all the sex appeal of a college term paper.

In most times and places, creating a perfect market would have seemed like an arcane exercise. But in Silicon Valley in the mid-

1990s, financial markets were as much a part of the culture as routers and microchips. New companies seemed to be going public daily, and freshly minted millionaires were everywhere. Omidyar kept hearing about company insiders, often friends and family of the founders, getting rich through stock purchases that were not available to average investors. This was standard practice for IPOs, but it struck him as unfair.

Omidyar had experienced the process firsthand. A few years earlier, he had been closely following a hot new video-game company called 3DO. Like many techies, Omidyar had been intrigued by its bold vision of creating a universal standard for the video-game industry. When 3DO announced plans to go public in May 1993, Omidyar placed an order for stock through his Charles Schwab brokerage account. What he had not counted on was that 3DO — whose high-flying CEO, Trip Hawkins, would later be named one of *People* magazine's "50 Most Beautiful People"— was about to become one of the most hyped IPOs of the tech boom. 3DO went public at $15 a share, but when Omidyar checked his account, he learned that the stock had soared 50 percent before his order had been filled. It all worked out in the end; Omidyar later sold his shares at a profit. But it struck him that this was not how a free market was supposed to operate — favored buyers paying one price, and ordinary people getting the same stock moments later at a sizeable markup.

Omidyar's solution was an online auction. He had never attended an auction himself, and did not know much about how auctions worked. He just thought of them as "interesting market mechanisms" that would naturally produce a fair and correct price for stocks, or for anything anyone wanted to sell. "Instead of posting a classified ad saying I have this object for sale, give me a hundred dollars, you post it and say here's a minimum price," he says. "If there's more than one person interested, let them fight it out." When the fighting was done, Omidyar says, "the seller would by definition get the market price for the item, whatever that might be on a particular day."

Since he was still working at General Magic, Omidyar had to do the programming for his perfect marketplace in his spare time. He was used to tinkering with Internet applications in his evenings and on weekends. He had already written a chess-by-mail program, which he was offering for free over the Internet. He had also completed the coding for a program he was calling WebMail Service, which allowed owners of small-screen computer devices like the Newton to get access to Internet pages through standard e-mail. More recently, he had created WebMail Watch Service, which monitored web pages users were interested in, and notified them when the pages had changed.

With Labor Day approaching, Omidyar made the program for a perfect marketplace his project for the long weekend. On Friday afternoon he holed up in his home office, a converted extra bedroom on the second floor of his modest town house, and began writing code. By Labor Day, he had created an auction website. The site was not much to look at. Its blocky blue-black text against a dingy gray background gave it all the graphic charm of a Usenet newsgroup. Omidyar had no real idea what people would want to sell, so he just created categories as they occurred to him—computer hardware and software, consumer electronics, antiques and collectibles, books and comics, automotive, and miscellaneous. The computer code Omidyar wrote let users do only three things: list items, view items, and place bids. The name he chose was as utilitarian as the site itself: AuctionWeb.

Since AuctionWeb was only a hobby, and he intended to offer its services for free, Omidyar tried to keep costs low. He wrote the program by patching together freeware he found on the Internet, and he ran the site from his home, off of a $30-a-month account he already had with Best, his Internet service provider. Rather than create a new website, he added AuctionWeb to one he was already operating. That spring, Omidyar had formed a sole proprietorship for his web consulting and freelance technology work, which he had named Echo Bay Technology Group. The name was not a reference to Echo Bay, Nevada, the wilderness area near Lake Mead, or to any other real-world Echo Bay. "It just sounded cool," he says. When he tried to register EchoBay.com, however, he found he was a few months too late. Echo Bay Mines, a Canadian company that mined for gold in Nevada, had gotten to it first, and was using echobay.com for its corporate home page. Omidyar registered what he considered to be the next best thing: eBay.com.

At the time AuctionWeb launched, Omidyar already had three other home pages running on eBay.com. One was for a small biotech start-up for which his fiancée, Pam Wesley, a management consultant, had been working. Another belonged to the San Francisco Tufts Alliance, an alumni group of which Pam was president. The third was Omidyar's own: Ebola Information, his offbeat tribute to the Ebola virus. The site had a photograph of the virus that he had found on the Centers for Disease Control website, and it linked to news stories and data about Ebola and Ebola outbreaks. If users typed eBay.com/aw into their browser, they would be taken directly to AuctionWeb, which the home page called "eBay's AuctionWeb." But if they typed in only eBay.com, they would have to wade through three home pages, including Omidyar's homage to a loathsome disease.

On Labor Day, when AuctionWeb was up and running, Omidyar got to work trying to publicize it. He posted an announcement on a Usenet newsgroup that tracked new sites, and another on the National Center for Supercomputing Applications' "What's New" page, where it ran alongside Battery World, "a one-stop source for all battery needs," and CARveat Emptor, a site that provided consumer advice about automobile sales and services. "The most fun buying and selling on the Web," Omidyar wrote in the "What's New" listing. "Run an auction or join the fun of an existing auction." But both listings were delayed. The moderator of the new-site newsgroup had taken Labor Day off; the AuctionWeb listing did not appear on it until the following day. And because the "What's New" page had a heavy backlog, the announcement did not go up until October. That meant that on AuctionWeb's first day, there was no publicity at all. Of course, even if there had been, many of the site's potential users were spending the last holiday of the summer outdoors. Given these obstacles, Omidyar was not discouraged when, at the end of AuctionWeb's first day of operation, it occurred to him that it had not attracted a single visitor.

◆

After its traffic-free Labor Day launch, AuctionWeb started to attract a slow trickle of visitors. Omidyar had none of the slick marketing devices other websites were starting to employ—no advertising budget, no public-relations advisers, no deals with other sites to drive traffic. But he was continuing to post announcements in Usenet newsgroups for what he was calling his "free web auction." In these early posts, Omidyar described the items on the site, lists that remain one of the earliest records of what was for sale on AuctionWeb.

The items that showed up for auction in the first few weeks were a strange mix of computer-related and noncomputer-related goods. In a September 12 post on misc.forsale.noncomputer, Omidyar listed the noncomputer items on the site, along with the current bids for each. It was a small, eclectic assortment:

Antiques, Collectibles

- Superman metal lunchbox, 1967, used good condition
  Current bid: $22.00

- Autographed Marky Mark Underwear
  Current bid: $400

- Autographed Elizabeth Taylor Photo
  Current bid: $200

- Autographed Michael Jackson Poster
  Current bid: $400

- Toy Power Boat, late 50's–early 60's
  Current bid: $60.00

- Hubley #520 Cast Iron Hook and Ladder Truck
  Current bid: $300.00

- Collectors Multicolor Reflection Hologram
  Current bid: $5000

■ Czech Vase
Current bid: $25.00

■ Cobalt Clear Cut Glass Rose Bowl
Current bid: $25.00

Automotive

■ Toyota Tercel (89)..64K Mi
Current bid: $3200

■ Yamaha '80 1100 cc Midnight Special Motorcycle (Chicago)
Current bid: $1350.00

■ Electronic Auto Stereo AM/FM/Cass—CD Ready w/130 Watt
Speakers
Current bid: $45

■ 1952 Silver Dawn Rolls Royce
Current bid: $38,500

Books & Comics

■ The Maxx issue 6
Current bid: $0.75

Consumer Electronics

■ Mattel Nintendo PowerGlove
Current bid: $20

■ 32x Genesis add-on system with 3 games
Current bid: $80

■ cd32 system amiga game console with 6 cd's
Current bid: $260

Miscellaneous

■ Chicago Health Club Presidential Premier GOLD Membership
Current bid: $400

The list was not a representative sample—it was every non-computer-related item on the site. A week later, Omidyar updated the list, which had grown from eighteen to thirty items, a 66 percent increase, in just seven days. Among the new listings: a 35,000-square-foot warehouse in Caldwell, Idaho, for which the bidding started at $325,000. In early October, Omidyar posted a notice on misc.for-sale.pc-specific.misc that listed the computer-related items. It was a larger, but less colorful, lineup, which included hard drives, antivirus software, and a used Sun-1 workstation.

Throughout the fall, both listings and traffic on AuctionWeb increased steadily. While Omidyar was putting up his newsgroup posts, AuctionWeb was also starting to benefit from the marketing force that would drive its growth for years to come: word-of-mouth publicity. Computer geeks and tech-savvy bargain hunters were e-mailing one another the AuctionWeb URL, and inserting hyperlinks on their websites that took web surfers directly to the AuctionWeb home page. By the end of 1995, AuctionWeb had hosted thousands of auctions, and attracted more than ten thousand individual bids.

Omidyar was still offering AuctionWeb for free. He could do it because his expenses were next to nothing—he was still running the site off of Best, his home Internet service. Toward the end of 1995, however, Best administrators were complaining that AuctionWeb was attracting so much traffic that it was slowing down their system. In February 1996, Best began charging him $250 a month, the rate for a commercial account, ignoring his protests that AuctionWeb was not a business.

Best's fee hike changed everything. "That's when I said, 'You know, this is kind of a fun hobby, but two hundred fifty dollars a month is a lot of money,'" Omidyar says. To pay the bills, he started to charge AuctionWeb users—"basically out of necessity," he says. Based on no market research, Omidyar decided he would not charge buyers at all, and that he would not charge sellers to list items. The only fees would be what he called final-value fees, which would be a percentage of the final sales price. The fees, he decided arbitrarily, would be 5 percent of the sale price for items below $25, and 2.5 percent for items above $25.

Omidyar had no way of knowing if users would be willing to pay to use the site. In fact, it occurred to him that fees could bring his little Internet experiment to an end. But Omidyar got his answer soon enough, when piles of envelopes filled with cash and checks started arriving at his front door. The amounts were not large, and the trappings were not fancy. Some of the envelopes contained dimes and nickels Scotch-taped to index cards. Still, when he added up the checks, the coins, and the crumpled bills at the end of February, he found that AuctionWeb had taken in more than $250—more, in other words, than Best was charging him. That put his fledgling little website in a category almost by itself: it was one of the very few Internet companies to be profitable from its first month of operation.

◆

In 1995, it was not clear that commerce would ever take hold on the Internet. A study by the Pew Research Center that year found that just 8 percent of Americans felt comfortable using a credit card online. The Pew study had no statistics on the percentage of Americans who would be willing to participate in auctions with strangers on a website that crashed almost daily, but it figured to be a lot smaller. If AuctionWeb was to have any chance of taking hold, establishing trust and confidence was essential.

Early on, Omidyar set out ethical guidelines for the AuctionWeb community to follow. In his experience, he said, people are generally good. He advised users to treat other people on the site the way they themselves wanted to be treated, and when disputes arose, to give the other person the benefit of the doubt. Omidyar's injunction was essentially the golden rule transported into cyberspace. It was the value system his mother had instilled in him, and one he tried to follow in his own life. "Some people say, 'Isn't that trite, it's like a Hallmark card,'" he says. "But I think those are just good basic values to have in a crowded world."

To a remarkable extent, AuctionWeb operated according to Omidyar's idealistic prescription. Trust on the site was so high in the early days, and the feeling of community so strong, that it was common for sellers to ship items even before they had received bidders' payments. Still, the harmony Omidyar hoped for did not always prevail. When buyers and sellers disagreed, they usually contacted Omidyar directly—easily enough done, since his e-mail address, Pierre@eBay.com, was prominently featured on the site. Omidyar got about a dozen e-mails a day from users complaining about each other. It almost always turned out, Omidyar says, that the dispute arose from a simple misunderstanding. "On the Internet, people forget that when they're dealing with an e-mail address there's an actual human being on the other side," he says. "Often their fears are manifested, or they jump to conclusions and think the most negative interpretations of that e-mail."

One thing Omidyar knew was that he did not want to arbitrate all these disputes. He was busy enough just keeping AuctionWeb up and running in addition to working at his day job. Moreover, true to his libertarian leanings, he believed people should be able to resolve their differences on their own. Omidyar's routine when he received an e-mail with a complaint about another user was to respond to the author, send a copy of the e-mail to the other person in the dispute, and tell them both, "You guys work it out." The parties usually resolved the matter on their own, but Omidyar realized he had to come up with a mechanism for enforcing good behavior. Unlike most companies, AuctionWeb was not able to control the quality of its service. "The brand experience" on AuctionWeb, Omidyar observed, was "defined by how one customer treats the other customer." If Omidyar wanted his customers to have a positive experience on AuctionWeb, he had to convince them to treat each other well.

In February 1996, Omidyar announced his proposal for how to do just that: the Feedback Forum. "Most people are honest," he wrote in a Founder's Letter posted on the site. However,

> some people are dishonest. Or deceptive. This is true here, in the newsgroups, in the classifieds, and right next door. It's a fact of life. But here, those people can't hide. We'll drive them away. Protect others from them. This grand hope depends on your active participation. Become a registered user. Use our Feedback Forum. Give praise where it is due; make complaints where appropriate. . . . Deal with others the way you would have them deal with you.

Remember that you are usually dealing with individuals, just like yourself. Subject to making mistakes. Well-meaning, but wrong on occasion. That's just human.

Through the Feedback Forum, the complaints that landed in Omidyar's e-mail in box would be brought out into the open. The entire community would know about them and have an opportunity to deal with them appropriately. Omidyar made clear from the outset that he wanted positive comments as well as negative ones, both to encourage people to say favorable things about one another, and because positive comments could be just as revealing as negative ones. "I was afraid it might just turn into a gripe forum," he says. "But as I watched it develop over the weeks, I was amazed to realize that people actually enjoy giving praise, too."

The rules of the Feedback Forum were straightforward. Users were allowed to give each other a rating of plus one, minus one, or neutral, and to include a written explanation if they wished. EBay's software then tabulated each user's score and put the total in parentheses after his or her name. The Feedback Forum played the same role on AuctionWeb that reputation plays in a small town. Through the numbers that appeared after users' names, the AuctionWeb community's opinion of them would follow them wherever they went. The new system did not entirely remove Omidyar from the role of enforcer. He decided that when users' Feedback Forum ratings got too low—negative four or less—they would be banned from the site. Omidyar arrived at the cutoff point of negative four without much deliberation—it just struck him as the point at which his assumption of goodness was sufficiently rebutted—and he did not reveal it to users. But even years later it would remain the number that caused eBay to "NARU" someone—to make him or her Not a Registered User.

Around the same time, Omidyar added another feature to the site: a message board called, simply, the Bulletin Board. Like the Feedback Forum, the Bulletin Board was designed to limit his role and place more of AuctionWeb's administration in the hands of the community. Omidyar did not have time to explain to each individual user how to write a listing in HTML, or to give advice on bidding strategy. The Bulletin Board was in the tradition of the Usenet newsgroups Omidyar had long used, a place for people to gather, share information, and ask for help.

As soon as the Bulletin Board went up, the questions poured in. What was the best way to ship? What should a seller do when a high bidder disappeared? The answers came just as quickly. "If someone came on and said, 'Please help me,' there were twenty-five people who would rush to help," recalls Steven Phillips, a retired naval petty officer from Dallas who sold chintz and pottery in the early days. A core group of regulars emerged who functioned as a de facto customer-service department. The site even had—in those innocent, spamless days—a directory of e-mail addresses, making it easy for users to communicate with message board regulars. Phillips alone got 100 to 150 e-mails a day from his fellow AuctionWeb users, and he answered all of them.

◆

With every day that passed, more cash- and check-filled envelopes arrived at Omidyar's town house. In March, revenues hit $1,000, once again more than the site's expenses. In April, revenues rose to $2,500, and in May AuctionWeb took in $5,000. The envelopes were piling up so fast that Omidyar literally did not have time to open them. He used some of the funds to make his first part-time hire. Chris Agarpao, the brother-in-law of a close friend, started coming to Omidyar's home twice a week to open the envelopes and deposit the money. In June, when revenues doubled for the fourth consecutive month, topping $10,000, Omidyar decided it had become a real business. "I had a hobby that was making me more money than my day job," he says. "So I decided it was time to quit my day job."

Omidyar thought when he left General Magic he would be able to reclaim his nights and weekends. But he found that all of his waking hours were now being taken up by AuctionWeb—keeping it running, writing code for new features, and answering user e-mail.

Having worked in start-ups, Omidyar knew that if AuctionWeb was going to keep growing, he would need a strategy that went beyond bringing in Agarpao to open envelopes and deposit checks. "I had a vague idea of what I needed to do as an entrepreneur," Omidyar says. "But I knew I wasn't going to be able to put together a business plan." He started looking for someone who could.

Omidyar thought immediately of Jeff Skoll, a Stanford MBA he had met through friends two years earlier. Skoll, a slightly built, hyperkinetic Jewish Canadian, was a born entrepreneur. His father sold industrial chemicals, and by age twelve Skoll himself was going door-to-door selling Amway products in Montreal. Skoll's youth coincided with a rising tide of separatism in Quebec, and he experienced the depth of French-Canadian nationalist sentiment firsthand when he was making the rounds selling electronic keyboards. He was often asked to demonstrate them, but the only song he could play was "O Canada," the national anthem. It went over well among the English-speakers, but not in French-speaking areas. One woman, on hearing Skoll's musical performance, sicced her dog on him. Not much later, Skoll's family joined the growing English-speaking exodus from the province and settled in Toronto, where he attended high school.

Skoll graduated from the University of Toronto in 1987 with an electrical engineering degree and a 4.0 GPA. He then founded two high-tech companies: Skoll Engineering, a consulting firm that helped corporate and government clients set up inventory management and accounting systems, and Micros on the Move Ltd., a computer rental company. Skoll's ambitions, however, extended beyond the comfortable life he was starting to carve out in Toronto. Six years after graduating from college, he headed to Palo Alto, California, to enroll in the Stanford Graduate School of Business. Skoll finished up his degree in 1995, at the same time Omidyar was wrestling with the idea for AuctionWeb, and found himself just as drawn to the Internet as his future partner. Skoll took his freshly minted MBA to Knight-Ridder Information, Inc., a unit of the large newspaper chain, which hired him to help direct its Internet strategy.

Skoll struck Omidyar as an "analytic powerhouse" whose skills would complement his own. But the attraction, at least initially, was not mutual. The previous Thanksgiving, when AuctionWeb was just a few months old, Omidyar had tried to interest Skoll in joining the company, but it had not gone well. "I told Jeff there were people buying and selling on the Internet who never see each other but actually send money and stuff back and forth," recalls Omidyar. "He said, 'That's ridiculous.'" Skoll had just come back from the first meeting of CommerceNet, a nonprofit symposium promoting commerce on the Internet. At the symposium, the moderator had asked the crowd of three hundred how many of them had bought or sold anything online, and only three people raised their hands. It seemed to Skoll that if e-commerce had made so few inroads in that tech-savvy audience, AuctionWeb was fighting a losing battle.

Since that Thanksgiving, however, Skoll had reconsidered. He could see, from his vantage point at Knight-Ridder, that the Internet had the potential to completely transform how goods were sold. One reason Knight-Ridder had established Skoll's unit was that the newspaper giant realized the Internet posed a significant threat to classified ads, one of its major sources of revenue. On the Internet, sellers could have considerably more space to describe their items and post photographs than they would in a print ad. The audience would not be limited to readers of a single newspaper, or of any newspapers at all. Online ads could be interactive, allowing buyers and sellers to contact each other by e-mail. Not least, the Internet allowed for dynamic pricing, which meant sellers did not need to choose a price in advance—they could charge whatever the market would bear. These advantages were, of course, all built into Omidyar's online auction model. Skoll eventually realized that "what Pierre was doing was a lot bigger than just a simple website." In February 1996, Skoll had agreed to do consulting work for AuctionWeb. By August, the site was so successful that Skoll quit his job and signed on full-time.

In Skoll, Omidyar found a yang to his yin. "It was the perfect balance," says Omidyar. "I tended to think more intuitively, and he could say, 'Okay, let's see how we can actually get that done.'" Skoll was the hard-driving one, the one focused on business development and fending off the competition. The more easygoing Omidyar tended the website and nurtured the AuctionWeb community.*

When Skoll reported for work, AuctionWeb was still operating out of Omidyar's home. Skoll wanted to move the company to Palo Alto, which he considered to be the "epicenter" of the Internet boom, or at least to nearby Santa Clara. But the Silicon Valley real-estate market was so tight AuctionWeb could not find office space in either city. While they looked for offices, Omidyar and Skoll moved AuctionWeb's headquarters from Omidyar's home to Skoll's, a group house in Los Altos Hills that he shared with a few of his former business-school classmates. Skoll's home had more room than Omidyar's, but it was still nothing like a real office. One of Skoll's housemates worked at the NASA Ames Technology Center, a NASA-funded high-tech incubator in Sunnyvale. He helped AuctionWeb get temporary offices there, a one-room space that could barely fit Omidyar, Skoll, and Agarpao. It was clearly not a long-term solution.

Omidyar suggested expanding the search for permanent quarters to the city of Campbell. A sprawl of suburban homes and office parks, Campbell paid tribute to its long-lost agricultural heritage every May, when it played host to California's largest prune festival. Campbell was not as fashionable as Palo Alto, and it was certainly not the epicenter of the boom. But what Campbell lacked in hipness and frenetic activity, it made up for with more practical attributes. Rents were lower and, more important, there might actually be some offices to be had. From Omidyar's perspective, Campbell had another advantage: he lived there.

The real-estate agent that Omidyar and Skoll pointed toward Campbell came back with a dentist's-office-sized suite on the second floor of 2005 Hamilton Avenue. The suite was located in the

---

*The Chinese book *I Ching* teaches that the yin embodies elements of the yang, and vice versa, and so it was with Omidyar and Skoll. Omidyar, the antimaterialist, was already a millionaire, and would become the wealthier of the two from his stake in eBay. Skoll, the corporate-minded MBA, would later assume a very different role at eBay, that of in-house champion of the community.

Greylands Business Park, a clump of low-rise brick buildings that cried out "business" far more than "park." Greylands was directly across the street from one sprawling shopping center, and diagonally across from an even larger one. The prospective headquarters were as blandly utilitarian as AuctionWeb's website, but they were a clear improvement over the room in the NASA incubator. Omidyar and Skoll told the agent they would take it.

There was just one problem. To evaluate AuctionWeb's financial situation, the landlord wanted Omidyar and Skoll to fax over a balance sheet. AuctionWeb did not have one, and it seemed unlikely the landlord would be satisfied with what the company did have: Agarpao's extensive list of cash deposits. Determined not to let the office space get away, Skoll sat down and began taking inventory. "What are the servers worth?" he asked Omidyar. They guessed about $5,000. Liabilities? They listed that month's phone bill, which had not yet been paid. When he was done, Skoll had a rudimentary balance sheet, which he faxed off. The landlord was unpersuaded. Before AuctionWeb could move in, Omidyar, the only partner who actually had some assets, had to personally guarantee the lease.

Skoll's other priority, after office space, was professionalizing the AuctionWeb site. Skoll argued that the San Francisco Tufts Alliance, the biotech start-up, and Ebola Information—which were all still on eBay.com—were distracting and, in the case of the Ebola page, more than a little creepy. Omidyar, perhaps partly to tweak Skoll, put up a defense of the Ebola page. McKinley's, an Internet search engine that rated websites, had awarded Ebola Information four stars, he reminded Skoll, while it gave AuctionWeb only three. It simply made no sense, Omidyar argued, to remove the one page that could be driving the most traffic to eBay.com. Skoll was not convinced. In the end, Omidyar gave in and reluctantly removed everything but AuctionWeb from the eBay site.

◆

In May 1996, Jim Griffith was sitting at a computer in an art studio in West Rutland, Vermont, shopping for computer parts.

Griffith, who has the bushy white beard, rounded physique, and biting wit of a mischievous St. Nicholas, had come to Vermont in a last-ditch effort to pull his life back together. He was coming off two hard decades of living in New York, where he had started out pounding the sidewalks of the casting-call circuit, struggling to make it as an actor. When his matinee dreams died, he threw his creative energy into a career as a decorative artist, doing ornate painting in the homes of the city's moneyed classes. His friend, Broadway director John Tillinger, introduced Griffith around, and in time his paintbrush was rubbing up against some of the toniest walls in Manhattan, including those of Lauren Bacall's home in the Dakota apartment building.

After ten years of painting upscale apartments, Griffith burned out. The combination of an especially disastrous work project and a head-on collision with middle age pushed him over the edge. He and his partner decided to get out of the city and start over in West Rutland. Griffith had planned to paint murals there and send them to clients back in New York, but he found it was too difficult to line up assignments from out of state. He ended up working as an administrative assistant for the Carving Studio, a nonprofit arts organization dedicated to teaching stone carving.

Working on a clunky old computer, a gift to the studio from a local bank, Griffith joined the information age. As his passion for art redirected itself to computers, he found himself spending countless hours on Usenet newsgroups. Griffith had been on an extended hunt for an obscure type of memory chip when one of his newsgroup contacts e-mailed him that the chip was up for auction at that moment on an online auction site called AuctionWeb. Griffith went to the site and placed a bid. He won it for $10, and he was hooked. Living in one of the most picturesque towns in one of the most beautiful states in the union, Griffith spent much of the summer of 1996 on AuctionWeb bidding on computer parts.

When he was not scrolling through computer listings, Griffith was spending time on the Bulletin Board. He was by now fairly proficient at using AuctionWeb and was happy to answer the technical questions that were being posted. Griffith soon became a fixture on the boards: Uncle Griff, a friendly source of advice for new users. One day, another board poster asked him what he looked like. "I don't know what came over me, but I said, 'I'm wearing a lovely flower print dress and I just got through milking the cows,'" he says. "That's how it started about Uncle Griff actually being a cross-dressing bachelor dairy farmer who liked to answer questions."

The legend of Uncle Griff grew quickly. On the Bulletin Board, Griffith referred to his AuctionWeb persona in the third-person: Uncle suggests you do this; Uncle would never do that. He also began to fill in ever more elaborate pieces of Uncle Griff's biography. Uncle Griff lived with his mother, but she was not available to post. He had duct-taped her mouth shut and stuffed her in a closet.

AuctionWeb lifted Griffith's spirits for a while, but by the fall he was spiraling downward again. In mid-October he stayed in bed for two weeks and thought about ending his life. Griffith forced himself to begin therapy and started taking Prozac, a drug that he says "should be in the water supply." Just as he was snapping out of his depression, he got a phone call.

It was Jeff Skoll. He wanted to know why Uncle Griff had stopped posting on the boards. Griffith was stunned that his absence had been noticed at AuctionWeb headquarters. Skoll had an assignment for Griffith. AuctionWeb was receiving fifty to one hundred e-mails a day from users, and it had no customer-support staff. Skoll was prepared to pay Griffith to answer the e-mails on a regular basis, and to keep up his presence on the Bulletin Board. Griffith was up for it, but he wanted to make sure Skoll knew what he was getting into. Uncle Griff was, Griffith pointed out, an unusual persona. "Yeah, we love it," Skoll responded.

Griffith became AuctionWeb's second part-time employee, at a salary of $100 a month, and its first official customer-support person. Skoll asked Griffith to select an alias to use as his AuctionWeb identity. That way, he could keep being Uncle Griff on the Bulletin Board without having his postings carry over to his official duties. When Skoll called, Griffith was looking through a book about one of his favorite movies, *Greed,* an eight-hour-long silent film directed by Erich von Stroheim. He came across a photograph of the actress Dale Fuller, who played the mad Mexican housekeeper. For his official AuctionWeb work, Griffith told Skoll, he wanted to be known as Dale.

Griffith returned to AuctionWeb with his two identities, Uncle Griff on the boards, and Dale@eBay.com to answer customer-support e-mail. Bulletin Board posters who knew both personas did not make the connection, and Griffith never let on. To help with the e-mail, Skoll sent Dale a Word document, much of it prepared by Omidyar, with suggested responses to frequently asked questions. In addition to handing out advice, Griffith spent a lot of time doing what Omidyar hated: stepping in and trying to resolve disputes. Griffith was amazed by how heated the controversies could get, and how seriously the participants took their online lives. He often got e-mail from posters saying that because of disputes on the Bulletin Board they had cried all night, sometimes all week.

To the noncombatants, the disagreements generally seemed wildly overblown. At one point, Uncle Griff had to step in to defuse an argument between a buyer and a seller of baseball cards that had started in private e-mail and moved onto the Bulletin Board. The fighting escalated until both men were on the boards every night, "screaming" at each other in capital letters. Griffith tried to persuade posters that hostility was counterproductive. "If you've got a bidder who is not honoring their bid, the last thing you should do is send them a nasty e-mail telling them they're a terrible person," he advised. "It may make you feel better for the moment, but in the end it doesn't serve any purpose at all."

When all else failed, Uncle Griff used his offbeat personality to defuse tension. Once, when a flame war was raging between two users, he cut in and announced that he had just been in his attic and had found a trunk that had not been opened for years. It contained a lot of his mother's old clothing, and he asked everyone to try an item on. Uncle Griff offered one board poster a feather boa, another an elaborate hat, and he declared that he himself was putting on a pair of high heels. He made a point of handing off virtual clothing to both of the posters involved in the fight. "Some people would re-spond, 'Oh, Griff, you're so silly,'" he says. "But what it did was break up the dispute without referring directly to the dispute."

Not long after Griffith got his call from Skoll in Vermont, Patti Ruby got one of her own in Indiana. Ruby owned an Indianapolis an-tique store with her husband and worked on the side as a computer programmer. Like Griffith, she had come to AuctionWeb early, and had become a personality on the Bulletin Board. Aunt Patti, as Ruby called herself, was knowledgeable about computers and antiques, and willing to take the time to answer users' questions about either. Ruby became eBay's second "remote," as its employees outside of Silicon Valley came to be known. She started out part-time, but within two weeks of Skoll's call she quit her programming job and began working for AuctionWeb full-time. Skoll asked Ruby, as he had asked Griffith, to choose an AuctionWeb identity. She became Louise@eBay.com and remained Aunt Patti on the boards, both per-sonas that would become famous in AuctionWeb's early days.

chapter two

Now that AuctionWeb had a real headquarters, it was ready for its first full-time employee. Skoll was at a Stanford business school party one Saturday night when he struck up a conversation with Mary Lou Song. Song, a stylish twenty-seven-year-old Korean American, was the perfect blend of eBay's two core values, commerce and community. The daughter of a University of Louisville economics professor, she had many friends who were MBAs, and had recently taken a job with a San Jose public-relations firm. But she was also a 1991 graduate of Northwestern University's Medill School of Journalism, and had worked briefly as a reporter for a chain of community newspapers in Michigan. Song had just earned a master's degree in communications at Stanford, where she had studied the ways in which public institutions foster popular debate and discussion. Song's family background was also a point in her favor — she would be a Korean American joining a Canadian Jew and a French Iranian American, trying to build a global marketplace.

When Skoll tried to recruit her, Song was willing to listen.

Her public-relations job did not feel right, but she still didn't know what she wanted to do with her life. In the circles she traveled in, the chatter about the Internet was endless, and Song had begun to think she should look into it. But the more Skoll talked about AuctionWeb, the more her reporter's skepticism kicked in. "This guy is going to be a lunatic," Song remembers thinking. Still, she was intrigued enough to tell Skoll that he could call her at the PR firm on Monday.

Skoll called on her that Monday—promptly at 9:00 A.M. He asked Song to come by for lunch the next day. Song had a chance to inspect AuctionWeb's offices before she, Skoll, and Omidyar went out for Chinese food at Fung Lum, a restaurant in a nearby shopping center. Song knew that start-ups often had a thrown-together look, but the cramped suite still struck her as a red flag. The two founders of the company she was being asked to work for were seated behind cheap particleboard desks, and the suite's largest room was furnished with a folding table and beach chairs.

Omidyar was not as intense as Skoll, Song observed, but he was unusual in his own way. He was an "old soul," Song says, and from the way he talked about AuctionWeb, he seemed to be operating on an almost spiritual plane. "What we're doing is building a place where people can come together," Omidyar told her. "They just happen to be coming together around trading." His description of what the company was trying to achieve had an idealistic quality that Song did not expect to find in a Silicon Valley office park. "I was so used to MBAs asking, 'What's the business model? How much money are you going to make from this?'" she says.

Song was no expert on the Internet, but she knew she at least had to examine the AuctionWeb site before she made a decision. Its dingy gray background and dull typeface made it look, she thought to herself, like "an old dirty newspaper." It seemed to her that the site was not even trying to be visually appealing. "It was just pure 'Here's the marketplace, here's the stuff, go at it,'" she says. The listings had by now expanded to thirty categories under three headings: Computer Hardware, Computer Software, and Antiques and

Collectibles. The two-thirds weighting toward computer products in the headings was an accurate reflection of the mix of items on the site, which Song remembers as being full of "geeky stuff."

Song found herself being charmed by AuctionWeb, almost against her better judgment. By week's end, she had accepted Omidyar and Skoll's job offer. When she reported for work on October 28, 1996, she was handed a prime piece of real estate: the third office in the suite, between Omidyar's and Skoll's offices. Her desk was a card table, and she was given a folding chair to sit on. Out in the suite's main room, Chris Agarpao sat at his own card table and computer, still processing payments.

Once she began work, Song realized that her initial impressions of Omidyar and Skoll had been exactly right. Omidyar may have grown up back East, but he was the ultimate laid-back Californian. He was "very even-keeled," she says, quietly managing the technical aspects of the site. He worked hard when he was in the office, but was philosophically opposed to long hours. The spiritual quality that Song had picked up on during her interview was real, and it influenced everything Omidyar did, from writing a letter to the community to developing rules for the Feedback Forum. "He saw things in a really digging-deep-down-into-your-soul way," she says. "Like, what are we doing with human nature here?"

Skoll was a more traditional e-commerce executive. He had the clean-cut look of a business-development guy, and he brought a laserlike focus to the smallest details. "He had this just bizarre knack for knowing what the numbers were," says Song. "You'd say, 'Hey, Jeff, when do you think we're going to hit fifty thousand items?' and he'd say, 'April 2, 1997.' And he'd be right." Skoll worked on the non-technical aspects of AuctionWeb: personnel, marketing, partnerships with other companies. He was also spending hours at a time locked in his office, toiling away on drafts of a business plan, trying to put into words just what AuctionWeb was, and what it was on its way to becoming.

◆

With just three full-time employees, life at AuctionWeb was informal and unstructured. There were no meetings or memoranda, and decisions were made instantaneously. If Song thought of a new feature she wanted on the website, she just walked into Omidyar's office and told him. He would usually write the code at home that night, and when Song logged on to AuctionWeb the next morning at work, her change would be on the site.

It did not take Song long to realize that there were some odd things about her new job. She was struck right away by the unusual relationship AuctionWeb had with its customers. For one thing, they were never called customers, always the "community." And their views seemed to carry an extraordinary amount of weight. When Song started, Omidyar told her to read the Bulletin Board daily and to be responsive to the community's concerns. Song read the boards, but she found it wasn't really necessary. From the moment her e-mail address appeared on the site, she never had a problem learning just what was on users' minds.

Song got a better sense of the community's role with one of her first assignments. The Feedback Forum had been in place for about nine months, and some of AuctionWeb's heaviest users were beginning to have fairly high feedback ratings. Skoll asked Song to create a series of colored stars that would appear beside users' names and feedback ratings, reflecting the amount of feedback they had. The stars would be a way for AuctionWeb to recognize its most outstanding buyers and sellers, while at the same time making it easier for users to spot other users with good reputations. The assignment itself seemed easy enough. "I know my colors," Song thought to herself. She developed a system of yellow, red, green, and purple stars for different feedback levels, culminating in a shooting star for anyone with a feedback rating over 10,000. As instructed, she posted her handiwork on the Bulletin Board for the community's consideration.

Song knew that most businesses made an effort to survey their customers and take their preferences into account. But the AuctionWeb community did not respond to her proposal like any focus group she had ever heard of. Song was flooded with irate e-mail. "I got e-mail messages like 'Are you insane? Do you know what you're doing?'" she says. Some of the criticism was aimed at her color choices—the shade of green she chose was, for some reason, especially unpopular. But most of the complaints concerned process. The community could not believe she would post a fully developed proposal for changing the site, even one involving something as inconsequential as Feedback Forum stars, without first soliciting their input. It was a level of entitlement Song was not prepared for. "If McDonald's unveils a new sandwich, people just decide to buy it or not," she thought to herself. "They don't say, 'Why didn't you talk to me?'"

But Song understood that the community's views were more important than her own. She apologized to Omidyar for upsetting AuctionWeb's users, and posted a new announcement on the Bulletin Board confessing her error and asking the community for its views about stars and colors. For the next two weeks, the boards resounded with opinions. Taking the community's comments into account, Song produced a new lineup with different feedback numbers for some of the colors. And the green star was gone. "It was my favorite," she says, still mystified by the reaction. "But people hated the green." Many users also railed against the shooting star, arguing that no one would ever reach a feedback rating of 10,000. But Song stuck with it, and in time her optimistic view of AuctionWeb's possibilities would be vindicated.

◆

It occurred to Song that there was something else peculiar about her new position. Although her title was public-relations manager, Omidyar and Skoll did not seem to want publicity. They were worried that a larger, better-funded company would learn what they were up to and jump into the online auction space. Publicizing AuctionWeb at this point, they felt, would only stir up the competition.

Even then, AuctionWeb did not have the online auction space totally to itself. There had been auctions on the Internet for years, long before Omidyar even thought of starting an auction website. But the

earliest ones, which took place on Usenet newsgroups, were struc-
turally flawed. Sellers put up posts describing their items, and buyers
sent in bids by e-mail. These auctions were labor intensive for buyers,
who had to look through countless newsgroups and extensive postings in each, searching for items for sale. Since bidding did not occur
in real time, it took considerable effort just to follow an auction and
keep up with the bidding. Newsgroup auctions were no better for
sellers, who had to review the e-mails by hand and post regular updates on the high bid. It was clear that Usenet auctions would never
be more than a historical footnote, and certainly no threat to
AuctionWeb.

There were, however, a few true online auction sites that posed a
more serious challenge. Most of these sites were smaller than
AuctionWeb, and were growing more slowly. But there was one that
was bigger and better-financed, and Omidyar and Skoll regarded it as
a significant threat. Onsale, launched in May 1995, was the brain-
child of Jerry Kaplan, a well-known Silicon Valley entrepreneur.
Kaplan had previously tried to make his mark with Go Corporation, a
start-up that sought to revolutionize computing through handheld,
pen-operated computers, much the same dream Omidyar had
chased in the first incarnation of eShop. Onsale was Kaplan's first
venture since Go, and he was intent on getting it right this time.

By most objective measures, Onsale was well ahead of
AuctionWeb. It had generous venture-capital funding, a slick site,
and a sizable staff that was aggressively striking alliances and marketing itself to the general public. Onsale had already received respectful coverage in mass market publications like the *Wall Street
Journal* and the *San Jose Mercury News.* In 1996, Onsale hosted more
than $30 million in transactions, nearly four times as much as
AuctionWeb. But there was a critical difference between the two
companies. Onsale took possession of the goods it sold, much of it
overstock or remaindered computers. It was a model that was super-
ficially appealing. Onsale could control the consumer experience by
examining the goods itself and making sure they were sent out to
buyers as promised. This model also allowed Onsale potentially

larger profits, since the company earned its revenue from the sale itself, not just by imposing a transaction fee. But Onsale's model also meant that it had an array of expenses—storage, shipping, inventory losses—that AuctionWeb, with its completely virtual business model, did not. It was not yet clear which model was more powerful, but at this point, Omidyar and Skoll were worried.

There was one looming threat that concerned them even more than Onsale: the prospect of a large Internet company moving into online auctions. The big Internet service providers had far larger audiences than AuctionWeb. AOL already had 8 million subscribers, and CompuServe had 5 million. They also had far greater financial resources and would be able to back their entries with aggressive marketing campaigns. Auctions were a logical next step, since the major ISPs had already developed online classified advertising services, which could easily have been converted into auction sites. It seemed to Omidyar and Skoll that the main reason the ISPs had not yet moved into online auctions was that it had not occurred to them. And that was how they wanted to keep things, until AuctionWeb got bigger. "We just wanted to fly under the radar," says Omidyar.

Fortunately, AuctionWeb was growing at breakneck speed entirely by word of mouth. In October, the month Song joined, it hosted 28,000 auctions, and it was adding new auctions at the rate of nearly a thousand a day. Each morning's mail brought "bags and bags of envelopes," Song says, so many that Agarpao, who had been coming in every other day, was now working full-time. He was not the only one having trouble keeping up. Omidyar feared the traffic would soon be more than AuctionWeb's patched-together software could handle. The flood of new users was also causing problems for Skoll, who was still trying to write the business plan. "We were growing, in terms of traffic, metrics, and everything, twenty to thirty percent a month," says Omidyar. "Every time we sat down to do the plan we'd say it couldn't last." It was hard to know how steep to make the upward curves.

◆

It would be an exaggeration to say that eBay was built on Beanie Babies, but not by much. The mass-produced plush toys, which were carefully designed to be both lovable and collectible, first showed up in stores in 1994. Upstart suburban Chicago toy manufacturer Ty, founded by colorful toy entrepreneur Ty Warner, introduced the original nine Beanie Babies: Flash the dolphin, Splash the whale, Legs the frog, Pinchers the lobster, Patti the platypus, Chocolate the moose, Brownie the bear, Spot the dog, and Squealer the pig. Sales climbed steadily for the next two years, as the company continually added new characters. Skeptics thought the fad would end quickly, but by 1996 Beanie Baby mania was still reaching new heights. Ty made headlines that year when it leased three 737s to fly an emergency shipment from its factory in Korea so they could be in U.S. stores in time for Easter.

Beanie Babies' success was due, in large part, to Ty's shrewd tactics for creating artificial scarcity. The company did not sell its plush toys through Wal-Mart, Kmart, and other discounters, which meant that buyers had to make an effort to find them. Starting in 1996, Ty also began "retiring" individual Beanie Babies. Every time the company yanked one off the market, as it did with Buzz the bee in 1996, it set off a buying frenzy. Ty was close-lipped about its finances, but before long analysts were putting the privately held company's revenues at more than half a billion dollars a year. The highly reclusive Warner, who rarely granted interviews, ended up on *Forbes* magazine's list of the richest Americans, with a fortune estimated at $4 billion.

It turned out that Beanie Babies, which were gaining popularity just as AuctionWeb was, were the ideal product to sell through an online auction. Auction theory teaches that auctions are not, in fact, an efficient way of selling most goods. They are too labor intensive and time consuming for items that are likely to sell at a price the parties could have anticipated in advance. But auctions excel when they are called on to set prices for items whose value is inherently indeterminate. Some of history's first recorded auctions were held at the gates of Rome by soldiers selling off war plunder—used, foreign, and one-of-a-kind goods whose worth was subject to debate. In modern times, land-based auctions have been used mainly to sell art, antiques, and other unique items. Beanie Babies, whose value rose and fell daily based on popular whim, could take full advantage of the dynamic pricing mechanism that auctions provided.

Beanie Babies and online auctions were also suited for each other in other ways. Much of the supply of Beanie Babies was in the hands of individual collectors who were scattered across the nation, and even the world. When they wanted to buy or sell, it was difficult for these far-flung Beanie Baby traders to find one another and negotiate a transaction. The ability to network geographically dispersed people was, of course, one of the greatest strengths of the Internet, and of AuctionWeb. It also helped that Beanie Babies were inexpensive enough that buyers and sellers were not afraid to trade them online with strangers, and small enough that they were easy and inexpensive to ship.

AuctionWeb quickly became the nation's leading Beanie Baby exchange. In April 1997, when more than 2,500 Beanie Babies were listed on the site, AuctionWeb gave Beanie Babies their own category. The new Beanie Baby category had the highest conversion rate on all of AuctionWeb, meaning that a greater percentage of items listed in it sold than in any other category on the site. The prices these fist-sized plush toys were drawing were also noteworthy. Beanie Babies that had only recently sold at retail for $5 were going for an average of more than $33. In May 1997, AuctionWeb sold $500,000 worth of Beanie Babies, and they made up a remarkable 6.6 percent of the site's total volume.

Beanie Babies were the most visible, but hardly the only, collectible flooding AuctionWeb. In fact, in late 1996 all the fastest-growing categories on the site were collectibles of one kind or another — coins, stamps, baseball cards. The same factors that made Beanie Babies ideal for AuctionWeb applied equally to these more traditional collectibles. A Robert Indiana "LOVE" postage stamp from the 1970s or a 1913 buffalo nickel had no more inherent value than a mint-condition Chocolate the moose. Internet auctions were the ideal way to determine the right price for all of them. AuctionWeb's ability to connect distant buyers and sellers also made it a far better market than the ones collectors had long been using—collector shows and flea markets.

Economics was not the only factor driving collectors to AuctionWeb. Collectors are people with a passion, and they seek out others who share their passion. Before the Internet, many collectors were geographically isolated. Someone in a small town with an interest in Depression glass or southern folk art might have trouble finding like-minded people nearby. But on the Internet, thousands of collectors with the same fascination were only a few mouse clicks away. It was no surprise that collecting communities were among the earliest and most enthusiastic posters on Usenet newsgroups. AuctionWeb provided a similar kind of gathering place, where collectors could speak to one another through e-mail and bulletin boards, but it had the added advantage of allowing them to do what they enjoyed most—add to their collections.

Collecting communities arrived at AuctionWeb en masse in its early days. When one member of a *Star Trek* or an antique jewelry newsgroup discovered the site, word spread quickly. "Barbie collectors went out and told their Barbie-doll friends," recalls Skoll, who watched happily as AuctionWeb's metrics soared. Sellers who had items listed on AuctionWeb had a particular interest in driving their fellow collectors to the site. Steven Phillips, the early chintz seller, posted announcements on Usenet newsgroups for antique collectors, directing people to his AuctionWeb chintz auctions. In late 1996, a single post that Phillips placed on rec.antiques.marketplace drove six thousand chintz buyers to AuctionWeb.

By the end of 1996, collectors were the driving force behind AuctionWeb's growth. In a four-and-a-half-month period starting in late 1996, antiques and collectibles listings on the site increased by nearly 350 percent. In response to requests from the new collecting communities that were showing up, AuctionWeb was adding new categories, such as antique toys and vintage sewing items, on a weekly basis. This deluge of collectors fundamentally changed

AuctionWeb's focus. As 1997 began, the computer-related items that had once dominated were just 14 percent of listings. Antiques and collectibles now made up nearly 80 percent.

◆

AuctionWeb was thriving, but its administrative operations were a shambles. Even with Skoll starting to exert some managerial discipline, the company had the feel of a casually run home business. AuctionWeb's financial records, such as they were, consisted entirely of the entries that Omidyar made in QuickBooks, an off-the-shelf small-business software package. The mundane tasks involved in keeping an office running—ordering supplies, filing, answering the phone—were no one's responsibility, and they were being done haphazardly. In December 1996 AuctionWeb took a small, but critical, step toward becoming a real business: it hired its first office manager.

Sandra Gaeta was the younger sister of Anita Gaeta, the operations manager at the NASA incubator that AuctionWeb had recently left. When Sandra, who was working in a finance job at a nearby hospital, heard about the opening, she leapt at the chance to join the new economy. But after the order and stability of her last job, AuctionWeb's overall chaos required some adjustment. After accepting Omidyar and Skoll's offer, she dropped by headquarters in the middle of the workday to make it official, only to find no one there. Nor was she prepared for just how small her work world had become. A few weeks before her official start date, Gaeta joined her future colleagues for AuctionWeb's first Christmas party, lunch at a nearby restaurant. "The five of us got in one elevator," Gaeta recalls. "We joked that nothing better happen to that elevator, because that would be the end of the company."

Gaeta's new "office" was a desk in the suite's main room, which she shared with Agarpao and his piles of money-filled envelopes. Omidyar, who was eager to end his bookkeeping career, trained Gaeta on QuickBooks and made her the head of finance. Omidyar and Skoll also put her in charge of customer service, billing, and filing—and since there was no director of human resources, they gave her that job, too. Not long after Gaeta arrived, Skoll announced a little morale-building contest: he offered a prize to whoever wore the silliest hat to work. Gaeta won with an entry of her own creation: a simple hat to which she had attached labels with phrases like "office supplies," "keeping the books," and "weekly checks." It represented, Gaeta says, the fact that she seemed to wear all the hats at AuctionWeb.

Just as Song's job had come with a philosophy that the community knows best, Gaeta learned that Omidyar had a guiding principle for her. It was a phrase he repeated almost as often as his homilies about people being essentially good. "Spend the money," he told her, "like it's your own." AuctionWeb's thriftiness, so rare in the heady days of the dot-com bubble, was largely a reflection of Omidyar's essential abstemiousness—another value he believed made sense in a "crowded world." It was strongly seconded by Skoll, who was already seeing the mistakes some of his Stanford business school classmates were making with their own Internet start-ups. "In every case, these guys went out right away and raised a lot of money and hired a lot of people, and within a year they were almost out of money and had to lay off all their staff," Skoll says.

In these early days, AuctionWeb raised thriftiness to an art form. Salaries were uniformly low. Song had gotten her master's degree from Stanford with the goal of getting a job that paid six figures; AuctionWeb was paying her less than half that. Gaeta took a substantial pay cut when she left her job at the hospital. Office supplies were tightly rationed. The Xerox machine was in the hallway, shared with other tenants on the floor, and AuctionWeb staff had to bring their own copy paper. When new employees were hired, they were issued $119 desk sets from Scandinavian Designs, which they had to assemble themselves. To save on delivery charges, Gaeta borrowed her uncle's truck to pick up the desks. To keep customer-service costs down, AuctionWeb encouraged its users to communicate by e-mail. There was only one phone line in the office, with an unpublished number. When it rang, the employees were instructed not to answer it. (In early 1997, the telephone policy was relaxed: staff could answer the phone, but if it was a user, the staff member was told to take a message and tell the caller to expect a response by e-mail.)

◆

In late 1996, Omidyar divided the Bulletin Board in two. A running debate had developed about whether the board's primary purpose was practical—to help users get answers to their questions—or social. To end the fighting, Omidyar gave each camp its own board. The existing message board was renamed the Q & A Board and officially limited to discussions about the use of AuctionWeb. A contest was held to name a new, more social board. Song posted a list of twenty nominees suggested by users. Spurning names like Backyard Fence and Kitchen Sink, the AuctionWeb community voted in favor of the eBay Café.

The two boards drifted in predictable directions. The Q & A Board met the needs of AuctionWeb users who wanted advice on using the site. The eBay Café, liberated from these mundane influences, became more outgoing than ever. The name "eBay Café" had a certain élan—and, of course, it rhymed—but its implication of European sophistication was misleading. The users who posted and lurked in the eBay Café were for the most part middle-aged, middle-class, and lived in Middle America, and they chatted as if they had known one another all their lives. They were, despite the vote, the sort of people who were far more likely to talk over a backyard fence than in a café.

EBay Café posters groused about AuctionWeb topics, like winning bidders who disappeared without paying up, but their chat could just as easily turn to boyfriends and husbands who had proven similarly unreliable. Instead of posting pictures of items for sale, they shared photos of their grandchildren and pets. And they thought up quirky ways of building community in their shared corner of cyberspace. When a poster wrote the word "pop," others would respond with "pop, pop" or "pop, pop, pop"—kicking off the eBay Café's hokey version of a popcorn party. The Café had regularly scheduled rounds of group "singing," where one poster started off with a lyric and someone else posted the next line. Reflecting the Café's demographics, there was, Song recalls, "a lot of seventies music and Shania Twain." But part of the board's appeal was that users never knew what they would find when they stopped by. It could be a poster named Armond asking which AuctionWeb category he should use to list a naked picture of himself. Or Song telling the board, as she did one year, what outfit she planned to wear when she went home for the Kentucky Derby.

Like a bad after-school special, the eBay Café had a way of shifting rapidly from the cloying to the throat-catching. In the early days of the Café, one woman wrote that an injured hummingbird had flown into her car and was refusing to come out. How, she asked her fellow posters, could she save the bird? A second poster gave her detailed advice. The bird died later that evening, and it turned out that the second poster was nursing a goat kid, which also died that same night. The two ended up ruminating over life and death into the early hours of the morning. "People's cats would die, someone's baby would be sick, and they'd post on the board asking what they should do," one early user recalls. "Someone would post that her husband was in the hospital, and everyone would lend their support and their prayers."

Board regulars lost sleep, and even missed work, because they stayed up all night on the Café. Personalities emerged and friendships formed. There was a breathless poster named Bubbles, whose messages had a flair for the dramatic. When she disappeared from the boards for a few days, which she often did, other posters clamored for her to return. Another poster named Darts could only use the board from work, because she did not own a computer. Members of the nascent eBay Café community chipped in parts of a computer, had them assembled, and delivered the full unit to Darts, so she could participate nights and weekends. In time, the boards developed their own cyberspace celebrities, posters with names like Jimbo, Twaze, and Queen Stacy, who through their frequent communications and engaging personalities quickly became board favorites. One longtime poster on the Café created an online eBay Café Scrapbook, with pictures of board regulars, some with family members. "We've had lots of 'firsts' in the Café . . . a first baby, a first marriage, and . . . sadly . . . a first death," one Café regular reminisced in an online discussion of eBay's history. "It's surely a microcosm of the world."

The AuctionWeb staff was also part of the eBay Café community. Omidyar, Skoll, and Song posted regularly. Their eBay IDs were their e-mail addresses, and users had no hesitation about writing to Pierre@eBay.com, Jeff@eBay.com, or MaryLou@eBay.com. Omidyar regularly fielded questions on the board and answered e-mail. Steven Phillips frequently exchanged e-mails with Song, suggesting ways of handling the heavy traffic, or pointing out auctions he considered suspicious. When Phillips spotted a seller who was using multiple IDs to bid on his own auction, he wrote directly to Skoll. Skoll, knowing that Phillips was an expert in pottery, once e-mailed him to ask his opinion about whether the pottery for sale in an ongoing auction was authentic.

The boards also developed an informal "neighborhood watch." If someone was being mistreated on AuctionWeb, board regulars often took matters into their own hands. "We used to band together and find the bad guys and make their lives miserable," recalls Phillips. "If we heard of someone who was defrauding people, we would all e-mail them and tell them if they didn't make it up we would go to the police." Jim Griffith, who was by now an AuctionWeb employee, led a posse of about twenty users who dedicated themselves to righting Feedback Forum wrongs. Claiming the motto "Only Do Good," Griffith's posse came to the aid of what he called "users-in-distress," who had received negative feedback unjustly. Once, the posse helped several Australian users whose feedback ratings had dropped from 67 to −4 as a result of "feedback bombing" from someone with whom they had gotten into a dispute.

What made the message boards so special, early users say, was that in the vast, cold expanse of cyberspace they were a convivial outpost, a place where users never felt alone. That feeling of connection was part of the overall appeal of AuctionWeb: unlike a traditional e-commerce transaction, an auction was an inherently social experience, with real people selling and real people bidding. But it was the warmth of the message boards, in particular, that set AuctionWeb apart. "EBay strips the anonymity away, and you actually feel like you're an important individual," says Song. "It's the exact opposite of television."

Omidyar liked to say that community was something that happened spontaneously—that it could not be imposed from the top down. Almost every city in the United States has a community center built by city hall, he used to point out, but most are empty, except for a janitor and someone working the front desk. Down the street, there could be a hole-in-the-wall diner where the easy rapport between the waitresses and the regulars makes the place feel like an extended family. The eBay Café was a setting in which community could take hold, but it was AuctionWeb's users, he insisted, who made it happen.

The community offered by the message boards, and by the site as a whole, was one of AuctionWeb's greatest assets—quite literally. In eBay's first business plan, Skoll wrote that the two key advantages the company had over its competitors were the number of users and the strength of the AuctionWeb community. "A few services have attempted to create a 'community-like' feeling by offering bulletin boards or asking users for their input on site improvements," Skoll explained. "The bulletin boards, however, are edited by the online auction companies, unlike the free-flowing conversation afforded AuctionWeb users." Later, when major competitors tried to move into the online auction space, it would become clear just how critical eBay's community was to its survival.

◆

AuctionWeb began 1997 with a single priority: overhauling its threadbare technology. Incredibly, the site was still operating on the same jury-rigged mix of shareware and handwritten PERL* code that Omidyar had cobbled together back in the summer of 1995. The demands being put on this creaky system were extraordinary, not

---

*Practical Extraction and Reporting Language, a relatively simple programming language.

just in traffic, but in the kind of technologically complex tasks it was required to perform. "Unlike other high-traffic sites like Yahoo! or Netscape, our system actually *does* something—bid processing, automatic updates, and billing amongst other things," Skoll wrote in an e-mail explaining AuctionWeb's predicament. With its existing architecture, AuctionWeb had little capacity to grow—or to "scale," as the programmers put it. "This is not a situation where you can simply plug in a new server or a communication line and scale the system," Skoll explained in his e-mail. "You cannot simply buy software off the rack to solve the problems." AuctionWeb had no choice, Skoll concluded: "in order to get to the next level of performance, *we have to build the tools ourselves*."

To head up the project, Omidyar reached back into his past and found Mike Wilson, an eccentric computer genius he had worked for at eShop. There was no mistaking that Wilson, with his unruly red hair and beard and his iconoclastic personality, was an Omidyar hire. Wilson's technical credentials were first-rate: he was one of the first one hundred employees at Oracle and had done Internet work for large corporations like Macy's and Chevron. But just as important, he had the appreciation for community Omidyar valued so highly. Wilson came to AuctionWeb from Well Engaged, the pioneering Sausalito, California–based online discussion group.

Wilson was a brilliant, quirky figure, part Bill Gates, part Lewis Carroll, part Abbie Hoffman. He demonstrated his whimsical side early on when he named each of AuctionWeb's servers after a different reptile. The community loved it, and iguana and gecko references became a staple on the message boards. (When the system crashed someone would invariably post that it was time to "kick the dragon.") Wilson was temperamentally incapable of corporate doublespeak, or of withholding what he knew from the larger AuctionWeb community. When the site's search engine went down, Wilson took to the boards and bluntly declared that the crash had been caused by "Microsloth" and its faulty software. "Microsoft promised us that their new search engine would be better (the 'Super Secret Search Engine'), and it was, except the durn thing fell flat on

[its] face last week," Wilson wrote in one post. "Microsoft has told us (again) they'd fix it, and we'll see how they live up to that tomorrow. But their you-know-whats are on the line, because if they don't, we're throwing them out the door and finding something else."

Wilson's assignment, according to Omidyar, was "to build our next generation from scratch." That required replacing Omidyar's old PERL script with a new architecture based on the more sophisticated C++ programming language. Omidyar wanted the new system architecture to be up and running by March or April, but there were some unexpected obstacles. Wilson was supposed to focus on writing the code for the new architecture while a second engineer kept AuctionWeb operating. But traffic on the site was increasing so rapidly that Wilson had to spend much of his time just warding off disaster. Wilson was also short on staff, and the tight market for engineers made it difficult to hire the help he needed. Still, with his all-nighters and unpredictable work habits, Wilson seemed to bring some of the chaos with him. Everyone at AuctionWeb was desperate to know when the new architecture would be finished, but whenever Omidyar asked how it was going, all Wilson would say was that it was almost ready.

◆

Traffic on AuctionWeb was so heavy in the first few months of 1997 that the period would later acquire a nickname: the Great eBay Flood. In January alone, the site hosted 200,000 auctions, compared with 250,000 auctions in all of 1996. In a single two-week period from mid-January to February 1, hits on the site spiked from 600,000 to more than 1 million. With the Flood, the site grew more unstable than ever. Things got bad enough that AuctionWeb posted an announcement to the community apologizing for the frequent crashes and the difficulty users were having posting new items, bidding, and conducting searches. The announcement explained that a system upgrade was under way and asked users to be patient and, if at all possible, to use the site in off-peak hours, anytime other than 5:00–9:00 P.M. PST.

The Great eBay Flood was partly due to a phenomenon larger than AuctionWeb: the extraordinary growth of the Internet as a whole. In the spring of 1996, fewer than 19 million people in the United States and Canada were using the Internet. By December, more than 50 million were. But there was also a more AuctionWeb-specific factor at work. AuctionWeb was seeing for the first time that its business cycle was different from traditional retailing. Department stores typically do one-third or more of their annual sales in the weeks leading up to Christmas, but AuctionWeb's strongest season, it turned out, was the start of the new year. AuctionWeb was not especially busy during the holiday season: buyers were reluctant to give "used" gifts, and many of AuctionWeb's hard-core sellers took time off for holiday shopping and family events. But in January, listings soared as sellers returned to the site, making up for lost time. There was another factor AuctionWeb's staff suspected might be behind the heavy January listings: unwanted presents. "A lot of people wanted to unload those fruitcakes they found under their trees this Christmas," Skoll figured.

There was one more reason for the Great eBay Flood: in early January, the company launched its first promotion of a specific auction. It had happened spontaneously, when a woman contacted AuctionWeb to say she wanted to sell an autographed Green Bay Packers' football from the 1960s, with signatures of Packer greats like Vince Lombardi, Ray Nitschke, and Bart Starr. With the Packers on their way to face the New England Patriots in Super Bowl XXXI, the timing could hardly have been better. Departing from AuctionWeb's general policy of operating under the radar, Song prepared a press release. The football auction was reported widely in the media, and it brought new waves of buyers to the site. But the auction also served as a reminder of the perils of attracting additional traffic. The ragtag AuctionWeb site, groaning under the weight of thousands of football fans, crashed repeatedly in the days leading up to the auction. It was beginning to feel, Skoll says, as if the site "was down more often than not."

While Wilson worked around the clock writing his C++ code,

AuctionWeb seemed to be drifting toward complete system failure. New listings were now taking as long as twenty-four hours to appear on the site. When users clicked on an item, it took a minute or more just to bring up the item's description. And AuctionWeb's search engine would go down for weeks, even months, at a time. Any more such success, it seemed, and AuctionWeb would be ruined. "The volume simply swamped our resources, both human and machine," Skoll recalls. "We spent most of February trying to dig out from the load."

Until the system overhaul was complete, Omidyar and Skoll decided there was only one thing to do: actively drive AuctionWeb's overly enthusiastic users away from the site. The problem was, they refused to be discouraged. "It was like holding back a hurricane," Song recalls. The first group AuctionWeb went after was deadbeat sellers, who were abusing Omidyar's trusting policy of granting unconditional credit. In February, AuctionWeb instituted a "credit approval" process that required sellers without strong payment records to provide either a credit card or a ten-dollar prepayment. The new procedures did little to decrease traffic, but they imposed an enormous administrative burden on AuctionWeb's small staff. Employees were inundated with e-mails protesting the policy, including twenty-five from a single irate user. AuctionWeb still had only nine staff members and it had to hire several more just to handle the paperwork generated by the new policy. At the height of it all, a computer crashed, wiping out several days' worth of billing records. Morale on the staff was declining rapidly. "You have no idea," Skoll told an online auction newsletter, "how a supportive message from a user can lift your spirits at three A.M., when you have barely slept in days."

Having failed to drive away users with "credit approval," Skoll and Song tried another approach: they started imposing limits on listings. At first, they decreed that only sellers with feedback ratings of 100 or higher could list more than four items a day, but the community rebelled, complaining that the rule was unfair to new users and low-volume sellers. Then Skoll and Song tried capping the total number of new items that could be listed on the site in a single day.

But West Coast sellers objected that sellers on the East Coast, who woke up three hours earlier, were getting all the listings. Finally, AuctionWeb imposed time-based limits. The site would only accept new listings for ten minutes out of every hour.

Time-based listing limits had an unintended effect. Sellers, desperate to get their items up on the site, sat at their computers with multiple web browsers open, ready to start listing the moment the ten-minute window began. The rest of the time, many of them went to the message boards to pass the time until they could try to list again. "For fifty minutes of every hour, they were talking, bonding, and really getting to know each other," says Song. Once again, community on eBay was forming in a completely unplanned way.

For all the grief it caused, the upside of the Great eBay Flood was that revenues were soaring. Over the previous year, the site had added some additional fees. Notably, since mid-1996, AuctionWeb had been charging a fee for listing items for sale, in addition to the final value fees. Omidyar insists that the purpose was not to bring in more money. Users had demanded the listing fees, he says, in e-mails and message board posts, because there was simply too much junk cluttering the site. "No one wanted to list their fine antiques," Omidyar says, "next to a pair of dirty socks." Omidyar decided, once again without benefit of market research or expert opinion, what the fee should be: $1 per listing. The community responded right away. One dollar was too much, they e-mailed him in frightening numbers, for listing low-cost items. Within a week, Omidyar had switched to a graduated scale starting at ten cents, based on the cost of the item. AuctionWeb had also added several new fees for value-added features. Sellers had the option of listing an item in boldface for an additional $2, or of having an item placed at the top of the listings as a Featured Auction for $39.95.

But it was the sharp increase in the number of sales on the site, more than the new fees, that was driving revenue growth. More items were selling, and an increasing number were the sort of high-priced items skeptics thought would never sell on the Internet at all, much less in an exchange between strangers. The sales in February

1997 included a check signed by Marilyn Monroe that sold for $1,995; an Andy Warhol *Dracula* artist's proof that went for $6,500; and a 1959 "Suburban Shopper" Barbie that sold for $7,999, a new record for AuctionWeb. In all of 1996, AuctionWeb had taken in just $350,000. Suddenly, it was on track to take in $4.3 million in 1997, an annual growth rate of 1200 percent.

The competitive climate AuctionWeb was operating in was also encouraging. There was no shortage of other consumer-to-consumer sites, with names like Auction Block, AuctionNet, and Auction Universe. But none had more than 3,000 listings a day, compared to AuctionWeb's 45,000. A few niche auction sites had also emerged, including Numismatics Online, and several antiques sites, but none were gaining any traction. Nor had any of the major Internet service providers—AOL, CompuServe, or MSN—moved into the space yet. For all Omidyar and Skoll's fears that their lead was about to be taken from them, AuctionWeb remained the un-disputed leader, with more than 80 percent of the consumer-to-consumer online auction market.

◆

One AuctionWeb employee spent more time on the message boards than any other, but the community did not even know he was an employee. It was not even clear if "he" was human. When AuctionWeb hired Mike Wilson, it also got "Skippy," the most leg-endary figure ever to post on the boards. The basic outline of Skippy's life was well known. Always referred to in a genderless third-person, Skippy lived in a cave, had a pet vole named Marta, and trolled the beach looking for dead things to eat. Skippy was a technology genius who always seemed to have inside information about what was going on with the computer system at AuctionWeb. Posters often asked if Skippy worked at AuctionWeb, and Skippy always answered no.

Skippy clearly had an ability to manipulate the AuctionWeb site. At one point, Skippy, who was fascinated with space aliens, filled the background of the message boards with aliens. Another time Skippy changed the e-mail address of AuctionWeb's staff on the boards. Louise@eBay.com became HarleyMama@ebay.com; another staffer's ID was switched to CamelSpit@eBay.com. And Skippy once changed the feedback ratings of a few users to −666. But Skippy's interventions were not always so whimsical. When there was a problem on the site, Skippy could make it right. If a user had paid off his account but it had not been credited, Skippy could take care of it. Users never knew for sure whether Skippy worked at AuctionWeb, but it was obvious that Skippy knew, and was in contact with, a lot of the staff. Song used to go on the message boards and complain about how bad Skippy smelled. Skippy responded by telling the community how hairy Song was.

Skippy became a growing presence on the boards at the same time that Omidyar stopped posting, and quickly became the voice — albeit a slightly twisted voice — of AuctionWeb. When the community asked for new features, Skippy would explain why they could or could not be added. When users asked about outages, or glitches in the system, Skippy gave them the view from headquarters. "The neatest thing about Skippy was that he was very honest," says Keith Antognini, an early AuctionWeb customer-service manager. "Skippy never tried to pull the wool over the user's eyes."

Members of the early AuctionWeb community say that Skippy was one of the best things about spending time on the boards. Although Skippy was usually playful and fun-loving, he also served as a semiofficial AuctionWeb enforcer. Skippy came down hard on message board abuse, especially abuse of AuctionWeb's support staff. Skippy's caustic comments were usually enough to make recalcitrant posters back down. But when they weren't, it helped that Skippy had a power the rest of the community did not: when posters went too far, Skippy could suspend them from the site.

◆

In January 1997, Mark Del Vecchio was at a computer in his basement in Prospect, Connecticut, catching up on the posts on bit.listserv.movie.memorabilia. Del Vecchio, who collected movie posters, had just come across what looked like a rare find: a classic *Breakfast at Tiffany's* poster with Audrey Hepburn in a black cocktail dress waving a long cigarette holder. This particular post had something he had never seen before: a hyperlink to AuctionWeb, where the owner had listed it for sale. The movie poster turned out to be a reproduction, and Del Vecchio didn't buy it. But the hyperlink was his first exposure to AuctionWeb, and he was instantly taken in. In those days, the site had few enough listings that it was possible to scroll through every item up for sale in a few hours, and Del Vecchio did just that.

Del Vecchio had more than just a hobbyist's interest in online auctions. He had kicked around as a reporter for years, moving up from covering Old Lyme, Connecticut, for the weekly *Old Lyme Gazette* to reporting on the Tiananmen Square massacre for United Press International. Del Vecchio was now back in Connecticut, working for the *Hartford Courant* as general manager of electronic publishing. In the notoriously change-averse newspaper industry, the *Courant* was that rare paper that embraced new technology. It was among the first newspapers to have a faxed edition, or a website. When Del Vecchio saw AuctionWeb, he realized its listings included just the sorts of items that would otherwise have been sold through newspaper classified ads. If online auctions took off, it occurred to him, they could pose a significant threat to his industry, which derived as much as 40 percent of its revenues from classifieds.

The thing to do, Del Vecchio decided, was to persuade his employers to partner with or, better yet, buy AuctionWeb. The *Courant* was part of Times Mirror, a sprawling old-media company that included major-market newspapers like the *Los Angeles Times* and the *Baltimore Sun*. Times Mirror was hardly rushing to embrace the Internet, and the online projects the company had backed so far were utterly conventional. Online auctions, Del Vecchio knew, would be a hard sell. Del Vecchio also understood that there was a powerful institutional force at Times Mirror that would have an interest in scuttling a deal with AuctionWeb: the newspapers' advertising departments. Seeing online auctions as a threat to their own classified listings, they could be expected to do everything they could to block an alliance with AuctionWeb.

Still, Del Vecchio forged on. He sent an e-mail to Skoll requesting a meeting. When no response came, he sent a second. And a third. Finally, Del Vecchio just announced he was going out to Campbell. He asked Larry Schwartz, an entertainment entrepreneur he had hired a few months earlier as a consultant, to come with him. Schwartz, a onetime rock-concert lighting technician with a degree from the Yale School of Drama, had started ArtSoft, Inc., a computer-based ticketing company that within a few years of its founding was selling more than 35 million tickets a year. In March, the two men arrived at Greylands Business Park ready to start negotiating.

Del Vecchio and Schwartz, who had seen their share of start-ups, were not expecting much in the way of infrastructure or amenities. Even so, they were not prepared for their first encounter with AuctionWeb's headquarters. No receptionist was on hand to greet them, and, Schwartz realized glumly, there was absolutely no chance anyone was going to offer him a cup of coffee. When they arrived, Skoll was working in his office, but Omidyar didn't seem to be around at all. Moments after they started talking with Skoll, Omidyar walked in with Mike Wilson, loaded down with two large plastic bags from CompUSA. Schwartz asked what was in the bags, and Omidyar replied that it was a few parts for a new server he was building to keep the site operating.

It was not the level of technological sophistication Times Mirror was used to. Nor could Del Vecchio and Schwartz help noticing that the offices were in utter disarray. Everywhere they looked, they saw overstuffed canvas bags. What, Schwartz finally asked, was in the bags? Envelopes filled with user fees no one had gotten around to opening, Skoll answered with a shrug. Del Vecchio and Schwartz noticed Chris Agarpao hunched over a computer typing in dollar amounts and looking completely overwhelmed. Suddenly, it clicked. "I'm thinking, what a great business to be in, where you can't even open the checks fast enough," recalls Schwartz.

The task of writing up a report fell to Schwartz. AuctionWeb was the leader in Internet auctions, which were growing at the staggering rate of 20 percent a month, he explained. This online auction phenomenon had so far eluded most analysts and Internet players, Schwartz advised, but that would not be the case forever. In addition to being a promising investment in its own right, Schwartz argued, AuctionWeb could provide Times Mirror with a line of defense against the fast-changing Internet. Rather than watch as its classified ads lost customers to online auctions, Times Mirror could buy AuctionWeb and give everyone who bought a classified a free auction listing. When they were out in Campbell, Del Vecchio and Schwartz had limited the discussion to the possibility of Times Mirror's making an investment in eBay——perhaps taking a 20 percent stake. But in his report, Schwartz urged Times Mirror to buy the whole thing.

Having received mild expressions of interest from Times Mirror's corporate offices, Del Vecchio and Schwartz continued their discussions with AuctionWeb. Skoll had a trip planned to New York, and Del Vecchio and Schwartz traveled down to the city to meet with him. For the first time, they broached the idea of Times Mirror's buying the entire company. Skoll was noncommittal, but he did not rule it out. In late April, Skoll and Omidyar flew to Los Angeles for a meeting with Times Mirror. In a windowless conference room in the Los Angeles Times Building, the two men sat down with a group of high-level Times Mirror executives. Omidyar and Skoll made it clear that they would sell the company if the price was right.

EBay's cofounders each had his own reasons for considering a buyout. Skoll, ever the cautious one, was convinced that no matter how well eBay was doing, its success could evaporate at any time. "We were a company of less than ten people, with flaky technology, hugely worried some bigger entity would come in, and we were still called AuctionWeb, with an ugly black-and-white logo," Skoll recalls. Omidyar, who was already thinking of moving on, was more concerned about not spending any more time on the company than was absolutely necessary. His position was straightforward: he and

Skoll should figure out what they thought AuctionWeb was worth, and see if Times Mirror would pay that much. "If you can get that value today, without taking that time out of your life, you should declare victory and go home," Omidyar believed.

There was, however, no easy way to arrive at AuctionWeb's value. Skoll, of course, was partial to mathematical calculations, but no matter how many spreadsheets he prepared, the key questions about AuctionWeb's future remained essentially unknowable. Would online auctions remain popular? Would the site be able to scale? Would a major Internet player move into the space? Omidyar, not surprisingly, had a more intuitive approach to valuation. "EShop traded for about forty million dollars," he says, recalling his first start-up venture. "I thought that's what a company sold for."

Times Mirror almost certainly could have bought eBay for $40 million, but it was not interested. Even with Schwartz's report in hand, and after meeting with Omidyar and Skoll, the media giant's executives were not enthusiastic about the future of online auctions. Their main objection was the one Omidyar had been hearing from the beginning: that strangers would never trade with strangers over the Internet in large numbers. Coming from the ink-stained world of old media, the Times Mirror management also failed to see what AuctionWeb had, exactly, that was worth millions of dollars. "They kept saying, 'They don't own anything,'" says Del Vecchio. "'They don't have any buildings, they don't have any trucks.'" Del Vecchio and Schwartz tried to explain that AuctionWeb had a community and a brand, and that they were fast building a prohibitive lead in the Internet auction space. And that not having buildings and trucks was actually an *advantage:* it was because AuctionWeb was a virtual business that it had gross margins above 80 percent. Most of these arguments were met, Del Vecchio recalls, with blank stares.

The discussion eventually came down to a scaled-back alternative. Times Mirror was considering investing $5 million for one-eighth of AuctionWeb. This deal had advantages for both sides. Times Mirror could claim some of the upside if AuctionWeb did well, while still limiting its investment in a field about which it remained dubious. AuctionWeb, for its part, would get a sizable war chest, and the credibility that came with having a major media company as a partner, without having to relinquish control. In the end, however, Times Mirror balked at even a limited investment. "The powers that be just didn't think it would be that big," says Schwartz.*

Remaining independent was, in retrospect, critical to AuctionWeb's success. AuctionWeb was quick and nimble, which it needed to be to survive in the fast-evolving world of e-commerce. If it had been sold, the company would have been paralyzed by Times Mirror's bureaucracy. Decisions that Omidyar and Skoll made in the hallway would suddenly have required elaborate levels of approval. Being part of a sprawling media empire would also have meant political battles and turf wars. The institutional opposition Del Vecchio feared from newspapers' ad departments would almost certainly have plagued AuctionWeb, blocking it from moving aggressively into cars, real estate, and other big-ticket items that would compete directly with classified ads. "For eBay, it was the best deal that never happened," says Del Vecchio. "If eBay had been acquired by Times Mirror, it would be nothing like what it is today." But for Times Mirror, not buying AuctionWeb for $40 million was a blunder of epic proportions.**

---

*While the negotiations with Times Mirror were under way, Skoll approached Knight-Ridder, his old employer, to see if he could get a bidding war going. Knight-Ridder was interested, but it was too slow to act. Before Knight-Ridder decided, Omidyar and Skoll had accepted funding from venture capitalists with the goal of taking the company public.

**In March 2000, Times Mirror was purchased by the Tribune Company for $8 billion. EBay was, at the time, worth more than twice that amount.

chapter three

The first AuctionWeb listings were dull-looking and plainly worded, closer to classified ads than to the glitzy, full-color sales pitches that would come later. But even in those black-and-white days, one part of the listing was critical to getting a decent price: the photograph. Buyers were reconciled to not dealing with an established retailer, not meeting the seller, and even to not touching the item. But at the very least, they wanted to get a look at what they were bidding on. The trouble was, posting photos on the Internet was not easy in early 1997. Digital cameras were expensive, and few nonprofessionals owned one. Even if a seller had a digital photo, AuctionWeb did not provide image hosting, and there were few websites that did.

Coming forward and meeting that need was what made Pongo such a revered member of the AuctionWeb community. Pongo—the only name she was ever known by on the site—was a message board regular who knew a lot about computers and image hosting, and she was generous about answering questions. At first, Pongo gave advice exclusively by e-mail. But eventually she wrote up tip sheets, which she made freely available to AuctionWeb users, on topics like how to upload pictures, how to resize them, and how to convert images from proprietary formats to standard ones.

But many sellers didn't want advice on photo hosting. They just wanted Pongo to handle their photos, and they were willing to pay her to do it. Arrangements like these were the genesis of Pongo.com, a small image-hosting business Pongo started running out of her home. Pongo began by charging fifty cents a photo, and trusted her customers to keep track of what they owed, paying her when their balances reached the point where it was worth sending a check. Before long, Pongo had a small but thriving business hosting hundreds of AuctionWeb photos at a time.

In addition to hosting photos, Pongo.com became an informal AuctionWeb drop-in center. AuctionWeb was crashing almost daily — the eBay Flood was hitting a high-water mark — and when it did, message board regulars were as upset about losing touch with their online friends as they were about the interruption of their auctions. To feed their addiction, Pongo opened Pongo.com/lockout, a place where message board denizens could regroup and wait together for AuctionWeb to be revived. This lockout board, which Pongo called the Emergency eBay Evacuation Center, or EEEC, quickly took on a semiofficial status, with AuctionWeb staff stopping by to give progress reports on how the recovery efforts were going.

Pongo designed elaborate fantasy sites within Pongo.com, dedicated to other personalities from the boards. The Queen's Round Room, which Pongo created for a prolific poster who went by the name Queen Stacy, included a dank dungeon, to which message board users were banished if they offended Her Highness. An area called Uncle Griff's Chapel featured a virtual church with stained-glass windows and an altar, with the caption "Confession Is Good for the Soul." Under the heading "Forgive Me Uncle for I Have Sinned," AuctionWeb users unburdened themselves to Jim Griffith about a wide range of misdeeds. The confessions were a reflection of the demographics AuctionWeb was attracting: in a typical post, a user named Maureen wrote, "Forgive me, Uncle, my sin is I would rather play on the computer than do housework."

Pongo, known off-line as Jane Dee, of Sitka, Alaska, was easily one of the most famous characters on AuctionWeb—the equal of Uncle Griff or Aunt Patti. If Pongo did a lot for the early AuctionWeb community, it also did a lot for her. A famous *New Yorker* cartoon shows two dogs seated at a computer, one saying to the other: "On the Internet, nobody knows you're a dog." The Internet is a great leveler, giving people with social disadvantages in the real world—the physically or mentally disabled, the unattractive, the shy—a place to shine. AuctionWeb's message boards did this for Dee. Pongo was popular not only for her good works, but because she was social and witty, the fun girl everyone wanted to know. "Pongo was a star; she tap-danced across the floors of those message boards," says Dee. "But I'm not really like that."

Indeed, Dee's off-line existence did not involve much tap dancing. Sitka was a fishing village of five thousand on Alaska's Baranof Island, accessible to the mainland only by airplane or ferry. Dee had bought her first computer in 1995, and taught herself web design through tutorials she found on the Internet. Struggling financially, she began reconstructing computers to make extra money. In early 1996, when she was looking for inexpensive parts for some computers she was trying to rebuild, she stumbled across AuctionWeb. Dee initially came for the ten-dollar hard drives and five-dollar video cards, but she ended up staying for the community.

Posting as Pongo, the name of her black-and-white spotted cat, Dee quickly became a fixture on the message boards. Like Uncle Griff and Aunt Patti, she made a name for herself by sharing her expertise. "A lot of the early users were retired antiques dealers who could barely turn on their computers," Dee recalls. "I had a knack for making people realize they could do things they didn't think they could." Before long, Dee was spending up to twelve hours a day on the boards.

By all appearances, Dee—a blond woman in her late thirties with two sets of twin girls—could have been a cheery soccer mom driving an SUV through the streets of any American suburb. But appearances, in this case, were deceiving. Like Griffith, Dee was often depressed in the off-line world, while she was shining on AuctionWeb's message boards. "It really gave me a reason to get up and face the world," she says. AuctionWeb also allowed Pongo to build relationships that would have been difficult for her to sustain off-line. "In my real life I'm an extreme hermit," Dee says.

Pongo's story was actually far more complicated than anyone who knew her on AuctionWeb would have imagined. Dee, who had grown up in the Pacific Northwest with the name Jody Roberts, had been a hard-driving reporter for the Tacoma, Washington, *News Tribune.* In May 1985, at the age of twenty-six, Roberts had simply disappeared. At first her family and friends thought she had gone on vacation. When she didn't turn up, they began to worry that an investigative piece she was working on might have gotten her in trouble. Roberts's family was desperate to find her, but none of the leads they pursued went anywhere. When they still had not heard from her after twelve years, they found it hard to believe she was still alive.

In fact, Roberts had been picked up days after her disappearance more than a thousand miles away, wandering around in a daze in a shopping mall in Aurora, Colorado. She had no identification on her and told the police she had no idea who she was. Roberts was taken to the Colorado Mental Health Institute in Denver, where she was diagnosed with psychogenic fugue, amnesia brought on by severe stress or trauma. Except for her psychological condition, the doctors found that she was perfectly healthy and that there was no reason to keep her. The hospital ran Roberts's photo and description through a police network, and released them to the media, but no one identified her. Before it discharged her, the institute gave her a new identity—a new Social Security number, a new date of birth, and a new name, Jane Doe. Roberts changed one letter, and started her life over again.

When Dee tried to find a job, she ran into a problem. Not discussing her amnesia was not an option: employers wanted to know something about her life that went back more than a few weeks. When she talked about her condition with employers, she found she had no trouble getting interviews—everyone, it seemed, wanted to meet the young woman with the soap-opera affliction. The trouble was, no one wanted to hire her. Dee enrolled in the University of Denver, reasoning that employers never ask new graduates about their lives before college. In 1989, she ran off to Sitka with a classmate, married a salmon fisherman, and had her two sets of twins.

Dee had forgotten her family and friends, but they had not forgotten her. At their prodding, the Pierce County Sheriff's Department in Tacoma launched a homicide investigation into Jody Roberts's disappearance. Years later, a former coworker in Alaska happened to see Roberts's picture on TV, and made the connection between Roberts and Dee. Dee and her family were reunited, and she brought her daughters down to meet their grandparents and extended family. The hardest thing about being discovered, Dee says—worse, even, than the reporters who stood vigil in her driveway for two full weeks—was being reunited with a family and past that meant nothing to her. Back in Washington, Dee's parents showed her old yearbooks, and her siblings reintroduced themselves, but Dee felt as though she was being given a tour of someone else's life. Dee, who was ending the relationship in Alaska, returned to the Pacific Northwest to live near her parents. It was good to be back, but she found it disconcerting that the people she called her "new relatives" expected her to relate to them as Jody. "There was an assumption I was going to pick up an old life that didn't mean anything to me," she says. Their stories about how she had been a reporter, and the articles they showed her that she had supposedly written, just perplexed her. "I couldn't imagine interviewing anyone or being that intrusive," she says. "It just didn't sound like the kind of profession I would choose, any more than I would be a Hollywood movie star."

Dee was a star, of course—on AuctionWeb. That was the word she herself used to describe Pongo, "tap dancing" her way across the message boards. In the real world, Dee was, for some reason, unable to hold on to her former personality. Her doctors told her she was repressing it because there was something painful lurking there. "It's probably just a door I don't want to open," she says. But somehow, on the AuctionWeb message boards, Dee felt comfortable expressing, through Pongo, her Jody Roberts persona—highly sociable, hyper-competent, a talented writer, and the willing center of attention. Dee's father was captivated by Pongo and loved going to Pongo.com and AuctionWeb to see the world she had created, and the positive feedback ratings and comments people left for her. His daughter Jody, as he once knew her, was lost to him in the real world. But when he missed her, he could visit her online.

◆

After the talks with Times Mirror ended, AuctionWeb began looking for other investors. In early 1997, Skoll finally emerged from his office with AuctionWeb's first business plan. As a blueprint for eBay's success, it still holds up well in many respects. In a section entitled "Philosophy," Skoll sketched out a vision of economic transformation that read more like an essay on economic history—a Fabian tract, even—than a mere appeal for financing. Before the industrial revolution, Skoll wrote, goods like chairs were custom-made for individual buyers. The craftsman and the customer had a personal relationship. The quality and service were excellent, but the personal attention also meant that goods were expensive, beyond the reach of most people. The industrial revolution ushered in a new era of mass production, in which goods were cheaper. But these efficiencies came at a cost: with large factories and elaborate distribution channels, buyers and sellers no longer formed personal relationships. The computer, Skoll argued, would make it possible to reclaim the old-style relationships. Internet auctions represented nothing less, he wrote, than "the opportunity for mankind to recapture the lost ambiance of the town market, when personal interaction and personal attention was the key to a trade and to life in general."

As insightful as this business plan was, it was misguided on a critical point. EBay, the corporate entity that owned AuctionWeb, was actually engaged in two distinct businesses. Its AuctionWeb auction site was getting all the attention. But Omidyar and Skoll had quietly put together a second business, called SmartMarket Technology, which licensed software to help other companies run their own auctions. In November 1996, eBay had entered into its first third-party licensing deal, with a company called Electronic Travel Auction to use SmartMarket Technology to sell plane tickets and other travel products. So far, almost all of eBay's revenues had come from AuctionWeb fees. But in the future, Omidyar and Skoll believed eBay would make most of its money licensing SmartMarket Technology and charging for technical support. In fact, the new business plan predicted that revenue from SmartMarket Technology would surpass the fees from AuctionWeb within two years. AuctionWeb would still be the company's "crown jewel," demonstrating to potential licensees the value of eBay's auction software, but it would contribute an ever-shrinking percentage of revenues. "Inasmuch as AuctionWeb represents the present for eBay," the business plan stated, "the service provider (technology licensing) arm of the company represents the future."

It was an analysis rooted in Omidyar and Skoll's excessive pessimism about AuctionWeb's prospects. They remained convinced that AOL and other Internet giants were on the brink of launching their own consumer-to-consumer auctions, and that with their financial resources and heavy traffic they would easily displace AuctionWeb. "EBay sees AuctionWeb as a twelve-to-eighteen-month gambit," the business plan concluded, "after which eBay will consider selling the service or paring back the investment." In hindsight, this forecast was a massive miscalculation: AuctionWeb's founders did not realize how valuable their fast-growing site was. But Skoll insists that their strategy was a reasonable one, given how small and vulnerable the company was. The focus on software licensing meant that even if bigger players moved into the online auction space, eBay could still survive by selling them software. Like the stores that prospered during the Gold Rush not by digging for gold but by selling equipment to the prospectors, eBay wanted to be, Skoll says, "in a position to provide the picks and shovels."

◆

Now that they had a business plan, Omidyar and Skoll were ready to hunt for venture capital. Most start-ups seek out venture capital firms for a simple reason: they need financing, either to keep operating or to fund necessary expansion. But eBay was not like most start-ups. Because of its unusual business model—the fact that it was an entirely virtual business, with negligible expenses—it was already turning a profit, not burning through cash the way most dot-coms were. Its virtuality also meant that, other than upgrading its technology, eBay did not have a lot to spend money on.

What eBay did need from a VC firm was strategic advice and credibility. In addition to writing checks, VCs generally take an active role—sometimes more active than founders like—in guiding the firms they invest in. Just as important, an investment from a top VC firm is an important imprimatur in the image-conscious world of Silicon Valley, which can help attract talent and corporate partners. Even with its enviable record of profitability and growth rate, eBay was still not being taken seriously. Omidyar and Skoll had seen this most recently when they tried to hire staff to work with Mike Wilson on AuctionWeb's new architecture. "The first question all the engineers would ask was 'Who is your funder,'" recalls Skoll. When the applicants heard that eBay was self-funded, most assumed it was because the company couldn't attract a VC. Not being able to hire skilled engineers was a problem, but Omidyar and Skoll were more worried about establishing credibility for their next major recruitment effort. "It was in our heads from the start to try to bring in a world-class CEO to grow this thing as big as it could possibly get," says Skoll. It was hard to see how eBay could attract a world-class CEO as long as it retained the stigma of being self-funded.

Omidyar and Skoll drew up a list of VCs they wanted to meet with, intentionally limiting it to no more than six firms. "The Valley is a very close community," says Omidyar. "The more VCs you talk to, the more chance you have to screw up your presentation, and then someone says, 'They really screwed up, they don't know what they're doing.'" Omidyar and Skoll had recently had an experience that made them think they would not have much trouble attracting investors. An East Coast venture capitalist, impressed by eBay's numbers, had cold-called and insisted on a meeting. "We said, 'Look, we really don't want to talk to you,'" Omidyar recalls. But the VC would not be put off. "One day he actually showed up at the office and said, 'I'm that guy you didn't want to talk to,'" says Omidyar, still incredulous. "So we had to talk to him."

EBay's biggest advantage in recruiting investors was that it had been profitable from its first month. Working against it, however, was a liability that had also been with it from the start: the perception that its business was just too offbeat. Skoll made a pitch to a partner at the Mayfield Fund, one of the oldest and most prominent VC firms on Sand Hill Road, Silicon Valley's famed avenue of venture capitalists. "The partner there didn't get it at all," Skoll recalls. "He said, 'Let me get this right, people are going to buy and sell antiques online. I gotta go.'"

Omidyar and Skoll hardly traveled in elite venture capital circles, but Omidyar had been quietly cultivating one powerful VC. Bruce Dunlevie, who had been at Merrill Pickard when the firm invested in Omidyar's old start-up, eShop, was now a partner at Benchmark Capital, one of the Valley's leading VC firms. Throughout 1996, Omidyar had been leaving Dunlevie monthly voice-mail messages keeping him apprised of eBay's progress. In early 1997, Omidyar called Dunlevie and said eBay was starting to look for VC money, and that he wanted to talk to Benchmark. Dunlevie did not immediately jump at the opportunity. EBay was "this sort of online flea market type of thing," says Bob Kagle, a Benchmark partner. "I think it was a little challenging to get Bruce's interest." But Dunlevie agreed to let Omidyar make a presentation. He invited Kagle, who had the most experience with e-commerce and consumer marketing of anyone at Benchmark, to join them for the meeting.

Omidyar dressed up for his visit to Benchmark—no T-shirt, no shorts—but even so, eBay's ponytailed leader bore little resemblance to the slick MBA types who hawked most of the business plans on Sand Hill Road. Omidyar came empty-handed, seemingly unaware that slides and handouts were an expected part of the start-up pitch.

And with Skoll out of town, Omidyar had to explain that he could not provide his would-be investors with much in the way of financial details. His plan was simply to talk a bit about eBay's history, and then take Dunlevie and Kagle through a brief tour of the site.

Omidyar sat down with the two men in a sleekly modern Benchmark conference room, and told them about how he had started AuctionWeb in his spare bedroom. Dunlevie and Kagle seemed interested, particularly in his description of the community and his efforts to imbue the site with his personal values. Omidyar reached for a laptop, hoping to close the deal by showing them the site. Unfortunately, AuctionWeb was down. Outages were a common enough occurrence in those waning months of the old system architecture, but this was the first outage to hit AuctionWeb in the middle of a $5 million investment pitch. As Omidyar tried again to make the site appear on the screen, Dunlevie broke the tension by saying the problem must be with Benchmark's Internet connection. "They were very gracious about it," Omidyar recalls.

The meeting ended inconclusively. Back in his own office, Kagle eventually managed to get on to AuctionWeb. "It really didn't have any sort of visual appeal," he recalls. Kagle was also troubled that the site was "brand schizophrenic," referring to itself both as eBay and AuctionWeb. But his opinion changed when he began examining the content. Kagle, who had grown up in a working-class auto-industry family in Flint, Michigan, was astounded by the range of items and users he found on the site. It struck him, he says, as "a gathering place for Main Street America." Kagle, an avid collector of hand-carved fishing decoys, typed "fishing decoys" into the eBay search engine, and was stunned by the vast array that appeared, including one by Bud Stewart, a renowned Michigan decoy carver. "I'd been looking for this stuff at trade shows for probably five years and hadn't come across it," Kagle says. Kagle bid on the Stewart decoy. When he lost the auction to a bigger Stewart fan, he was even more impressed.

Benchmark deliberated for nearly two months after Omidyar's presentation about whether to invest. Kagle went down to Greyland

Business Park to meet Skoll and talk with him about his ideas for the future. Kagle was sold on the AuctionWeb story. Bringing the world together to trade in a single market, individual to individual, struck him as "a very grand vision." And while Benchmark was considering what to do, several of his partners made a point of stopping by his office to tell him how impressed they were with the items they were finding on the site. But what clinched the deal, in the end, were the numbers. EBay had just gone through the Great eBay Flood, and auctions on the site had increased nearly tenfold in the past six months. Skoll, never one to leave things to chance, was sending Kagle regular e-mails highlighting every upswing in eBay's metrics. "People say to me now, 'How did you know that an online flea market would be successful,'" Kagle says. "But the proof was in the pudding—it was already working at the time that we invested."

By June 1997, Benchmark was in. It paid $5 million for 21.5 percent of the company. Omidyar had insisted all along that eBay did not need VC money, and when Benchmark's first $5 million arrived, he proved his point by depositing it in the bank, where it remained untouched. Benchmark's stake would eventually be worth more than $4 billion, making it one of the most richly rewarded investments in the history of business.*

Considering that eBay did not need the money—the do-or-die condition that forces most start-ups to sign over a large part of their company to VCs—it could be argued that eBay overpaid for the tactical advice and prestige it received. But Omidyar insists that Benchmark's behind-the-scenes work on recruitment, its strategies for negotiating with other companies, and its guidance on issues like branding and consumer marketing were critical to eBay's success. "It's unfair to ask whether it added up to four billion dollars of guidance because no one could ever have anticipated just how valuable

---

*Benchmark's offer put the value of eBay at about $23 million. Knight-Ridder, with which Skoll was still negotiating, was considering paying as much as $50 million, but Skoll could not get a commitment. Benchmark's was the best firm offer eBay had—far richer than the roughly $10 million valuations two other VC firms, Orchid Holdings and CMGI, had placed on eBay earlier in the year.

eBay would become," he says. "But when I think about whether their contribution was worth one-quarter of the company—a real partnership stake—the answer is absolutely."

◆

As summer drew to a close, all of eBay was obsessed with a single question: Would Mike Wilson complete the second-generation site architecture by the new Labor Day deadline Omidyar had given him? The official line was that Wilson was on schedule, but sightings of the sleep-deprived, somewhat crazed-looking chief engineer were hardly reassuring.

With site traffic continuing to soar, AuctionWeb's creaky old architecture was now crashing almost daily, often for hours at a time. Buyers and sellers could not count on auctions proceeding on schedule—or on the site even being up and running when their auction was scheduled to end. The community was becoming increasingly outspoken about the site's instability. Some posts on the boards were "totally uncalled-for and full of anger," recalls Sonny Wagner, a user who would go on to become an eBay customer-support employee. It didn't help that Skippy, who could usually be counted on to placate the community, had gone AWOL, a casualty of Wilson's round-the-clock work schedule. Members of the community testily demanded to know what had become of their eccentric champion. "Have you ever been around Skippy when he hasn't slept in seventy-two hours because he's working so hard on the improvements that he forgets to eat, sleep, and occasionally shower?" Song replied. "He looks bad. He smells bad. And he gets mean. Skippy's been that way for three weeks."

In the weeks leading up to Labor Day, the staff met daily at 4:00 P.M. to plan the transition to the new architecture. The engineers had created a transitional site, eBay Beta, which they launched while AuctionWeb continued to run. The switchover would require moving 3.8 million individual records from AuctionWeb to eBay Beta—and persuading roughly 200,000 registered users to reregister manually. "We were trying as gently as possible to shove people over to the new site," says Patti Ruby. "But people are resistant to change." It was also difficult persuading users to start selling on eBay Beta, which had to happen for the transition to work. As an incentive, eBay offered free listings, but sellers were still reluctant, because there were few buyers, and items were selling for far less than they would have on the old site.

For the community, which monitored the switchover intently, no aspect was too small to evoke questions or protests. Song experienced the depth of user feeling firsthand when she was given the task of redesigning the category listings, which, with the new site architecture, were being increased from forty to one hundred. Song developed what she thought was a good list and posted it. The community's response was a repeat of the Feedback Forum stars fiasco. What astonished Song this time was not only the vehemence of the objections, but the level of detail. Button collectors, a group whose existence had escaped her until now, excoriated her for being so ignorant about buttons. "Did you know there are vintage buttons, antique buttons, and modern buttons?" one irate button-seller lectured her. "That buttons don't belong in Sewing Collectibles? That they belong in their own button category? Did you know that you can have plastic buttons, or metal buttons? Did you mean pin-back buttons or did you mean four-hole buttons?" Once again, a chastened Song bowed to the will of the community. She drew up the list again, and worked with the button collectors to develop AuctionWeb's first category for buttons.

To help with the transition, eBay opened the eBay Beta board, eBay's first live customer-support board. Instead of throwing out questions to the community on the Q & A Board, users could post their questions on the Beta Board and get answers in real time from Mike Wilson, Jim Griffith, Patti Ruby, or another member of the eBay staff. After the transition, Ruby successfully lobbied for the board to be made permanent. It was, for eBay, a small step toward becoming a real business. For the first time, when AuctionWeb users had a routine service problem, an employee was available to help in real time.

The switchover also gave the company a chance to address

a significant branding problem that had plagued it from the beginning: the auction site was called AuctionWeb, while the domain name remained www.eBay.com. Making matters worse, eBay did not even own the domain name AuctionWeb.com. People who typed www.AuctionWeb.com into their web browsers ended up at the Internet equivalent of a wrong address.* Omidyar had noticed, even in the early days, that when users e-mailed him about the site, they invariably ignored the official AuctionWeb logo at the top and referred to it as eBay. When Song surveyed users, they confirmed Omidyar's observation: most thought the auction service was called eBay. Omidyar and Skoll decided to use the switchover as an opportunity to rebrand. When Mike Wilson's newly scalable site debuted on September 1, 1997, the name AuctionWeb was retired. Both the auction site and the domain name were now eBay.

◆

Every successful start-up has a *Paradise Lost* moment, when it casts innocence aside and embraces a more complicated adult identity. For eBay, that moment came in August 1997 when it hired Steve Westly as vice president for marketing and business development. Westly, a Stanford MBA, had the buttoned-down look and careful speaking style of an old-economy executive. His title alone mapped eBay's coming of age. Cyberspace was fast filling up with corporate Internet sites built by slick web-design firms, which were attracting visitors by forging corporate alliances and buying traffic. But eBay had always been different: it was a grassroots community, built on word of mouth and sustained by people's feeling of belonging to something special. If Westly was going to be in charge of business development,

---

*Omidyar tried to register AuctionWeb.com just months after he created the website, but he discovered it had already been claimed by one Eric Poole, a New Hampshire software consultant. Poole, who was trying to set up a website for auctioneers, was not cybersquatting. He had thought up the name himself, not having heard of Omidyar's fledgling site. When Omidyar contacted him, Poole said he did not want to sell, but the two men made a deal. Each site would include a disclaimer saying the site was not affiliated with the other AuctionWeb, and each would include a link to the other site.

that meant that eBay would be signing deals, cobranding, and pay-ing for traffic. It would, in other words, be a real business.

EBay's staff could feel the culture changing when Westly came in to interview. For one thing, he didn't have the kind of eclectic re-sume most early eBay employees did; he was, in fact, strikingly qual-ified for the precise job he was applying for. Westly had taught public management at Stanford business school before leaping into the world of Internet start-ups. As vice president of WhoWhere?, the largest directory of people and businesses on the Internet, he had a track record of putting together deals, and he knew many of the key players in Silicon Valley. Westly brought two young men with him who would be part of his team: Tom Adams and Richard Rock. Adams and Rock were younger versions of their mentor: well-dressed, carefully groomed Stanford MBAs, who had learned their way around cyberspace with Westly at WhoWhere?

Even the interviews had been a tip-off. Hiring at eBay had always been a collaborative process. The whole staff participated, and eBay prided itself that an applicant who charmed the top executives but slighted the customer-support reps would not get an offer. When the Westly team showed up, everyone was allowed to talk to them, but it was clear that they were going to be hired no matter what most of the staff thought of them. And in a corporate culture where creden-tials mattered little—Omidyar had barely eked out his own under-graduate degree—it seemed to the current staff that there was a troubling uniformity to the Westly team's prestigious educational backgrounds. "Oh, man, this is where it starts to go," Song told her-self at the time. "Three Stanford MBAs."

The old-timers' fears turned out to be well-founded: the new guys really were different. Stanford business school had taught them to fill in spreadsheets, but nothing in their past prepared them for a business built on Beanie Baby trading and message board chatter about cross-dressing farmers. Keith Antognini went to lunch with two of the new arrivals early on, and came back in despair. "They wanted to know why this whole community thing was so impor-tant," he says. "They did not buy into it at all."

In biblical times, the Gileadites and the Ephraimites could tell each other apart by how they pronounced the word *shibboleth,* the Hebrew word for stream. The Westlyites, it soon became clear, had no end of shibboleths that set them apart from eBay's indigenous tribe. In a T-shirt-and-shorts office, they came to work in jackets, crisp blue shirts, and dark dress pants. While old-timers like Omidyar and Mike Wilson talked endlessly about "community" and "empowerment," the Westly team packed their conversations with phrases like "cash flow" and "click-through rates." If the Westlyites had an idea, they didn't pop their heads into Omidyar's office, as Song or Wilson would have. They developed a mathematical model that made their case and put together a PowerPoint presentation. "They definitely had their slides together," Sandra Gaeta says with a sigh. That Halloween, some of eBay's more bohemian early employees came to work in boring blue shirts and black slacks—and went as Westly, Rock, and Adams.

If the arrival of the Westly team was a shock to eBay's ecosystem, it also proved critical to eBay's success. In the fall of 1997, eBay was ready to grow. With a scalable site in place, eBay could handle considerably more traffic, and now that it had $5 million in the bank, Omidyar and Skoll were less worried about being overtaken by better-funded competitors. "It was the first time," says Omidyar, "that we felt comfortable enough to actually go out and bring more members in." Before Westly was hired, marketing and business development didn't exist in a formal way at eBay. Now there was a group in place whose focus was forging development deals to drive new traffic to the site. Westly, Rock, and Adams were all well versed in the arcana of banner ads and pricing clicks per thousand, and they got right to work.

Within days of starting, Rock had hammered out eBay's first major business-development contract, a pact with Netscape for ads that would drive traffic to eBay's site. Some longtime employees, particularly Wilson and Song, thought the deal took the company in precisely the wrong direction. It was a point of pride for them that eBay had always grown organically—it had never paid for traffic.

This antibusiness-development camp objected, but Omidyar and Skoll weighed in on the side of the Netscape deal; it was precisely the sort of alliance the Westly team had been brought in to develop. In the next few months, over the continuing objections of the organic-growth faction, eBay signed deals—negotiated by Westly, Rock, and Adams—with Excite, Angelfire, and Lycos to drive traffic to the site.

◆

In November 1997, as part of its new effort to raise its profile, eBay launched a public-relations offensive that its PR firm was calling, somewhat grandly, the Fall Vision Tour. The idea was to unleash Omidyar on reporters and industry analysts on the East and West coasts to spread the eBay gospel. The fact was that outside of its passionate user base, eBay was still hardly known. There had been few press stories about the company, and since it was still private, no analysts followed it. As he had for his Benchmark appearance, Omidyar dressed up in a suit and tried his best to transform himself into a salesman. Omidyar had prepared himself for tough questions, but on many of his stops there were hardly any questions at all. "People didn't really know what to ask," says Johnny Wong, a PR agent who went along on the tour. "It was such a totally different animal, they didn't know what to make of it." And now that Omidyar was forcing them to think about online auctions, they weren't sure they liked them. "Their reaction was mainly, 'My God, people are actually doing business with strangers over the Internet, how can that be?'" says Omidyar.

Omidyar had come armed with statistics and overhead slides. He had charts showing eBay's rapid growth: listings were up 20 to 25 percent a month, and the value of the items sold in 1997 was projected to increase eightfold over that of 1996. The slides, prepared by the PR firm, trumpeted the core message of the trip: that "eBay is proven, fun, and safe." Omidyar discussed the mechanics of the Feedback Forum and how it provided users with an incentive to be honest. When buyers reported that they had been defrauded, Omidyar explained, eBay asked them to file a complaint with the

National Fraud Information Center or the U.S. Postal Service, and to provide eBay with a copy so it could suspend the offending user. In a recent month, as one overhead slide illustrated, there had been 1 million auctions, and fewer than thirty complaints filed with the fraud information center or the Postal Service. Of course, there were more actual cases of fraud than were reported to eBay, Omidyar conceded. But the number of complaints was so low, he insisted, that eBay compared favorably to traditional off-line retailing.

The eBay Vision Tour was at best a limited success. It introduced Omidyar to East Coast opinion makers, and prepared them for the day when eBay would become too big to ignore. But as a vehicle for generating immediate coverage and for driving more traffic to the site, it was a disappointment. Fox Television abruptly canceled its meeting with Omidyar. The newspaper and magazine reporters he met with were polite but cool. "*Fortune* said it sounds kind of neat, keep us posted, but we're not going to write about it anytime soon," says Wong.

Back in Campbell, Song was running into similar problems. Now that eBay was ready to grow, and she was authorized to pitch the eBay story as aggressively as she wanted, it turned out that the media was not interested. Song tried dangling different angles in front of reporters—the novelty of online auctions, the community forming on the message boards, Omidyar and Skoll and their start-up dreams. But the reporters she spoke to, already stretched thin covering the tech explosion of the late 1990s, did not consider a fledgling online auction site especially newsworthy.

Song was feeling particularly discouraged one day when she was visiting her friend Pam Wesley, Omidyar's fiancée. As it happened, Wesley had a frustration of her own: since she had moved to Silicon Valley with Omidyar, she had been having a hard time, she told Song, finding people who shared her interest in collecting and trading PEZ dispensers. That was when Song came up with eBay's creation myth.

Song decided to tell reporters that Omidyar had invented eBay to help Pam trade PEZ dispensers. "Nobody wants to hear about a thirty-year-old genius who wanted to create a perfect market," she thought to herself. "They want to hear that he did it for his fiancée." When she mentioned it to Omidyar, he was game to go along with it. Song called a reporter she knew and told him that the official story of eBay's founding was all the stuff about perfect markets, but the real inspiration had been trading PEZ. "Sure enough, we were in the paper the next day." With that brief write-up in a local newspaper's tech pages—the first of countless eBay feature stories to relate the PEZ anecdote—a legend was born. And a small irony: that a company built on a philosophy of openness and honesty toward its community was finally noticed with the help of a well-crafted lie.

◆

In October, Karin Stahl, employee number thirty-five, was hired to work with eBay's highest-volume sellers. Stahl, frizzy-haired and partial to Birkenstocks and hippie dresses, was typical of many of eBay's early employees. That is, she was a lot like Omidyar. The daughter of German immigrants, Stahl grew up in Silicon Valley back when it was still orange groves. She had always planned to be a teacher. But she graduated from college during the recession of the late 1980s, when California's public schools weren't hiring. Stahl bought some time with a two-year stint teaching English in Venezuela, but when she returned to the Bay Area and schools still weren't hiring, she decided to go where the jobs were: technology.

Like Omidyar, Stahl was drawn to Apple. She, too, was a natural fit for its iconoclastic culture. She got a job in the developer-relations department, but not long after she arrived the company began undergoing a transformation. Steve Jobs was on the way out, and layoffs were starting. Stahl decided to get out before the ax fell on her. She had a cousin working at a dot-com job, and she kept hearing that the Internet was the next big thing. Since she did not have an MBA, Stahl thought it made sense to try to get in early. But when she sent out feelers, the only job opening that came back was one at eBay. Stahl was not enthusiastic. "I had this impression of what an auction was," she says. "A high-end, snooty thing." But since it was her sole Internet prospect, she decided to go for an interview.

When Stahl arrived at eBay headquarters, she could see right away that snootiness was not the problem. This was one auction house, it turned out, that conducted its interviews in a large room called "the Beach," furnished with beach chairs. Most of the staff worked at desks in that same large room, which gave the office an open, communal feeling. Work stopped every day at 3:00 P.M. for a companywide game of Nerf soccer, and when things were slow, someone would run out to the nearby Century Theater to buy tickets, and the whole office would spend the afternoon watching a bad movie.

Nor, Stahl quickly realized, was she underqualified. Her insecurity about not having an MBA disappeared when she realized that neither did her two interviewers, Song and Antognini. In fact, if Stahl had known how desperate eBay was to attract workers, she might have worried she was overqualified. EBay was still largely unknown, and the whole idea of online auctions struck many people as vaguely disreputable. "Gosh, for the first year I was employed, my mother was convinced I worked for an Internet porn site," recalls Sonny Wagner, an early customer-support representative. With the Silicon Valley labor market as tight as it was, Omidyar and Skoll were grabbing new employees anywhere they could find them. Kristie Reed, who started at eBay the same day as Stahl, had been working for a water-purification company in the same building when Chris Agarpao urged her to submit a résumé. Debbie Bailey, who joined the billing department as employee number thirty-nine, had been styling the hair of an eBay employeé, who suggested she apply. When the mailman arrived at the office each day, the running joke was about asking him if he could upgrade to e-mail. If he could, they would have hired him away from the Postal Service.

Stahl took to the eBay culture immediately, and accepted the company's job offer. When she reported to work, however, she was still a little puzzled about exactly what her new position entailed. Her job description said she was responsible for working with eBay's high-volume sellers. EBay had been hearing anecdotal reports that people were quitting their jobs to sell on the site—a development the company was eager to encourage. Omidyar and Skoll believed eBay's top sellers must have special needs, and they wanted Stahl to find a way for the company to address them. Stahl began by designing a survey, but she found that Mike Wilson's staff was too busy working on site maintenance and adding new features to help with her research assignment. It took her months of quiet lobbying to get them to produce a list of eBay's top sellers. When she got it, she began calling them personally.

Back in the fall of 1997, eBay's top users were not a fancy group—there were none of the car dealers or jewelry sellers who would come later. Most of the people Stahl reached by phone went to garage sales and Goodwill stores, bought up boxes of miscellaneous junk, and listed it on eBay, working out of a den or a spare bedroom. The few who specialized at all mainly sold low-end collectibles like Beanie Babies or dolls. Stahl found in her informal survey that eBay's top sellers were doing fine on their own. The biggest complaint she heard was a minor one: that, not infrequently, eBay's credit card verification company wrongly rejected their fee payments, and they were temporarily prevented from listing. The top sellers also wanted help getting through to eBay customer service, which always had a significant backlog. Stahl worked out the problems with the verification company, and she came up with a low-tech solution to the problem of customer-service delays. When a top seller needed help, Stahl walked over to the customer-support department, tapped a representative on the shoulder, and got him to take the call.

For its first year, the program Stahl was running did not have a name. She asked the top sellers for suggestions, but the ones that came in—Premium Sellers, Premiere Sellers, and Top Sellers—all struck her as too hierarchical for a company committed to providing a level playing field for all of its users. In the end, Stahl came up with a name herself: Powersellers. It suggested, she felt, that the top sellers had been empowered by eBay, but not that they were superior to those who sold less.

Her colleagues did not know it when she was hired, but Stahl had come to eBay with an ulterior motive. Despite her flower-child appearance, Stahl was an evangelical Christian. Through her faith, she had become deeply concerned about poor children around the world. In the summer of 1997, just before she started at eBay, Stahl had traveled to Guatemala to visit a child she was sponsoring through a charity called Compassion International. Compassion had asked her, while she was in Guatemala, to make a delivery to a struggling school it was working with in another part of the country. In the final days of her Guatemala trip, Stahl took a ferry across Lake Atitlán and found her way to San Pedro La Laguna, a Mayan village of twelve thousand.

As Stahl walked the dusty, rock-strewn roads of the village she was struck by how untouched it was by modern times. The locals still spoke Tz'utujil, an ancient Mayan language, and many still wore brightly colored traditional garb. Families were packed into crumbling adobe homes and wood huts, most without electricity or running water. There was no health clinic, and witch doctors still did a brisk business whispering incantations and dispensing herbal remedies in the darkness of the forest. Disease was rampant, and many children died of preventable illnesses. Stahl struck up a quick friendship with the husband-and-wife team who ran the school Compassion had sent her to visit. Although she had not yet figured out how, she told them that when she got back to Silicon Valley and settled into her new job, she would find a way to help them.

◆

During the September switchover from AuctionWeb to eBay, the site got a new home page. With all the effort the engineers expended keeping eBay running during the transition, no one had paid much attention to the niceties of designing the new page, and it showed. This was the first home page to have the name eBay on it, and the first to be in color, but it was strikingly ugly. The word *eBay* was written out in simple block letters, and the two most elaborate graphic touches were a steaming cup of coffee to signify the eBay Café, and an open book that was intended — for no obvious reason — to illustrate the phrase "list an item for sale." The new logo was better than the boxy black-and-white AuctionWeb logo, which was so sinister the eBay staff had taken to calling it the "death bar," but not by much. Steve Westly implored Skoll to come up with a redesign soon. The current home page, he complained, was scaring away potential corporate partners.

In fact, a redesign was in the works. Benchmark had been advising eBay on the importance of building its brand. On Bob Kagle's suggestion, eBay had retained Bill Cleary of CKS Interactive, Silicon Valley's leading branding expert, to reposition the eBay brand and redesign its website. CKS conducted customer surveys and came back with good news. Users had strongly positive feelings about eBay, and the brand did just what branding consultants want brands to do: it conveyed a crisp, clear message about what the company was trying to be. EBay had always stuck tightly to its mission of being an online trading platform, and that focus had helped it avoid the trap so many other dot-coms had fallen into—being a vague solution to a vague problem. "It was probably the smartest thing we did, not selling ourselves as the 'Backbone of the Internet,' or something like that," says Maria Lee, one of eBay's first marketing employees.

But eBay clearly needed a new logo. In about a month, CKS designed five or six prototypes for eBay to choose from, including the one that would eventually become famous: the letters e-b-a-Y written out in bright primary colors. It was the most fun choice, certainly, but it was also intended to suggest larger themes. The primary colors, engaging in an almost childlike way, had a retro feel, harking back to the psychedelia and flower power of the 1960s, a formative era for eBay's many baby boomer users. The four letters of the logo overlapped with each other, suggestive of the ties binding the eBay community together. The letters also had what graphic artists call "baseline shifts," meaning the letters were not on a straight line. That quirky lineup gave the logo an offbeat feel, reflecting that eBay was not Nieman-Marcus or Tiffany's. Then there was the issue of capitalization. The Cleary designers first tried the logo with a capital B, the way eBay was spelled out in print. But as one of the designers says, they found that the B was like an enormous roadblock in the middle of the name. Instead, they capitalized the Y, another way of being quirky and different. Branders like to say that branding is about personality, and the new logo was an attempt to capture eBay's distinctive personality—and Omidyar's. "It was friendly, open, and accessible," says Cleary. "And it had a little bit of the pony-tail about it."

The new home page called for a white background, rather than the existing dull gray one. Now it was Mike Wilson's turn to be whimsical. Instead of changing the background from gray to white at the same time as the new home page was launched, he decided to alter the color one hexadecimal value at a time. The background would gradually become more white day by day, until it was completely white on Christmas—eBay's version of a white Christmas, as Wilson put it. The transition snuck up on the eBay community, but by mid-December, posts began appearing on the message boards from users wondering which was changing, eBay's home page or their eyesight.

◆

In October 1997, eBay yielded to the inevitable: it hired its first lawyer. True to its thrifty nature, eBay was not looking for high-priced legal talent, which was just as well, since the nation's leading lawyers were hardly clamoring to make the move to Greylands Business Park. EBay retained a headhunter, who proceeded to call the young associates at Cooley Godward, one of Silicon Valley's top corporate law firms, in alphabetical order. She made it as far as the H's without encountering anyone willing even to consider taking the job. Then she reached Brad Handler, a corporate lawyer two years out of the University of Virginia law school, who took the call only because he thought it was someone else. As it happened, Handler had worked at Apple before law school, and had spent a few hours on eBay looking for computer parts. He was intrigued enough to agree to an interview, and then to accept a job offer.

When Handler showed up as employee number thirty-six, he had the same reaction many early eBay employees did: a sinking feeling he had made a terrible mistake. Coming from the plush world of corporate law, Handler was more chagrined than most to be pointed in the general direction of a desk kit, handed some tools, and told to get to work. Some of his new colleagues, he noticed unhappily, were working in beach chairs. In deference to his professional status, Handler was given $150 to go out and buy an office chair. Then there was the matter of an office. He had assumed that as someone who had to deal with confidential information on a regular basis he would naturally be given one, but all he got was a cubicle. "I thought to myself, I don't know if this is going to work out," Handler recalls.

After he settled in, Handler was amazed at how chaotic eBay's legal situation was. As an intellectual property lawyer, he was particularly pained to see that eBay had not bothered to patent a single aspect of its site. It seemed to him that the Feedback Forum, the bidding algorithms in AuctionWeb's code, and other early Omidyar innovations "cried out for patents." If eBay had bothered to apply, it was likely the U.S. Patent and Trademark Office would have awarded it quite a few.* But when Handler arrived, the damage had been done: patent law requires an application to be filed within one year of disclosure.

Patents on eBay's most important innovations would have been enormously lucrative, and would have made it far more difficult for rivals to move into the online auction space. Many of eBay's key features, from feedback ratings to the way in which categories were laid out, were freely copied by virtually all of its competitors. It was not just carelessness and the general chaos of AuctionWeb's early days that prevented eBay from applying for patents. The libertarian Omidyar, who had founded AuctionWeb to keep the Internet open and accessible to all, was just not the sort to lock up intellectual property rights by patenting key technology.

*The patent office was liberal in allowing patents of Internet technology—some said too liberal. There would be a firestorm in September 1999, when Amazon.com announced it had been awarded a patent for its one-click ordering technology, and that it was suing Barnes & Noble for infringement. Critics argued it was too generic an application—and too important for e-commerce—for any one company to have the exclusive rights.

Handler was too late to fight the patent war, but he was in time for another battle, which would ultimately prove more important for eBay's long-term success. It was critical that eBay establish the principle that it was "only a venue," and therefore not legally responsible for items sold on the site. This was, at the time, far from a settled question of law. The Telecommunications Act of 1996 gave ISPs like AOL safe haven, recognizing as a matter of law that they were like telephone lines, mere conduits for the information they transmitted. But eBay was in a legal netherworld. If it was functioning like newspaper classifieds, as eBay argued, it should not have been responsible for illegal and misrepresented listings. But if it was more like a land-based store, as its critics maintained, it might have had an obligation to investigate and stand behind the items it sold.

In Handler's first weeks on the job, eBay got a letter squarely raising the issue of its legal duties. It was from a luxury watchmaker complaining about knock-off watches being sold on the site. The watchmaker wanted to know what eBay planned to do about this infringement on its intellectual property rights. Pulling down illegal auctions sounded like a reasonable enough request. But eBay wanted to avoid taking responsibility for actively vetting its millions of auctions in advance—an undertaking that would be so labor-intensive it could have put eBay out of business. Handler's response to the watchmaker was that eBay had no duty to look for infringing items itself, but if the watch company notified it of a specific illegal item being sold, eBay would end the auction.

The watchmaker agreed. Handler wandered into eBay's three-member customer-service department and asked for a volunteer to be the watch company's "buddy," someone it could report infringing items to and ask questions of by e-mail. It was the start of eBay's "Legal Buddy" program. Eventually, companies like Louis Vuitton, Disney, and Planet Hollywood, and individuals like the rock group Hanson and actress Jennifer Love Hewitt would sign "Buddy Agreements," and conduct their own searches of the eBay site, looking for infringing items. EBay, for its part, kept its promise to remove illegal items that it was notified about. Microsoft would eventually become one of the most active members of the program, fighting aggressively to prevent the sale of pirated software on the site.

EBay worked with law enforcement to track down buyers and sellers who engaged in fraud of all kinds — misrepresenting items, accepting payment and not sending the goods, or bouncing checks. In his first month on the job, Handler spoke to the director of the local FBI office about joining forces to fight online auction fraud. In time, eBay would also cooperate with the U.S. Postal Service, and with prosecutors and police departments around the country. Users who were taken advantage of often argued that eBay bore some responsibility and had the financial resources to compensate them. But as with pirated goods, eBay insisted that in cases of fraud or theft it was a witness, not a responsible party. "If a deal goes bad with someone from the *Washington Post* classifieds, you don't go to the *Washington Post* and say 'make me whole,'" says Handler. "What you do is go after the bad guy."

chapter four

In October 1997, Omidyar and Skoll's greatest nightmare came to pass: eBay was confronted by its first large, well-funded competitors. EBay was no longer the fledgling site it had been in its early AuctionWeb days. There were now 300,000 registered users, twice the number of just six months earlier, and it was hosting 115,000 auctions a day, up from just 45,000 in April. But Auction Universe and Onsale Exchange had powerful backing, and each had a real chance of knocking eBay out of first place.

The Auction Universe threat came from old friends. Mark Del Vecchio and Larry Schwartz had failed to persuade Times Mirror to pay $40 million for eBay, but they had succeeded in piquing the media giant's interest in online auctions. In August, Times Mirror had gone bargain hunting and quietly picked up Auction Universe, the number two person-to-person auction site, for just $200,000. The company then installed Schwartz as Auction Universe's new CEO. Times Mirror got what it paid for with Auction Universe: the site had only about a thousand auctions going at any given time, and its technology was a mess. After the purchase, the company closed Auction Universe down for two weeks to give it a badly needed overhaul.

Auction Universe's site was in many ways similar to eBay's. It offered its own version of the Feedback Forum, although it decided against allowing users to actually import their ratings from eBay. Auction Universe even offered a few things eBay did not. Among these was BidSafe, a $19.95-a-year service that allowed sellers to accept credit cards, which the company would process and credit to a user's account. But Schwartz's big idea for wresting the lead from eBay was editorial content. He believed that as a media-company-owned site, Auction Universe could distinguish itself by including articles about auction strategy and collecting on the site. Schwartz hired a colorful North Georgia journalist named G. Patton Hughes, who had been producing an online newsletter about online auctions, to do the writing. There was, however, one area in which Auction Universe was notably deficient: community. The site started out with no message boards. In time, it added boards that were hosted on another website, but these distant boards, which required clicking away from the Auction Universe site, never became popular.

The other major threat to eBay came from Onsale. Onsale was no newcomer to online auctions; it had been auctioning off excess computer parts even before Omidyar created AuctionWeb. With 400,000 registered users, Onsale was the leader in online auctions, and as a publicly traded company, it had access to money and media. But Onsale had, of course, always been a "merchant site," which took possession of goods—mainly remaindered and close-out items—and auctioned them off itself. It had never competed directly with eBay in the person-to-person auction space. Lately, however, Skoll had been hearing through the Silicon Valley grapevine that Onsale was up to something. Not long after the rumors started, Onsale approached eBay to ask about buying the e-mail addresses of its registered users. EBay refused. But after it did, Mike Wilson noticed "bots," or automated data harvesting devices, crawling across the site and collecting the same users' e-mail addresses eBay had declined to sell. Wilson traced these electronic intruders back to Onsale. EBay sent a letter to Onsale's cofounder and CEO, Jerry Kaplan, asking him to desist. But the bots kept coming.

On Halloween, eBay's suspicions were confirmed. Onsale launched OnSale Exchange, a new person-to-person auction site. Using the e-mail addresses harvested by its bots, Onsale spammed eBay's users, inviting them to try the new site. As an incentive, Onsale Exchange would be free for the month of November. While the spam ricocheted through eBay's networks—threatening to lure away its most loyal users—eBay management anguished over how to respond. Their mood was somber, but the scene was surreal. In typical eBay style, the staff had decided to come to work that day in Halloween costumes. So Skoll was dressed as Sonny Bono while he worked with Brad Handler, made up as a Denver Broncos fan, on a sharply worded cease-and-desist letter to Kaplan. Keith Antognini, who played an important role in the discussions because he had previously worked at Onsale, offered strategic advice while dressed as a cow, complete with udders. Omidyar, ominously, had come to work that day outfitted as the Grim Reaper.

Across the country in Vermont, Jim Griffith was spending Halloween at home monitoring the eBay boards. An agitated Song called him to say that someone named AuctionGal had appeared on the eBay Café to announce that she had just discovered a great new auction service called Onsale. AuctionGal included the Onsale URL, and urged eBay users to check it out. It was considered bad form to promote a rival auction site on the eBay boards, and by the time Griffith checked in, some of the other posters were already flaming AuctionGal.

EBay's engineers looked up AuctionGal's user information and found that the ID belonged to Michelle Pettigrew, Onsale's vice president of marketing and public relations, who also happened to be Kaplan's fiancée. Griffith went on the boards and told the community who AuctionGal was, and why she was promoting Onsale. Then he declared that he was getting out his "virtual paddle" to administer "bottom reddening sessions" to Pettigrew. When he put up a post saying he was serving her "a piece of spam pie," other posters joined in, throwing virtual blueberry pies at her. Antognini, who knew Pettigrew from his Onsale days, watched happily as Griffith completed the humiliation. "He made a complete fool out of her," Antognini says.

◆

Humiliation alone, however, would not be enough to hold back competitors from the now hotly contested person-to-person online auction space. EBay had suddenly gone from peace to a two-front war. As commander of the eBay army, Skoll set up a war room in a spare office at eBay headquarters. The walls were covered with army camouflage; mosquito netting dangled from the ceiling. Old bazookas were casually strewn around. The troops who reported for combat— Skoll, Omidyar, Song, Handler, and Wilson—were issued military helmets and dog tags. On a more practical note, Skoll had set up two computers in the room, one to monitor Onsale, the other to track Auction Universe. EBay's army kept a close watch on the two enemy sites, bidding on them to see how well they operated, and tabulating and posting the number of listings on Auction Universe and Onsale on a daily basis.

As part of the war effort, eBay launched a public-relations attack on Onsale. "The spin was, here was a big company trying to crush a little community," recalls Skoll. EBay charged that Onsale's unsolicited e-mail promotions flouted the unwritten ethical code of the Internet. "We're shocked that Onsale, a public company with a responsibility to its shareholders, would stoop to such desperate tactics," Omidyar told reporters. Onsale tried to argue that the e-mails it sent out were not spam at all. "We collected those publicly displayed addresses and did a one-time message, suggesting that people might want to take a look at our related offerings," Kaplan said. "The e-mail was targeted to an interested audience." Then, playing right into the bully's role eBay had cast it in, Onsale threatened to send its lawyers after eBay if it complained about the spam anymore. "Their attempts to damage our reputation are inappropriate and likely a libelous interference with our business," Kaplan said.

Onsale's spam, which at first seemed like a shrewd marketing tactic, proved to be a major blunder. It was exactly the wrong way for a person-to-person auction site, which depends on its reputation as an honest broker, to market itself to new users. "In a single act they demonstrated in a way we never could that this would not be a very good community if it was based on deceit and taking something that wasn't theirs," says Westly. The spam also turned out to be representative of a larger problem: Onsale's complete tone deafness on issues involving community. An important factor in eBay's rise was the upbeat, trusting environment Omidyar fostered on the site. Kaplan, by contrast, set a tone of competitiveness, even ruthlessness, on Onsale Exchange. "We're creating a whole new way to sell goods that appeals to male hunting instincts, to male gamesmanship, competition, and skill," Kaplan boasted in an interview.

Another problem with Onsale Exchange was that it failed to convince users that it was the sort of fair, neutral broker eBay had always been. In Omidyar's model, eBay was no more than a middleman. It had no reason to favor buyers or sellers; its only economic interest was encouraging listings and completed transactions. Onsale, which was itself a seller on the merchant part of its site, seemed to be more interested in high prices for sellers than bargains for buyers. Its version of a "Dutch" auction, notably, was more weighted toward sellers than eBay's. In an eBay Dutch auction, multiple identical items are listed for sale, and once all the bids are in, all of the highest bidders get the item for the lowest successful bid. But in Onsale's "Yankee Auction," the highest bidders paid the amount they actually bid. It was a subtle difference, but one that clearly favored sellers. If fifty items were up for sale, and the top fifty bids ranged from twenty-five dollars to seventy-five dollars, on eBay all of the top fifty bidders would pay just twenty-five dollars; in Onsale's Yankee Auction, they would pay up to seventy-five dollars.

On the second front in eBay's war, Auction Universe seemed at first like an even more formidable adversary. As soon as Times Mirror acquired it, listings began to shoot up—by March, there were as many as five thousand listings at a time—and there were a few product categories, including Beanie Babies, where it was especially strong. Enough buyers were finding their way to Auction Universe that its sell-through rate, the percentage of listed items that actually sold, was nearly 55 percent, not much less than eBay's. And the number of listings continued to build, rising over the summer to some fifteen thousand. That was still far fewer than eBay had, but from the vantage point of the war room, this steadily growing site, backed with the money and resources of one of the nation's largest media empires, was a cause for alarm.

Then something surprising happened: Auction Universe's listings and registered users began to level off. In part, the problem lay with the site itself. There was no mistaking its corporate orientation—it was slick, lacking eBay's quirky charm. One online reviewer, who rated all the major auction sites operating at the time, gave Auction Universe high marks for site mechanics but faulted it for having "no distinct personality." EBay had always understood the virtue of keeping things simple; the site still offered little more than listings, a search engine, message boards, and the feedback forum. By contrast, Auction Universe's well-funded, overly planned site had a frenetic quality: it bombarded visitors with escrow services, a frequent buyers program, an elaborate powersellers area called Merchant Central—and, of course, many articles written by G. Patton Hughes. Users complained that it was hard to find the auctions.

At the same time, the advantages of being owned by a major media company—the attribute Omidyar and Skoll had always feared most in a competitor—proved to be overstated. Times Mirror's plan was to promote Auction Universe in its nationwide chain of newspapers, using well-placed advertisements and editorial content to steer readers to the site. On the day of the launch, full-page ads appeared in the *Los Angeles Times*, the *Baltimore Sun*, the *Hartford Courant*, and *Long Island Newsday*. The company's internal projection was that the ads would generate at least 35,000 new registered users. In fact, they produced just 200.

In the end, what hurt Auction Universe most was simply a lack of users. When buyers showed up at the site, they found that there was not much for sale—certainly far fewer items than on eBay. Sellers, for their part, found that there were few buyers. A reviewer from *PC Magazine* compared the photo equipment categories on eBay and Auction Universe. EBay listed 2,500 cameras and more than 1,300 lenses. Auction Universe had 8 cameras and no lenses. The reviewer liked the mechanics of the Auction Universe site, but he recommended that his readers go to eBay, because that's where the cameras were. It was Auction Universe's undoing. "We were advertising and promoting the online auction experience," says Hughes. "Then people would come to Auction Universe, do a search, and end up going to eBay."

The key to eBay's defeat of Auction Universe and Onsale Exchange, it turned out, was its first-mover advantage. "First-mover advantage" was perhaps the most oversold catchphrase of the Internet bubble. In the then prevailing e-commerce metaphor, cyberspace was a high-tech land rush, whose riches would belong forever to whoever claimed territory and put down stakes first. At the height of the bubble, Wall Street analysts drew up complex financial models purported to show that the company that was first to market was worth at least twice as much as a similar company that got into the space later. Adherents of the first-mover doctrine liked to point to online bookstores: Amazon got in early, and Barnes & Noble and Borders, despite their enormous land-based presence and financial resources, found it hard to catch up. But the truth was that first-movers were left behind as often as they prevailed. AOL pulled ahead of CompuServe and Prodigy; Microsoft's Internet Explorer web browser passed Netscape, which had itself unseated Mosaic, the first-mover. After a few years of seeing first-movers lose out, some Internet consultants began to reverse the presumption and talk, with no more hard evidence, about a "second-mover" or "fast-follower" advantage.

In the case of online auctions, however, the first-mover advantage was real. In part it was because "switching costs" were so high on eBay. Consumers will stay with a given provider, economists explain, when the cost of switching is more than the gains they are likely to achieve from the switch. People rarely switch primary-care doctors, for example, because of the time and effort involved in locating a good doctor, transferring medical and billing records, and educating the new doctor about their medical history. But people switch long-distance carriers often, in exchange for a small financial incentive, because the inconvenience involved is minimal. In general, switching costs in e-commerce are lower than in off-line retailing. With a few mouse clicks, a buyer can move from one online seller to another.

But with eBay, registered users had a significant investment in remaining on the site. They had reputations, in the form of Feedback Forum ratings reflecting months, even years, of online activity. If they switched to Onsale Exchange or Auction Universe, they would have to leave those ratings behind. It would be like a businessman closing up shop in a town where he was well known and starting over somewhere new. The strength of eBay's online community also made switching costs high. The friends community members made on message boards, and the connection they felt to people like Uncle Griff and Pongo, would all be lost. "It's not so much that our users were that loyal to eBay," Song says. "EBay was part of the equation, but they were really loyal to each other."

The other reason eBay's first-mover advantage was so real was that its rise was a product, as Omidyar and Skoll liked to say, of a "virtuous cycle." Buyers came to eBay because it was where all the sellers were; sellers came because it was where all the buyers were. Once eBay achieved critical mass, which it did early on, it would have made no sense for users to go to any other site. Buyers who did were less likely to find what they were looking for; sellers were less likely to get a good price. The virtuous cycle does not operate for traditional, one-to-many e-commerce sites—a company selling books, say, or toys. The products and prices offered by those sites do not depend on who else is shopping there. But for online networks like eBay, where the user experience is almost completely determined by the other users of the site, being the first to build up a large network gives a site a critical edge. It was the difference, as the *PC Magazine* reviewer observed, between being able to offer 2,500 cameras and 8.

EBay's virtuous cycle was a specific instance of an Internet phenomenon called "network effects." An interactive technology has value only if many people use it: when one person has a telephone, it is worthless; the more people who have phone service, the more useful phones become. Robert Metcalfe, the founder of the Internet networking company 3Com, quantified—and immortalized—that concept in Metcalfe's Law, which holds that the utility of a network equals the number of users squared. A network that has twice the number of users as another network is actually four times as valuable. When a traditional e-commerce site adds a new user, it is adding only one new relationship: the site can sell products to that new user. But every new member added to a network like eBay represents not just a single networked relationship, but a relationship with all other eBay users. Those eBay relationships work in both directions: anyone in the network can buy from or sell to the new user.

It is not hard for a would-be competitor to create a traditional "one-to-many" e-commerce business: all it takes is a website, a product, and a delivery system. But it is considerably more difficult to build up a network that can compete with an existing one like eBay. In October 1997, eBay had 300,000 users—a small fraction of what it would later have, but more than enough to constitute critical mass. "We had a big magnet, which was eBay, and all these little magnets came along and tried to pull people away," says Omidyar. "But eBay's magnet was so powerful it was hard for them to get started."

Auction Universe stuck it out for a while, but it was unable to resume its upward trajectory. Times Mirror sold the site to Classified Ventures, a consortium of eight newspapers that hoped to use it to sell more classified advertising. Auction Universe, which changed its name to Auctions.com, never again posed a real challenge to eBay.

Onsale, for its part, eventually sued for peace. Jerry Kaplan approached eBay about combining into a single company, which he proposed to call eSale, and he offered to let eBay's management run the combined company. The one appealing aspect of joining forces was Onsale's vastly superior technology. Its back-end operations looked, according to one eBay executive who inspected them, "like the cockpit of the starship *Enterprise*." But in the end, eBay decided the answer was to buy more servers and upgrade eBay's technology—not to join forces with the hated Onsale.

◆

From the moment they arrived at eBay, Steve Westly and his team dreamed of the Big Deal. There were a few Internet companies— starting with America Online, Yahoo!, and Microsoft—that had access to the kind of traffic that could completely transform eBay. But it was AOL, above all, that the Westly team had set its sights on. Like eBay, AOL was a true online community, with registered members and proprietary chat and hobby areas. At the time, Internet snobs liked to look down on AOL users as the rubes of cyberspace, but AOL's solidly middle American users were, in fact, just the kind of people who were also flocking to eBay. EBay and AOL started talking, but Westly was wary. AOL's negotiators were notorious for driving hard bargains, and there would be a lot to fight over: price, of course, but also critical issues about where to place ads on the AOL site so they would reach eBay's ideal prospective customers. "One of the mistakes a lot of Internet companies made when they did deals with the larger companies was to assume that all traffic is equal," says Tom Adams.

The negotiations, which were held at eBay headquarters, were contentious from the start. The two sides were at odds on a basic point. EBay wanted to start with a small contract, then evaluate how it was working before making a long-term, high-priced commitment, but AOL did not like to enter into tactical deals with the possibility that they might develop into broader strategic relationships. "Normally we believe you can't live together; you have to get married," says Myer Berlow, who headed up the AOL negotiating team. Berlow's marriage proposal called for a $1.5 million dowry from eBay, in exchange for which eBay would gain a long-term relationship, with significant ad placements and hand-holding by AOL's marketing staff. Westly countered that the most eBay could possibly afford was $300,000 for a thirty- to ninety-day deal. In that case, Berlow said, eBay would just get some relatively ineffective banner ads, and it would not be allowed to work with the A-team in AOL's marketing department. "You get the banner guy," Westly recalls the AOL negotiators saying. "I think he has a college degree, but maybe not."

It was, of course, bluster on both sides. Westly believed a deal with AOL was critical for eBay, and he was willing to pay more if he had to. AOL was just as eager to work out a relationship with eBay. In part, it was simply that AOL was in the business of selling ads, and did not want eBay to walk away from the deal. But, AOL was also in the business of spotting Internet up-and-comers, and Berlow says that AOL's higher-ups sensed that eBay was on the verge of breaking out. "We could see that Omidyar's vision was massive," Berlow says. "And eBay had a spirit about it. Like we used to say in the early days of AOL, 'It's not a job, it's a jihad.'" In the end, eBay and AOL met in the middle: $750,000 for a six-month deal. Westly could return to eBay's management team victorious.

Or so he thought. The three most powerful people at eBay at the time were Omidyar, Skoll, and Mike Wilson. Wilson's status was something of an anomaly. Based on his position as head of technology, he should not have had much say in business-development deals, but influence does not always follow an organizational chart. Wilson's power derived in large part from the weight his views carried with Omidyar. The two men had a friendship that predated eBay, and they shared a worldview. They were the company's two nerdy, countercultural code writers, with a similar idealism about what the Internet could be. When Wilson argued against "selling out" to the corporations, Omidyar was his most sympathetic audience. Wilson was also powerful because of the sheer force of his personality. He could be charming, as any Skippy fan from the message boards could attest, but he was also a fiery advocate for his views, outspoken, even combative, in discussing company policy with his fellow executives. Not least, Wilson's influence derived from his absolute control over eBay's technology. EBay's site was still highly unstable, and Wilson was the one who decided what stresses it could tolerate.

When Westly came back with the AOL deal, Wilson led the charge against it. Wilson saw eBay as a unique cybercommunity— like his former employer, Well Engaged—that had always been allowed to grow organically. But the business-development department wanted eBay to start paying corporate partners enormous amounts of money for new traffic. Wilson, backed by Song and a few other employees who were skeptical of corporate influence, argued it was simply unnecessary. If eBay's short history demonstrated anything, he insisted, it was that the site was perfectly capable of continuing to grow virally, as sellers and buyers referred each other to the site. Worse, he argued, the AOL deal would change the voluntary, grassroots nature of the eBay community, turning it into something crass and commercial.

The AOL deal was backwards, in Wilson's view. EBay was a special enough community that AOL should be paying to link its site to eBay's, not the other way around. When Westly boasted to the senior management team that in the deal with AOL he had "negotiated them down to twenty-five cents a click," Wilson chimed in acerbically, "Oh, great, they are going to pay us twenty-five cents a click." Westly was not amused.

As a fallback position, Wilson and his adherents argued that this particular deal was simply too expensive. Later in eBay's life, $750,000 would look like a rounding error, but at the time it struck many eBay employees as exorbitant. The staff was still following Omidyar's injunction to spend every dollar like it was their own. Scrimpers like Sandra Gaeta, who was still picking up desk kits in her uncle's truck, were especially outraged. Even eBay senior managers who were sympathetic to business-development deals worried it might be a mistake to blow almost one-quarter of the company's cash reserves on a single deal to drive traffic to the site. Skoll, normally one of Westly's strongest internal champions, was one of the waverers. "Good business fundamentals say you don't pay more than a customer is worth," says Skoll. "And we just weren't sure if the AOLs and Netscapes of the world were cost-effective."

But the Westlyites responded forcefully that the Wilson camp was being hopelessly naive about the Internet. "People were saying, 'eBay's so cool they should pay us,'" says Westly. "It doesn't work that way." Wilson's stand in favor of organic growth was equally unrealistic, according to the Westly team. Much of eBay's past viral growth, they argued, was based on hard-core collectors finding the site. The supply of these passionate buyers and sellers would eventually dry up. Deals to drive traffic were necessary if eBay was to continue its explosive rate of growth.

The Westly team had one last argument in favor of the deal: it would likely prevent AOL from getting into online auctions itself. EBay's senior managers were more worried about AOL than any other potential competitor, both because of AOL's skill at e-commerce, and because of the large overlap between the two companies' registered users. For people on the fence about the deal, like Bob Kagle, keeping AOL out of the auction space was the decisive consideration. "I thought in some ways we were paying that amount of money to keep AOL from entering the business," says Kagle. And he thought it was worth it. In the end, even Omidyar broke with Wilson and supported the deal.

When the debate wound down in late December, eBay signed a contract with AOL. Its duration, six months, was a compromise, arrived at after a series of intense negotiating sessions. Although it was longer than eBay wanted, it would give the company a wealth of data to review in deciding whether to make a longer-term commitment. Westly was under instructions, Omidyat says, to "measure [the deal] like hell to make sure we know if it's working."

Two months in, eBay found that it wasn't. The AOL ads were not delivering the amount of traffic, or generating the number of registrations, eBay was expecting. Westly approached his contacts in

AOL's marketing department—the good ones, with the college degrees—and asked them to fix it. Under the terms of the contract, AOL did not need to make any changes, and after the knockdown, drag-out negotiations they had just been through, Westly thought AOL might refuse. But AOL did exactly what eBay asked. "[Bob] Pittman always said, 'Write a contract, but put it in a drawer,'" Berlow says of his boss, who oversaw AOL's online service at the time. "You do what it takes to make the relationship work." In this case, AOL increased the number of banner ads and improved their placement on the AOL site. The changes resulted in 30 percent more traffic being driven to eBay. It was good news for eBay, but also for Westly and his team. In a few months they would have to go back to senior management all over again, and the modifications would help them make the case that the AOL relationship was working.

◆

David Irons, a Northampton, Pennsylvania, antiques dealer, was following the eBay revolution from his quaint country antique store, built on the site of a 1760s mill. Irons, a thoughtful man with the look of a humanities professor, has an academic's knack for extracting broad themes from everyday life. Many in the antiques community were rushing to eBay, and Irons could see right away that in the new order, dealers like him were in danger of being swept away.

The first sign came in the fall of 1997, when Irons stumbled on a rare fluter. A specialized kind of iron, fluters were once commonly used to make ruffles in clothing and pillowcases. They "were patented and in use long before women had the right to vote," the author of an informal history of these labor-intensive devices observes, "and given the choice I imagine most would have voted against it." David Irons knew quite a bit about fluters, but he was taken by surprise when, at an antiques show in Holland, a seller offered to sell him a 1950s Swedish chrome fluter for $40. Irons had never seen anything like it, and he knew he would have no problem reselling it for considerably more back in the United States. He bought the fluter and said he would pay $60 for any others the seller could find.

When Irons got home, he went on eBay and saw something that amazed him: a 1950s Swedish chrome fluter just like the one he had bought in Holland. The bidding for it was lively, and it sold for $475, which he considered an excellent sign. Irons e-mailed the underbidder—the buyer who had the highest losing bid—and succeeded in selling him his own identical fluter for $400. By now Irons's Dutch connection had come through for him, and he had several more 1950s Swedish chrome fluters. He sold another one to a fluter collector he knew personally, also for $400. Irons was acting in the time-honored role of a middleman. He was making a sizeable profit buying fluters for $60 and selling them for $400, but all parties to the transaction were benefiting. The Dutch seller was getting more money for his fluters from Irons than he could get in Holland. And Irons's buyers were getting an item they wanted, at a price they were willing to pay.

Then something odd happened. It turned out 1950s Swedish chrome fluters were not rare at all—there were plenty in Sweden, but no one in Sweden knew American collectors would pay $400 for them. When word got out, they began showing up on eBay regularly. Predictably, the increased supply drove down the price. Within a year of seeing the first 1950s Swedish chrome fluter sell for $475, Irons bought one on eBay, in its original box, for just $95. Economists would say eBay had made an inefficient market efficient. But from Irons's perspective, the 1950s Swedish chrome fluter market, which had been giving him more than a 500 percent rate of return, had crashed.

Irons had been disintermediated. At the height of the dot-com bubble, disintermediation was a favorite buzzword of business consultants and business journalists. The Internet, they predicted confidently, would wipe out middlemen of all kinds. Businesses and individuals who relied for their livelihood on buying undervalued merchandise in one place and selling it for a markup in another would be, as the title of an influential book put it, "blown to bits." The intellectual forebear of disintermediation was Joseph Schumpeter, the Austrian economist who argued that capitalism is inherently a force for "creative destruction" of existing institutions and distribution patterns. Disintermediation was wildly oversold: dot-coms were projecting that Americans would soon be buying almost everything—groceries, drugs, pet food—online, and that bricks-and-mortar retailers would wither away. But disintermediation was also, to a limited extent, real.

The reason was simple economics. Commerce has always been eased along by dealers, agents, and other assorted middlemen, but not every transaction requires a middleman. In 1937, Ronald Coase explained, in "The Nature of the Firm," an article for which he would win a Nobel Prize more than half a century later, that intermediaries made sense only for certain kinds of exchanges. The crucial factor, Coase argued, was whether the parties to the transaction could save more money by hiring the middleman than it cost to hire him. The Internet was driving down the value of middlemen because it was making it easier—and therefore more economically efficient—for individuals to carry out their own transactions. Europeans who owned 1950s Swedish chrome fluters, for example, could use eBay to find American collectors who wanted to buy them—without the help of David Irons.

EBay was also hurting dealers like Irons by bringing creative destruction to their traditional methods of doing business. Antiques dealers have historically relied on "pickers," buyers who go out to estate sales, flea markets, and country auctions, hunting down antiques. Pickers resell what they find to dealers, who have the expertise to know what a piece is worth, and who have retail stores from which to sell the antiques to the general public. Like many dealers, Irons had spent decades cultivating his personal network of pickers, who were an important source of inventory for his store.

But with the arrival of eBay, pickers did not need dealers like Irons to sell to the public. Anyone who listed an item on eBay had access to a retail market of millions. Having a bricks-and-mortar store, and contacts among collectors, was suddenly unimportant. Nor did pickers need a dealer's expertise to know what a particular piece was worth: they could list it on eBay, and the market would set the correct price. "It took us thirty-something years to get where we are," Irons says glumly. "But now nobody has to know anything." It did not take most pickers long to figure out that with eBay, they could do better on their own. "I know dealers who had a route; they would go to this picker, and this picker, and this picker, and they always came back with such great stuff," says Irons. "Now they tell me, and this is the honest truth, that pickers won't even open the door for them, and they bought from them for twenty years."

Ordinary sellers were abandoning dealers for the same reason pickers were. Before eBay, it was common for a dealer to show up after someone died and buy up an entire estate for a modest sum. Now, when dealers showed up, they often found the heirs in front of a computer, pricing individual items on eBay, and demanding market value. Even older sellers were increasingly computer-literate and familiar with eBay. Irons had a dealer friend who recently went to the home of an elderly man to examine his toy collection. When the dealer made an offer, the older man rejected it as too low and said he would be listing the toys on eBay.

Flea markets and antiques-and-collectibles shows were also starting to be hurt by disintermediation. At a meeting of the National Flea Market Association in Orlando, more than a hundred flea market owners jammed into a hotel ballroom for a panel discussion on the topic "The Internet: Friend or Foe?" The participants tried to see the "friend" side — the flea market association was planning to start its own online auction site — but the mood was grim. "It has the potential of absolutely destroying the business," warned Joe Spotts, the panel's organizer, who had seen the number of vendors at one trade show he owned, the Denver Collectors Fair, slump 30 percent.

Antiques stores were also feeling eBay's impact. The most resourceful had begun installing PCs on the premises and listing the contents of their stores on eBay. Some were reporting that their eBay sales were making the difference between profitability and being forced to shut down. But other antiques store owners complained that eBay was driving them out of business. A dealer from Seattle explained on an eBay message board why he was forced to close his store. "A couple years or so ago my best buyers started spending their money at eBay," he wrote. "Then my pickers started selling on eBay instead of selling to me. Then when I went to the flea market and asked how much an item was, I got quoted what one sold for on eBay, not what the seller wanted for the item. I have a toy show that sold out for years, but nowadays all my vendors sell on eBay, and all the buyers are spending their money on eBay. I used to buy and sell a lot in the toy magazines before they got reduced to mere pamphlet-sized rags. . . . Get my drift?"

EBay was not driving Irons out of business. He was fortunate to have a picturesque antiques store in a heavily touristed area; the experience his customers had buying from him could not be replicated over the Internet. To acquire inventory, he had begun marketing himself more aggressively, speaking regularly about antiques and collectibles to civic groups whose members might have items they wanted to sell. And he devoted more time to high-end products that do not sell well online. Still, Irons could see that in the age of eBay, his business would never be the same. "I get hurt, all of the dealers get hurt, but what are you going to do?" he says. "It's like selling the buggy whip for the buggies. Now you sell the tires for the cars. You adapt."

◆

Founders who will not step aside in favor of more seasoned management are a familiar Silicon Valley story. But Omidyar and Skoll were the rare exception: founders who were clear-eyed about their own limitations. "We were entrepreneurs and that was good up to a certain stage," says Omidyar. "But we didn't have the experience to take the company to the next level."

In Omidyar's case, it wasn't just a lack of business acumen that held him back. In the hard-driving world of the Internet start-ups—

where mainlining caffeine and sleeping under desks was the norm—Omidyar stood out as a passionate believer in the balanced life. He had always made a point of leaving work at the end of an eight-hour day, and expected his employees to do the same. He took vacations, and found time to enjoy the outdoors—often going snowboarding, and bringing a laptop with him to check on the site. Technology's upper ranks were filled with men like Bill Gates, Larry Ellison, and Michael Dell, who had built multibillion-dollar corporations and could not imagine handing them off to others to run. But Omidyar always insisted that he did not want to remain at the helm for the long haul. "I didn't even want to be CEO for the short haul," he says.

With a scalable site and a venture capital firm in its corner, eBay began looking for its next CEO in the fall of 1997. There was a broad consensus, both at eBay and at Benchmark, about the qualities an ideal candidate would have. Because eBay sold directly to consumers, everyone agreed that a consumer-marketing background was critical. Given how chaotic eBay's internal structure was, how much it still resembled a start-up, solid management experience was also considered important. No one particularly cared if the new CEO had a background in technology and the Internet. That could be learned. But everyone agreed that eBay's new leader had to have a deep understanding of the company's unique culture and community—had to be, in the word that Omidyar used throughout the process, eBaysian.

EBay's headhunter generated a list of candidates that was eventually whittled down to fewer than ten, and the interviews began. One Fortune 500 executive tried to show off his knowledge of online auctions by saying that although Onsale was the leader in the space, there was no reason eBay shouldn't be able to copy its success. He didn't get the job. Another candidate, with an important position at a large East Coast company, insisted on flying first class and staying at San Francisco's aristocratic Fairmont Hotel, and pulled up to eBay's threadbare headquarters in a stretch limousine. When he submitted a bill for $8,000 in expenses, Omidyar declared him the least eBaysian person he had ever met.

Then there was Meg Whitman. At first glance, she did not seem particularly eBaysian, either. Whitman had grown up on Long Island, New York, the youngest of three children in a well-to-do family. All four of her grandparents came from old Boston stock. Whitman's father made a comfortable living as a factor, someone who lends businesses money on accounts receivable. Her mother was "a mom," Whitman says, but one with latent entrepreneurial spirit. In 1973, when her children were nearly grown, Mrs. Whitman traveled to China with a women's delegation led by the actress Shirley MacLaine, one of the first groups to visit China after it was opened to the West. In her memoir of the trip, *You Can Get There from Here*, MacLaine wrote that she already had a Native American activist, a twelve-year-old volunteer in the United Farm Workers grape boycott, and a "two-hundred-pound, coal-black woman of mammoth heart" who was a voting-rights worker in Issaquena, Mississippi. MacLaine needed a "conservative Republican housewife person," she explained, but since she didn't know any, she had to ask around. Mrs. Whitman "swept into my New York apartment as if she were about to ride to the hounds," MacLaine wrote. " 'My name is Whitman, and I'm just what you're looking for,' " she said. " 'I'm conservative, tweedy, self-sufficient, and way over thirty.' " Mrs. Whitman was given the Republican housewife slot, and became one of the most popular members of the delegation. After the trip ended, she wrote a letter to MacLaine declaring herself "newly liberated" and turned travel to China into a late career, leading more than seventy government delegations and tour groups to Asia.

Meg Whitman attended Princeton, where her plans to be a doctor faltered during sophomore year organic chemistry. "That was the end of that," she says simply. She sold ads for *Business Today*, a Princeton magazine, and found that she liked it. By spring of her junior year she had decided on a career in business. After graduating in 1977 with a degree in economics, she got an MBA at Harvard. Whitman took a job with Procter & Gamble working on consumer branding, and in 1980 married Griffith R. Harsh IV, a brain surgeon. When he accepted a residency at the University of California–San

Francisco, she signed on as a management consultant in the San Francisco office of Bain & Company. One of Whitman's early projects was helping Saga Foods improve performance in the division that handled college meal service. She toured universities, talking to food service directors and students. "It was an early introduction to the importance of talking to customers," she says.

After Bain & Company, Whitman worked her way up through the ranks of corporate America, still focusing on marketing. At Disney, as senior vice president of marketing in the consumer products division, she helped Disney's theme stores move overseas, at one point spending a week of every month in Japan. When her husband was offered the directorship of the brain tumor program at Massachusetts General Hospital, Whitman became president of Stride Rite shoes, and then of Florist Transworld Delivery (FTD), which she helped transform from a voluntary association into a private business. When eBay's search was under way, Whitman was general manager of Hasbro's preschool division, in charge of global management and marketing for the Playskool and Mr. Potato Head brands. Playskool had fallen on hard times—it had lost millions the year before Whitman came in—and she was hard at work redesigning the product line and changing the advertising in an attempt to turn it around.

Whitman was "the perfect person," says Omidyar. But there was a hitch: she initially had, she says, "no interest" in the job. Whitman knew the Internet was becoming increasingly important, but she had barely used it, except to send e-mail or make an occasional travel reservation. She was happy at Hasbro, and her husband and her two sons, ages thirteen and ten, did not want to move. When David Beirne, the Benchmark partner coordinating the search, called to recruit her, Whitman turned him down.

Two weeks later, at the urging of eBay's management team, Beirne called Whitman again. He tried to explain to her why she and eBay were a perfect fit. Whitman still wasn't interested, but she was reluctant to alienate one of Silicon Valley's leading headhunters. "Mostly not to make David Beirne angry, I decided to come out and spend the day with Pierre and Jeff," she says. Whitman looked at the eBay website to prepare for the interview and, like so many before her, was not impressed. "But I had already committed," she says. "So I got on the plane."

As impressive as Whitman was on paper, eBay's search team liked her more in person. Tall and blond, with an easy smile and a direct manner, she charmed everyone she met. Whitman looked and acted the part of a CEO —she was charismatic, confident, and articulate—and had no trouble holding her own in a conversation with Omidyar and Skoll. No less important, this scion of the East Coast establishment fit in well with the quirky little start-up founded by a French Iranian and a Canadian Jew. Whitman impressed the eBay contingent, Steve Westly says, by the fact that "she didn't have a lot of airs about her." During her interview, Whitman asked a question that impressed Kagle. "If this is something I decide to do," she said, "Pierre isn't going anywhere, is he?" Just as Omidyar and Skoll were not the typical founders, intent on leading the company no matter how large it grew, Whitman was not the usual new CEO, eager to push the original management out. "She was very cognizant of the fact that this was a special thing and that Pierre had been the father of it," says Kagle. There was no real debate—a consensus formed quickly around Whitman.

Whitman, for her part, was far more impressed by eBay than she had expected. She was particularly struck that it was no ordinary e-commerce website: Omidyar had created an entirely new business, one that could not have existed without the Internet. Whitman called Beirne from the airplane to say that she was interested in talking more. If eBay still wanted her, she was willing to come back for a second visit to delve into its financials, which she had not done the first time, and meet more of the staff.

The day before Thanksgiving, Whitman returned. If the eBay search team knew the chaos she had left behind in Boston, they would not have doubted her interest. Forty people would be arriving at her home for Thanksgiving dinner the following day. Kagle picked Whitman up at the airport and drove her to Greylands Business

Park. It was raining hard, and when she arrived at eBay's building, it struck her as dark and dingy. The elevator clanked its way to the third floor, and when the door opened Whitman was relieved to see an actual receptionist sitting at a desk. Had she known that eBay had hired Kristie Reed a few weeks earlier, expressly to give eBay a professional look when CEO candidates showed up, she would have been less sanguine.

Whitman spent two hours reviewing eBay's financial records. The 30 percent month-to-month growth rate was astonishing, far greater than anything she had ever seen in the old economy. But what really amazed her was eBay's cost structure: its gross margins were 85 percent. Omidyar, for his part, was struck by Whitman's ability to make sense of eBay's books. When she pointed out eBay's gross margins, he remembers asking himself, "What are gross margins?" Whitman left this time "pretty sold on the idea," she says, of joining eBay.

That December, eBay held its holiday party at the Tech Museum of Innovation in downtown San Jose. It was a festive affair, far larger than the previous year's celebration, when the attendees had fit in a single elevator. Mike Wilson, in his persona of Skippy, invited Patti Ruby to fly in from Indiana to be his mystery date. The museum had Internet hookups, and Griffith, Song, Ruby, Wilson, and even Omidyar logged on to the eBay message boards to give the community a running commentary on the party. Griffith posted that Ruby was wearing a too-short dress and was dancing on tables. "None of it was true," Ruby says with a laugh. "But the members loved it." As a holiday gift, Omidyar had ordered forty denim-and-khaki eBay jackets. Although it was looking increasingly likely that Whitman would be eBay's next CEO, Omidyar, ever the egalitarian, made a point of not ordering a jacket for her. They were only for eBay's current staff.

After Christmas, Whitman came out to visit eBay one more time, this time with her husband and two sons. At this point, she had only one hesitation about signing on. It occurred to her that if she was going to make the leap to an Internet company, she might want to do a broader survey of the industry to make sure eBay was the right company for her. She had not had time to do that, but the eBay position just felt right. That evening, Kagle hosted a dinner at his home for the Whitman family, Omidyar, and Skoll. The mood was upbeat, and it seemed that Whitman was on the brink of accepting the CEO position. There was only one down note at the meal: eBay's growth had slowed in recent weeks, and Whitman and her husband worried out loud that eBay might turn out to be a fad. Omidyar and Skoll explained the unusual pattern to eBay's seasons—that December was always a slow time—and the Whitmans seemed to be satisfied.

When Whitman finally decided to take the job, her husband was, she says, "incredibly game." They had traded off moves in the past for each other's careers, and he was willing to let her have a turn. They both liked northern California, and thought it would be good for their boys to be exposed to technology. The only hitch was finding a job for Whitman's husband. When she came for her first interview, a few of the eBay staff members had been put off by how casually she suggested that if she accepted he could probably just join the faculty of Stanford medical school. Typical East Coast elitism, they grumbled to themselves, assuming that Stanford was an academic backwater desperate for professors. What they did not realize was that Whitman's husband was one of the nation's leading brain surgeons. When he called up the chairman of the Department of Neurology, it turned out that the department was about to post the position of head of the brain tumor program, for which he was instantly the leading candidate. "The stars aligned," says Whitman.

◆

In December 1997, David Eccles was hunched over an old PC in his wood-paneled home office in rural Mount Aukum, California, an hour's drive northwest of Sacramento, watching the final minutes of an eBay auction. Eccles stared at his monitor, making no effort to bid, as the clock ticked down toward zero. With just nine seconds left in the auction, he watched as a new high bid suddenly appeared on the screen. Before the previous high bidder could react, the final nine seconds wound down, and the last-minute bidder had won.

The final bid had come from Eccles himself, though he did not need to touch his keyboard to place it. It was delivered through a piece of "sniping" software he had just designed and was testing for the first time. Sniping, or placing a winning bid just as an auction is ending, takes advantage of an odd fact about eBay auctions: they are not true auctions at all. In a classic auction, the auctioneer yells, "Going once, going twice, sold!" before he slams down the gavel, a final invitation to anyone who wants to place a higher bid to do so. There is no time limit; the auction continues until the price goes as high as any participant is willing to pay. EBay auctions, in contrast, have fixed durations: three, five, seven, or ten days. When the official clock runs out, they end, even if someone desperately wants to place a higher bid. This quirk of eBay's auction format—which emerged, with no real planning, when Omidyar created AuctionWeb—was about to give Eccles a whole new career.

Eccles was an unlikely software entrepreneur. He conformed to none of the stereotypes: he was not young, urban, overeducated, or afraid of sunlight. With a mop of white hair and a bushy white beard, he looked like Ernest Hemingway with an Internet connection. In fact, Eccles was living a Hemingway-like existence in rural northern California, in a home that looked like a hunting lodge. When he was not writing code, he was often shooting wild birds or boar. On the floor of his home office, amid the computer disks and programming manuals, were a few double-barreled rifles and a gun that, under the strict letter of the federal law, qualified as an assault weapon.

Eccles came to the sniping software business in a roundabout way. After graduating from high school, he moved to the Caribbean to trap tropical fish for American pet stores, using a chemical, given to him by his fish-trapper father, that stunned the fish, making them easy to catch. But Eccles did not like catching fish, and he heard the fish-stunning chemical caused cancer. He returned to the United States and entered the restaurant business. After a career that took him from washing dishes at a Sambo's to managing a Western-themed family restaurant, Eccles realized he hated restaurants, too.

adam cohen

After a brief stint in construction, another bad experience, Eccles decided to support himself as a picker, buying antiques and collectibles at flea markets and garage sales, and reselling them to dealers. While he was eking out a living picking, a friend in the trucking business offered him a part-time job keeping the company's books, and Eccles taught himself computers so he could run an accounting program. In early 1997, when he was working in both antiques and computers, he stumbled across eBay. He tried taking a few of the antiques and collectibles he had been reselling to dealers, and put them up for auction on eBay.

Eccles's first items—mainly glassware, because it was cheap and easy to ship—sold easily. The prices were low, but the markups were remarkably high. Pieces of glassware he paid five dollars for at a flea market easily sold for twenty-five dollars to buyers back East. The eBay sales were soon going so well that Eccles brought in a partner, George Sedelmeir, an old prospector friend who had spent a lifetime looking for gold in abandoned mines that had been built around Mount Aukum during the Gold Rush. Eccles and Sedelmeir were doing a new kind of prospecting, and they got it down to a science: Eccles went out to flea markets with a cell phone, and before he made a purchase he called Sedelmeir, who priced it on eBay. Eccles set up a shipping station in his garage, and scheduled daily UPS pickups. The two men spent days, nights, and weekends working out of Eccles's home, buying inventory, taking digital photographs, writing listings, closing out auctions, charging credit cards, packing, and shipping. It was a living, but not an easy one.

Like many eBay sellers, Eccles had started buying things on the site, in his case, mainly copper pots for his wife, who collected them. He figured out right away that sniping was the most strategic way to bid. A well-timed snipe allowed him to win auctions with lowball bids—bids that another buyer wanted to top, but did not have time to. In those early days, Eccles sniped by hand, since there was no other way to do it. He sat at his computer with the eBay bid page open, typed in his bid, and hit the send button just as the auction was about to end. Over time, Eccles became more adept, keeping as many as fifteen browsers open at once, with different bid amounts in each. In the final seconds of an auction, he could use one browser window to snipe, and the others to respond instantly if anyone sniped back.

Eccles knew enough about computers to realize that the sniping process could be vastly improved with software. Sniping software would mean that buyers would no longer need to watch the clock, bidding manually in the final seconds of the auction. And by automating the process, sniping software would liberate snipers from their PCs: with it, they could even snipe in auctions that ended while they were at work or asleep.

All Eccles knew about computers was the little he had taught himself, to do accounting. He had never taken a formal computer class, and did not know any programmers. But working from books he bought on Amazon, Eccles taught himself how to write a sniping program that synched itself with eBay's official clock and allowed bidders to place bids up until the final seconds. In tribute to the insect whose chirping broke his concentration as he tried to write the code, he called it Cricket Jr.

Eccles's motivation for creating sniping software was purely mercenary. He had been looking for something to sell on eBay that did not require as much work as the antiques and collectibles he had been laboring over. In fact, sniping software turned out to be the perfect product. It could be copied endlessly, so his one program could be sold to thousands of buyers. Delivery was easy. He could make it available for download from a website, or slip a computer disk into an envelope and send it by regular mail. When Eccles began listing Cricket Jr. on eBay, he soon found himself selling three hundred to four hundred copies a month, at ten dollars each. The income was steady enough that by the spring of 1998 he quit the antiques-and-collectibles business to sell software full-time.

Eccles had the field to himself at first, but he knew it would not last. "I told my wife, give it three months before the competition comes," he says. Sure enough, within months a product called TurboBid appeared. More snipeware followed, with names like Winning Bid Pro, and Bay Town's Bidmaster. The competition forced

Eccles to be more aggressive about marketing. He enlisted his brother, a professional diver in the Channel Islands, to sell Cricket Jr. on a website to supplement his eBay sales. Eccles developed more products to sell—an improved version of Cricket Jr., a new software product called Cricket Master, that helps sellers manage their auctions, and Power Chat, which helps users navigate the eBay message boards.

Eccles found himself becoming more than just a software entrepreneur; he was increasingly becoming a sniping consultant. Cricket Jr. allowed the user to decide how many seconds before an auction closes to send in a bid, and Eccles's customers wanted advice about how to make that key strategic decision. "Everybody wants to snipe in the final second of an auction," says Eccles. "But I advise against it." It is too difficult, he says, to gauge how quickly a computer will send the signal, how fast it will travel over a particular Internet connection, and how efficiently the bid will be processed when it reaches eBay. Eccles recommended that his customers allow at least ten to fifteen seconds. A powerful computer or a high-speed Internet connection could shave a few seconds off, he told them, but it was risky to cut a snipe too close. One of Cricket Jr.'s competitors warned its users that 4.5 percent of snipes sent out arrived after the auction had closed.

Sniping was good to Eccles, but it also made him enemies. He got hate mail, easily delivered since he kept his e-mail address on the Cricket Jr. website. Sniping was a bitterly divisive issue on the eBay message boards, where critics attacked it as rude, unsportsmanlike, and duplicitous. Bidders who were sniped said it violated the spirit of an auction: items ended up selling not to the person who was willing to bid the most, but to the one who most deftly gamed the system. They also complained that it unduly rewarded bidders with sniping software and high-speed Internet connections over less technologically advanced users. At the same time, many sellers opposed sniping because it kept prices down. They urged eBay to follow the lead of Yahoo! and Amazon Auctions and permit a "soft close," in which auctions could be automatically extended if there was a bid in the final minutes.

EBay officially takes no position on sniping. Its answer to the complaints from buyers is to encourage them to use proxy bidding, a feature on the eBay bidding page that allows bidders to enter the maximum amount they are willing to pay for an item. EBay then acts as a proxy for the buyer, automatically bidding as much as is needed—but no more—to keep him the top bidder. Because a buyer who uses a proxy loses an auction only if the item sells for more than the maximum he has authorized, eBay says sniping is rendered ineffective. But sniping's critics respond that eBay's answer ignores the dynamic nature of an auction. The amount a buyer is willing to pay for an item is determined in part by what other buyers bid for it. It is possible, they say, for a buyer using a proxy to lose to a sniper who has bid more than his maximum bid, and still have been wronged. He has been deprived, they say, of an auction participant's inalienable right to counterbid.*

Despite the criticism, sniping—by hand, or with software—remains popular, especially with hard-core eBay buyers. One study of a thousand auctions found that of those with more than one bid, fully 18 percent were won in the final sixty seconds. Sniping was most common in categories that attracted the most sophisticated and competitive buyers. In the category Antiques: Ancient World, 58 percent of the auctions the researchers examined ended with a bid in the last minute. But in Collectibles: Weird Stuff: Totally Bizarre, none did. Another study found a direct correlation between the time a bidder had spent on eBay and the likelihood he would snipe.

Eccles has sold more than ten thousand copies of Cricket Jr., and his competitors have sold tens of thousands of their own. Eccles's home page contains testimonials from customers explaining what Cricket Jr. has meant to them. Some, improbably enough, tug at the heartstrings. One user with a tremor from Parkinson's disease told of not having a steady enough hand to win contested auctions before

---

*EBay's format implicitly acknowledges the limits of proxy bidding. EBay could require every bidder to make a single bid by means of a proxy. But what excited Omidyar about AuctionWeb from the beginning was that it would be dynamic, and real-time—a social experience in which bidders interacted with each other to produce the final price.

sniping software came along. Some of the testimonials are a bit creepy, like the customer who "smoked three other snipers bidding on the same items . . . almost like NAM . . . three shots, then move." But most focus, unsentimentally, on the bottom line. "If I use Cricket to snipe, I win," a buyer from Maryland wrote: "If I don't, I don't."

◆

As 1997 drew to a close, eBay still had fewer than fifty employees, and it retained the informal feel of a start-up. There were still Nerf soccer games and movie outings. And the staff gathered every other week in the office's large main room for a companywide meeting. As a large jar of Sweet Tarts was passed around, Omidyar or Skoll delivered a progress report and encouraged everyone to share their ideas. There were still few rules, and decisions were often made on the fly. Kristie Reed, the newly hired receptionist, recalls walking by Song's cubicle and being enlisted in a project. "Hey, give me some bad words that we need to ban from the site," Song told her. The two young women sat down at Song's workstation and made a list of dirty words that users would be prohibited from posting.

But these informal times were drawing to a close. Now that eBay was on its way to becoming a real company, Omidyar and Skoll decided the time had come to replace the beach chairs and employee-assembled desks with real furniture. EBay could easily have afforded the $650 Herman Miller Aeron chairs, $1,500 workstations, and 42-inch televisions that many dot-coms were splurging on. But a few million dollars in venture capital had not changed Omidyar's philosophy about spending. Omidyar had heard that Apple had over-ordered cubicles for its headquarters, and was willing to sell some of the extras cheaply. He drove to the warehouse himself, and when the cubicles passed his inspection, he ordered seventy. The arrival of the cubicles at the end of the year seemed like a small thing, but it completely changed the atmosphere at eBay. Employees who had worked in sight of one another were now separated by cubicle walls. And the midafternoon Nerf soccer games ended, since the playing field was now filled with workstations. The suite's main room began to feel less like a college dorm and more like an office.

Along with the cubicles, something else showed up in December — Gary Bengier, eBay's first chief financial officer. Bengier, like Westly, was a new kind of employee: he was a grown-up, and he came with relevant experience. A Harvard MBA, Bengier had worked for two decades in financial management, much of it in the tech industry. Microsoft had just swallowed up his last employer, VXtreme, a start-up that made products for streaming video over the Internet, putting him back in the job market. In deference to his high station, Sandra Gaeta informed him on his first day that she had taken the unprecedented step of assembling his desk for him.

Bengier had to rebuild eBay's finance system from the ground up. The records were still being kept on QuickBooks, and on a cash basis, not the more sophisticated accrual basis most businesses use. Other than Gaeta, who was being pulled in so many directions, eBay's financial staff consisted of a single temp from a small accounting firm, who came in every two weeks to reconcile the books one check at a time. EBay's funds were being kept in a small-business account at Wells Fargo, designed to meet the needs of an average dry cleaner. Soon after Bengier arrived, Wells Fargo cut off eBay's banking privileges: its credit card deposits were so heavy they had triggered the bank's antifraud warning system.

But what brought Bengier to eBay wasn't its sound financial infrastructure; it was levels of profitability and growth he had never before encountered. "From a CFO's point of view, this thing was gold," he says. Like Karin Stahl, Bengier had come to eBay with a hidden agenda. He had watched his last start-up, VXtreme, bungle its chance to go public, and he had vowed not to let that happen at eBay. As soon as he arrived, Bengier began quietly mapping out a schedule to take eBay public. His painstakingly prepared time line had specific dates for hiring lawyers and investment bankers, filing papers with the Securities and Exchange Commission, and launching the road show, culminating in an initial public offering on

September 24, 1998. Bengier knew he would have to show his time line to the rest of eBay's management team if it was going to have any chance of becoming a reality, but he did not want anyone outside the company to know about it. "I had this image of a submarine launching a cruise missile," says Bengier. "You make sure that it breaks the surface at just the right trajectory so it has so much speed by the time it hits the radar that it's too late for the enemy."

chapter five

In early January 1998, eBay's senior management convened for a daylong strategic off-site at Quadrus, a conference center on Sand Hill Road. Omidyar, Skoll, Bengier, Westly, Wilson, and Bob Kagle were there, along with John Thibault, eBay's first head of off-line marketing. With eBay on the brink of the first leadership change in its short lifetime, this was the last chance for the old guard to develop its vision for the future, one they could present to Whitman when she took over as CEO. The old guard had a specific idea in mind: taking eBay public by September, following Bengier's detailed timetable.

Start-ups go public for many reasons. The first, and often the overwhelming one, is money. In a hot IPO market—and early 1998 was one of the hottest—selling stock to the public is generally the best way for a company to raise money, and the most lucrative exit strategy for anyone with an equity stake. Glory is often a factor. In the great Silicon Valley entrepreneurship race, going public is the ultimate victory lap. EBay's management had those motives, but also one more: they were convinced that an IPO would be a powerful branding event for a company that was still little known to the larger world. "No one was paying any attention to us," Omidyar says. "Primarily for me it was, if we take the company public, it will be a lot easier to get the word out."

Whitman started work on February 1, unaware that her arrival was itself an item on the IPO schedule that senior management had agreed to at Quadrus. She had arranged to work only part-time the first month, and to commute back to Boston on weekends through June, when her family could join her. At Bengier's first meeting with Whitman, he took out a sheet of paper and delivered the news. "Here's the time line," he told her as tactfully as possible. "What time line?" Whitman asked. The entire management team, he told her, was committed to going public by September 24. Whitman knew when she was recruited that eBay was almost certainly headed toward an IPO, but based on what she had seen of the company, she thought it would take at least eighteen months to prepare for it. Still, after she reviewed Bengier's time line, Whitman gave it her endorsement. As it turned out, eBay would follow it for the next nine months, almost to the day.

It was not hard for Whitman to identify the flaws in eBay's internal operations. When she arrived, she bought a paper calendar for her desk and asked her senior staff to start signing up for meetings. "It seemed like the normal thing to do, but they looked at me like I'd lost it," she says. "There was a little bit of pushback." (Who pushed back was a good indication of how people felt about eBay's new direction. Bengier, Westly, and others with a corporate outlook did not object to signing up for meetings; Mike Wilson, not surprisingly, did.) It also seemed to Whitman that too many decisions at eBay were being made based on instinct, rather than on thoughtful analysis. She told Westly and Wilson she wanted to receive regular reports on "click-throughs," "reach," and other common measures of Internet performance. Whitman also began to hold regular senior management meetings.

The eBay hierarchy changed with Whitman's arrival. Omidyar, who had been CEO, moved up to chairman. Skoll, the president, became vice president of strategic planning and analysis. The other positions remained the same at first: Bengier as chief financial officer, Westly as head of business development, Wilson as head of product development, and Thibault as head of off-line marketing. As soon as she got a feel for the personalities, Whitman began to make some changes, notably combining Thibault's off-line marketing and Westly's online marketing departments into a single marketing division, under Westly's direction.

Mike Wilson, it was clear, was going to be a problem. No one questioned Wilson's brilliance, or the importance of the new architecture he created to eBay's success. But as marketing and corporate alliances—two things he detested—became more central to eBay's strategic plans, Wilson was increasingly viewed by his critics as an obstructionist force. The marketing department was convinced that Wilson was using his control over technology to block changes he did not want made. Westly was eager to develop a cobranded site with AOL, which would include both companies' logos, but Wilson opposed cobranding on philosophical grounds. Whether by coincidence or not, whenever marketing asked Wilson about the feasibility of a cobranded site, he had a reason it could not be done anytime soon. One top manager was particularly exasperated when he approached Wilson about a change in the site, a change Wilson did not favor, only to be told, "Skippy is tired."

Not surprisingly, Whitman and Wilson did not get off to a good start. Omidyar and Wilson had a strong working relationship, built on their common experiences. But Whitman did not share Wilson's love of code writing, or his fear of corporate entanglements. Wilson, for his part, could not bond with Whitman over her own area of expertise, consumer marketing. In fact, it represented everything he was working against. Despite the distance between them, and some tense early interactions, Whitman kept Wilson in his job and resolved to try to make it work.

One problem Whitman had anticipated took care of itself. Despite the slow December, the site was not losing momentum. Omidyar and Skoll had been right when they assured her, at Bob

Kagle's dinner, that eBay's traffic would surge when the holidays were over. On February 5, days after Whitman's arrival, Skoll sent around an e-mail reporting that eBay had just recorded its 6-millionth listing, a mere twenty-five days after its 5-millionth listing. "Personally, I am amazed that all those fancy numbers dancing in our business plan from way back when have become real," he wrote. EBay now had nearly 500,000 registered users, and it continued to command more than 80 percent of the consumer-to-consumer online auction space. In the first quarter of 1998, more than $100 million in goods changed hands on the site, and eBay was bringing in more than $3 million in revenue a month.

◆

In February 1998, Crystal's No Complaint Board appeared in cyberspace. Crystal was Crystal Wells-Miller, who ran an antiques store with her husband, Jim, outside Rochester, New York. Crystal and Jim had discovered eBay the previous summer, and were soon putting some of their antiques up for auction. They found, as many antiques dealers did, that most things sold better online than they would have in their store. "Sitting-on-the-shelf time was down to nothing," says Jim. "You put something up on eBay and instantly found the right buyer." Jim and Crystal did the logical thing—they shut down their store and moved their business onto eBay.

EBay made economic sense, but Crystal missed the social aspects of selling at the store. In search of human contact, she made her way to the eBay message boards. Crystal became a fixture on the Q & A Board, but she found much of the online conversation draining. Too many of the posts were complaints about eBay and other users. She told her husband she wished there were a less contentious board, one more like an online watercooler.

Jim built Crystal's No Complaint Board in response. He ran it from isplaza.com, short for Internet Service Plaza, a domain he had been using to sell antiques online. Many people, it turned out, were looking for the sort of upbeat online gossip session Crystal had in mind. It was soon flooded with posts. The format was informal: it did not require users to register their names, or to use passwords to post. Like the eBay boards, it was "scrolling," rather than "threaded," which meant the posts scrolled down the message board, and eventually disappeared entirely as new ones were added. The technology was so primitive that after a few hundred messages were posted, Jim had to delete them by hand to make room for new ones.

Crystal's No Complaint Board was popular enough that in June, Jim and Crystal decided to take it to the next level. They dropped the clumsy isplaza domain and replaced it with another one Jim already had, otwa.com, left over from On the Web Antiques, a sales project that had never really gotten off the ground. To take advantage of the new domain name, Jim and Crystal renamed Crystal's No Complaint Board the Online Traders Web Alliance. The OTWA board was threaded, which meant that messages could now be sorted by subject and could remain on the board indefinitely and, equally important, that Jim no longer had to delete posts by hand. The board was divided into categories for different online auction services, including eBay and Auction Universe, and for subject areas, like antiques and collectibles. OTWA grew rapidly by word of mouth, much as eBay had. Controversy in the eBay community invariably caused traffic to pile up on OTWA. "Any firestorm on eBay was at least a firestorm on OTWA," says Jim.

Jim and Crystal did not have the space to themselves for long. In July 1998, Mark Dodd, a freelance computer consultant in Amherst, New Hampshire, started a message board of his own. Dodd was a tinkerer—as a child, he had taken his parents' TV and microwave apart and reassembled them—and a computer fanatic. He had started out buying and selling computers and accessories on Onsale, and later on eBay. He eventually branched out into a lucrative sideline, buying *Star Wars* figures at a Wal-Mart near his rural New Hampshire home and reselling them to buyers in places like northern California, where people lined up to buy them. Dodd bought the domain AuctionWatch.com for $100, and began e-mailing online auction users to spread the word. Like OTWA, AuctionWatch had separate categories for eBay and Onsale, and for various topics, including fraud. But most of the postings were about eBay.

Unlike Jim and Crystal, Dodd was thinking about the commercial possibilities from the beginning. He talked it over with his friend Rodrigo Sales, who was getting an MBA at Stanford. The two men met in New York, where Sales had a summer job with Credit Suisse First Boston's technology group, and over pizza in Sales's apartment they brainstormed about how to turn AuctionWatch into a business. They briefly considered creating their own auction site, but competing with eBay seemed hopeless. The e-commerce buzzword of the moment was "portal," and Dodd and Sales decided they would turn AuctionWatch into a one-stop site for online auction users.

Dodd returned to New Hampshire and continued working on AuctionWatch. In November, the site registered its one-thousandth user. At first, most of the posts contained advice for buying and selling and for dealing with fraud, much like on eBay's Q & A Board. But AuctionWatch quickly gained a reputation as a place where eBay could be discussed more critically than on eBay's own boards. Some of the most outspoken AuctionWeb posters had actually been suspended from eBay's boards. But many other users were eBay supporters, and even eBay staff.

That fall, Dodd moved to the Bay Area to work with Sales on turning AuctionWatch into a business. In January 1999, they incorporated, and got their first round of funding from an individual investor. The following August, they received $9.6 million more from venture capitalists. AuctionWatch's business plan followed the pattern of many of the specialized portals that were emerging at the time. It would sell advertising, but also make money by offering escrow, insurance, and other services targeted to online auction buyers and sellers. To attract traffic, Dodd and Sales established a news and information section on the site, and they hired two reporters from CNET News, an Internet news site, to cover online auctions.

◆

In April, Whitman scheduled an off-site to discuss marketing. Now that she had settled in, she wanted to take a step back and think big thoughts about eBay's direction. But when the senior managers gathered, their first item of business was the highly specific question of what to do about AOL. The six-month pact eBay had signed in late 1997 was about to run out, and Steve Westly wanted management to agree to a larger deal. Given how hard it had been to persuade the company to spend $750,000 in December, he knew getting approval would not be easy. Mike Wilson, of course, was as strongly opposed as ever. But this time Omidyar, Skoll, and Kagle were also dubious, put off by the high price tag. "I'm not sure a lot of people wanted to do the deal besides Steve," says Whitman.

But the more the eBay management team talked about how to market the company, the better an AOL alliance looked. The group was now convinced it made sense to spend money to drive traffic to the site, and to shore up eBay's dominant position. If eBay was going to do a major marketing buy, everyone agreed Internet ads were the most cost-effective because, unlike print and television ads, they would reach only Internet users. And although Mike Wilson had not persuaded his colleagues not to pay for traffic, his cautionary words about upsetting the equilibrium of the eBay community had made the management team skeptical about rushing into television. "We were quite worried that we had this thing that was growing organically, and that if you shocked the system by mass-market advertising you potentially disrupted what was so wonderful about eBay," says Whitman.

Westly had done his part, coming up with numbers to show that the AOL deal was paying off in terms of traffic and registrations. It always amused Omidyar to see Westly's painstakingly prepared charts, since he knew the numbers for them had to be mined from eBay's database, and he could only imagine the Herculean efforts Westly must have made to get Wilson to hand them over. Westly was also able to argue that the relationship had succeeded in keeping AOL out of auctions, and for that reason alone it was worth renewing. In the end, when Whitman went around the room asking the staff to rank possible Internet partners, everyone said that if there was going to be a deal, it should be with AOL—of course, whether to sign on with AOL would depend on what terms Westly could extract.

The other major decision that came out of the off-site meeting was a renewed focus on the collectibles market. Collectibles were still a core component of eBay's business, but the company's commitment to them had been wavering. Average sales prices for collectibles were low, certainly far lower than prices for computers or electronics, and faddish collectibles like Pokémon and Beanie Babies went through cycles of popularity that were hard to predict or plan for. There were also pride issues: it hurt to be dismissed in the media as a Beanie Baby exchange, or as FleaBay. But Whitman spoke out strongly in favor of collectibles, arguing that eBay's success at the moment depended more on keeping and expanding on the hard-core users than on reaching out to the "periodic buyers" who were stopping by other, more expensive, categories.

When the off-site discussion was over, eBay's marketing department compiled a long list of collectors' publications and began buying ads in them. In addition to being targeted at likely eBay users, ads in these offbeat periodicals were cheap—a few hundred dollars could make a big splash. By September, eBay had taken out ads in ninety "vertical publications," as these highly specialized magazines and newsletters were known, including *Mary Beth's Beanie Baby World, Toy Trucker and Contractor, Postcard Collector,* and *Elvis World.*

◆

With the IPO approaching according to Bengier's timetable, eBay began preparing itself for Wall Street's scrutiny. QuickBooks was finally abandoned on May 1, replaced by higher-grade financial software suitable for the audits that were certain to come. In June, eBay selected its first board of directors: Whitman, Omidyar, Kagle, Intuit founder Scott Cook, and Starbucks CEO Howard Schultz. EBay also hired a general counsel, a vice president of finance, and a director of investor relations. At the end of the summer, eBay brought on Brian

Swette as senior vice president of marketing. Swette came to eBay after a seventeen-year career at Pepsi, where he had risen to chief marketing officer, in charge of all of the Pepsi brands. To the anti-corporate camp, Swette's arrival was yet another sign—as if one were needed—that the marketers had taken over. But to Wall Street, which would soon be asked to put a value on the company, Swette was an impressive hire. A year later, Whitman would elevate Swette to chief operating officer, eBay's number two position.

As the IPO drew near, it was critical that traffic and revenues on the site remain strong, and the numbers were more than holding up. In early May, eBay was hosting 375,000 auctions at a time, and it had 750,000 registered users—a 50 percent increase since early February. On June 30, Skoll sent out an e-mail to the staff announcing that late the previous night, eBay had hit a once unimaginable milestone: its one-millionth registered user.

Despite the strong numbers, eBay went into the IPO market with some trepidation. The company had always been nervous about how it would be received by the East Coast financial establishment. But everything had changed since the eBay Vision Tour a year earlier, when Omidyar's earnest attempts to explain the company had been met with yawns and cancellations. Now, when eBay sent its business plan out to the ten investment banks it wanted to meet with, all ten said they wanted to compete to take the lead on the IPO.

As with the search for a CEO, eBay was concerned about finding an investment bank that understood the company and its unique culture. EBay decided to give the prospective bankers an assignment: by the time they came to make their pitches, they had to have purchased something on the site. What they bought, and how they talked about the experience, would be a formal part of the scoring sheet eBay had drawn up to evaluate the bankers. Michael Parekh of Goldman, Sachs, the investment bank that ended up as lead underwriter, impressed the eBay team with the four or five items he bought on the site, including a Parcheesi game for his mother. Goldman beat out tough competition, including Morgan, Stanley, whose Internet analyst, Mary Meeker, was the closest thing the analyst community had to a superstar. The eBay management team was impressed, Whitman says, by how well the Goldman bankers understood the online auction business. EBay was not yet calling itself a consumer-to-consumer site, but Goldman told eBay that was exactly what it was. The eBay team had asked the ten competing investment banks to prepare fake analyst reports as part of the selection process. Whitman had been particularly taken by Goldman's title: "From C to Shining C."*

In mid-July, eBay formally filed an IPO registration statement with the Securities and Exchange Commission. Omidyar posted a letter to the community setting out eBay's future plans, and acknowledging the critical role they played in eBay's success. "You can all be proud of the fact that you helped create this, and when your friends hear about us in the news, or see us at trade shows, or see our ads, don't hesitate to tell them, 'I knew those eBay guys when they were little,'" he wrote. "You discovered us. You helped shape eBay." The letter was classic Omidyar: friendly, empathetic, and keenly in touch with the community. He addressed head-on the community's concerns that eBay would never be the same again. "Will eBay change after it becomes a public company?" he wrote. "I'm sure things will get even better." But "our core beliefs and vision won't change, and that's because you all have a part in it," Omidyar promised. "EBay is what you have made it, and it will always reflect your attitudes and your activities." The letter was signed, simply, "Pierre." But if the community was worried that eBay was undergoing a fundamental change, the conclusion of Omidyar's post could not have been reassuring. He was forced to tack on, at the end of his breezy letter, a "word from our lawyers," which included a lengthy and distinctly un-Pierre-like morass of legal technicalities.

---

*That eBay went with Goldman, the most blue-chip of investment banks, was no great surprise. But many in the financial world had expected Meeker to end up with the IPO. EBay was reportedly turned off by Meeker's presentation, which struck some of the management team as un-eBaysian. "She was on her pager a lot and getting calls from the CEO of Hewlett-Packard," one eBay director told *Fortune* magazine.

◆

The day after eBay registered to go public, it announced that it was acquiring Jump, Inc. Jump ran Up4Sale, a fast-growing person-to-person auction site. With 50,000 registered users, Up4Sale was the second-largest of the 150 to 200 online auction sites, trailing only eBay. What worried eBay's management was less Up4Sale's size and growth rate than its philosophy. The company founders—four recent graduates working out of the attic of a Victorian house in Cincinnati—had an eBay-like understanding of the importance of community. And they shared eBay's sense of whimsy, a spirit embodied in Auction Arnie, Up4Sale's winsome mascot. Not least, advertiser-supported Up4Sale was free for users—a business model eBay considered a threat to its own fee-based approach. EBay's real concern was the prospect that a larger Internet company might buy out Up4Sale and use it to launch a competing online auction service. These concerns were well founded. EBay did not know it, but Yahoo! was making just such an overture to Up4Sale at the time.

Omidyar made the first contact, online-auction entrepreneur to online-auction entrepreneur, suggesting a discussion about how the two companies might work together, and in the spring of 1998, he and Skoll flew to Cincinnati to meet the founders. They explained that eBay was interested in buying the company, and that they wanted to move quickly. After a few days of due diligence, eBay and Up4Sale shook hands on an all-stock deal. Part of the reason for the rush was that eBay's management was about to file its financials with the SEC, and they did not want to have to amend them.

When eBay announced the acquisition, the official line was that Up4Sale was going to be integrated into eBay's operations. "We believe that the long-term relationship between eBay and Jump will ultimately bring a great deal of value to our communities," Whitman declared. But the truth was, integration made little sense. Unlike acquisitions eBay would make later, Up4Sale did not bring a new area of competency. The auctions that were occurring on Up4Sale could just as easily occur on eBay. And Up4Sale's pricing model—free auctions—clearly could not be integrated into eBay. It soon became clear that the acquisition was little more than an attempt to keep a competitor out of the space. The impulse to buy Up4Sale "was as much defensive as it was offensive," concedes Bengier. In time, eBay closed Up4Sale, and Auction Arnie was given a new job: smiling at visitors to Up4Sale's old site and directing them to eBay. EBay did, however, appreciate the talents of the Up4Sale founders, and put them to work on a variety of projects, including Mister Lister, a bulk listing program for high-volume eBay sellers.

Around the time it acquired Up4Sale, eBay found itself being courted by a corporate suitor of its own, Amazon. Since it had filed to go public and circulated its business plan to the top investment banks on Wall Street, eBay's corporate profile had been raised considerably. EBay figured that some of the buzz from the financial community must have made its way to Amazon CEO Jeff Bezos. Whitman and Omidyar flew up to Seattle, hoping to talk about a strategic alliance of some kind, which they were prepared to argue would benefit both companies. At the least, they figured, the trip would be good opposition research.

But Whitman and Omidyar found out when they got to Seattle that Bezos was interested in acquiring eBay. The two sides never got to the point of talking price. Whitman and Omidyar were deep into the IPO process and were not interested in selling out. Bezos, always a tireless cheerleader for his company, argued that Amazon had the resources to help eBay reach its full potential. But Whitman was not impressed by Amazon's bricks-and-mortar assests. "They have all these warehouses and inventory they're so proud of," she told her management team when she returned to Campbell. "I'm glad we don't have to deal with any of that."

◆

In mid-August, while fifty thousand fans descended on Memphis for the candlelight vigils and karaoke contests of Elvis Week, eBay launched its first Elvis site. "All the King's Things," which included an online Elvis museum, an Elvis chat room, and page after page of auction listings, owed its existence to a one-woman campaign by Rockin' Robin Rosaaen, an Elvis groupie who believed the King had personally intervened to get her a job at eBay processing payment checks.

Rosaaen, a perky mid-fifties brunette with the intensity of a true believer, dates her infatuation to a single night: Elvis's legendary '68 Comeback Special. Growing up in Oakland, Rosaaen had twisted her childhood away to the beach anthems of Jan and Dean, Frankie Avalon, and Fabian. But none of those pop warblers had prepared her for the pulse-quickening sight of a leather-clad Elvis strutting before the cameras in his first TV appearance in eight years and snarling: "If you're looking for trouble, you've come to the right place." Rosaaen never looked back.

Rosaaen spent her twenties following Elvis and "dating a couple of fellas that worked for Colonel Parker." In the seventy-two times she saw Elvis in concert, she had a few brushes with greatness. After bribing the Sahara Tahoe maître d' one night, she worked her way up to the stage, waving an "I Want Your Body" sign from the health spa where she was working. Elvis strode over and said, "You've got it," and—in a knees-into-jelly moment she captured on film—leaned down and kissed her. At another show, Rosaaen gave Elvis a water gun, and during the concert they had a water-gun fight. But Rosaaen's finest hour came one night when Elvis spotted her in the audience and serenaded her with the song "Rockin' Robin." She has kept the nickname ever since.

Rosaaen's Elvis memorabilia collection started in her groupie days. At first it was just common things—ticket stubs, concert programs, LPs, and magazines. But she acquired her first true relic in 1988 at an auction in the Bay Area sponsored by the Sisters of the Holy Family, where she paid eight hundred dollars for a blue suede jacket that had once belonged to Elvis. Rosaaen started hitting the record stores in San Francisco's Haight-Ashbury neighborhood, picking up old Elvis albums, and she bought anything Elvis-related she could find at swap meets and auctions. In the early 1990s, she wrote *All the King's Things: The Ultimate Elvis Memorabilia Book.*

Rosaaen's expertise did not help her in the job market. While she was assembling her forty thousand Elvis items, perhaps the largest collection outside Graceland, she toiled away for eighteen years at Pacific Bell, part of the time as a 411 operator. When Rosaaen submitted her résumé to a personnel agency—and here's where she saw Elvis's hand—it landed with a receptionist who was also a fan. Seeing *All the King's Things* on Rosaaen's résumé, the receptionist decided Rosaaen would be wasted in an ordinary job. She passed the résumé on to another agency that was trying to fill a position at eBay.

EBay needed someone to help Chris Agarpao open the check-filled envelopes that were pouring in faster than ever. A few days after her interview, Rosaaen, who became employee number forty-one, was slicing open envelopes with a letter opener and manning the eBay fax machine. At the holiday party a few months later at the San Jose tech museum, Rosaaen gave Omidyar a signed copy of *All the King's Things.* Having thus laid the groundwork, she approached Omidyar back at the office about her idea for an Elvis category. There were millions of Elvis fans, she told him, and a lot of Elvis collectors, but there were only about 150 Elvis items up for sale on eBay at any given time. She wanted permission to promote Elvis memorabilia on eBay on her own time, by reaching out to the Elvis collecting community. Omidyar agreed, and Rosaaen got to work.

As it happened, Rosaaen's Elvis obsession fit in with two of eBay's corporate priorities. Elvis collectors were just the sort of hard-core collectors Whitman and the management team had decided at the off-site meeting to make a priority. Rosaaen's goal of creating a separate Elvis category was also consistent with eBay's new emphasis on professionalizing its categories. In April, eBay had launched home pages for computers, coins, stamps, and several other areas, along with category-specific discussion boards. The marketing department had also begun what it called its Vertical Trade Show Program, a coordinated outreach to niche markets. The idea had started informally with George Koster, a longtime employee and *Star Trek* fan, who had been going to *Star Trek* conventions and talking up eBay. Now the marketing department was sending representatives to gatherings like the Doll & Teddy Bear Expo, the American Numismatic Society World's Fair of Money, and the National Barbie Convention.

But the key to eBay's new campaign was the new position of category manager. EBay had begun hiring specialists—Jill Finlayson in Toys and Dolls, and Eric Moriarty in Antiques, Sports, Coins/ Stamps, and Pottery and Glass were two of the first—to organize and actively promote specific categories. Category managers were expected to build relationships with experts, clubs, dealers, and major collectors in their areas, and to encourage them to think of eBay as a place to buy and sell. They were also told to monitor eBay's boards, to track what the community was thinking about their categories, and to follow trends in their areas elsewhere on the Internet and off-line.

Without realizing it, Rosaaen had asked to become one of the first category managers. While keeping her job in the billing department, she began to do for Elvis collectibles what the official category managers were doing in their areas. She reached out to people who might have Elvis collectibles to sell—actors who had starred in Elvis movies; alumni of Humes High School, from which Elvis graduated, who might have a yearbook with the King in it; and members of the Memphis Mafia, who might have memorabilia packed away. With Rosaaen's active promotion, Elvis listings quickly climbed from fewer than five hundred to more than two thousand.

The quality of the listings also started to improve. EBay's Elvis category still contained plenty of schlock—Love-Me-Tender music boxes, Hound-Dog clocks, and Elvis oven mitts ("Don't be cruel to your hands"). But Rosaaen was proudest of her success in getting sellers to list items with a connection to the historical Elvis. One of his television sets—important because of Elvis's well-known love of the medium—sold on eBay for $7,000. A nativity scene used at Graceland went for $10,000. And a Tennessee woman got $12,500 for a previously unknown four-minute black-and-white home movie, taken in 1961, of Elvis leaving a Florida hotel. Memphis Mafia member Joe Esposito sold his personal ID card, one of a small number

Elvis issued to members of his inner circle, for $1,600.72. And a lucky Elvis fan beat out forty-six other bidders to pay $811 for the pest control agreement from Elvis's home on Hillcrest Road in Beverly Hills.

Rosaaen was one of her own best customers. She sold a Xerox copy of the floor plan of Graceland, making clear in the listing that the five-page document was a copy. She expected to get about ten dollars for it, but after a heated bidding war between a Florida woman and a California man, it went for $454. She acquired one of her most prized pieces of Elvis memorabilia on eBay—Elvis's dental records. A dentist in Palm Springs inherited them when he took over the practice of another dentist who had treated Elvis. The records were everything Rosaaen hoped they would be and more: three X rays of his teeth, a patient information chart he filled out and signed in 1967, a chart of his bridgework, and a list of the medications he was taking. Rosaaen got the lot for $4,000, but she would have paid more. "How much closer can you get to the King," she says, "than having his X rays and dental chart?"

In the spring of 2000, Rosaaen was promoted from billing to assistant category specialist for Elvis collectibles. The promotion gave her more time to tend the category, including answering the flood of e-mail she received through its "Ask the Expert" feature. Rosaaen dispensed advice about how much an Elvis autograph is worth. ("I try to educate them that it matters if it's a photograph, an album cover, or a signed piece of paper.") She told users how to know if Elvis hair is authentic. ("You have to have the history, and find out if they know who the haircutter was at the time, since there were only three or four people Elvis let cut his hair.") And she scoured the listings for phony items. Rosaaen once had to e-mail a seller that an autographed photo of Priscilla Presley was clearly inauthentic, since the photo was actually of Cheryl Ladd. She also kept order in the chat area, at one point ejecting a participant who refused to stop posting that Elvis had had an affair with Marilyn Monroe and had planned the assassination of John F. Kennedy.

Rosaaen helped make the Elvis chat room one of the closest com-

munities on eBay, posters regularly sharing their personal recollections of Elvis. One woman, in a fairly typical post, recalled the time
she chased Elvis through a parking lot. Another told about talking
the cleaning crew on Elvis's private plane into giving her the trash,
only to have her mother throw it out while she was at work.
Members of the Elvis chat group met off-line several times. A contingent of twenty-five descended on Memphis in 2000 for an Elvis pil-
grimage, and another came to San Francisco to meet Rosaaen and
join her for "Elvis in Concert," a tribute show featuring the Sweet
Inspirations, backup singers who toured with Elvis, singing in front
of a video of Elvis performing, which was shown on a two-story-high
screen. It was, in a way, what eBay was all about.

◆

As the IPO approached, eBay had to choose between two potential
allies, Yahoo! and AOL. Yahoo! and eBay had been talking for much
of the year about entering into an alliance of some kind. EBay
wanted an agreement to share traffic, but Yahoo! was interested in
buying eBay. The driving force pushing for an acquisition was
Masayoshi Son, chairman of Japan's Softbank Corporation, the
Internet-investment powerhouse that held a 31 percent stake in
Yahoo! Son liked to put his money in market leaders in every area he
invested in, and for online auctions that meant eBay. The acquisition
made strategic sense for Yahoo! Auctions were a logical extension of
Yahoo!'s brand, and Yahoo! would be able to increase eBay's value by
steering millions of its own users to the site. But eBay was no more
interested in being bought by Yahoo! than it had been in selling out
to Amazon. No one at eBay wanted to give up so close to the IPO, and
in any case, Omidyar argued, going public was the eBaysian thing to
do. EBay had always been about free markets, he pointed out, and the
IPO would let the market, not two teams of negotiators, decide what
the company was worth.

That left AOL. EBay's management had agreed in principle at the
off-site that if it made an alliance with any Internet company, AOL
would be its first choice. And Whitman believed that having a deal

with AOL would be a sign of strength as eBay put itself on the IPO market. But the two companies had yet to agree on terms. AOL's negotiators flew out to eBay headquarters, and a contentious round of talks began. "We camped out for nearly three weeks," AOL's Myer Berlow recalls. AOL had heard the rumors that eBay was talking to Yahoo!, and throughout the negotiations AOL was worried that eBay might fold its tents and sell out. In the end, Berlow and Westly agreed on price and terms: eBay would pay AOL $12 million over the next four years for prominent placement on the AOL site. The old debate about whether eBay should pay for traffic was now, undeniably, over. EBay would not only pay for traffic—it would pay a small fortune.

◆

Few entrepreneurs have anything good to say about the antiquated institution known as the road show. In the weeks leading up to an IPO a company's management team has to stop managing and start selling itself. The company going public pays investment bankers to haul its top executives to meetings with St. Louis pension-fund executives and Boston mutual-fund managers, where the executives try to persuade the money men to invest in the company. Most executives regard road shows as an irritation, but for eBay the experience had an added level of annoyance. EBay's great innovation was that it had created an ideal, frictionless marketplace. But now it was being forced to sell itself the old-fashioned way—tromping around the country, making in-person sales calls. Worse yet, the whole point of the road show was to meet with big investors behind closed doors and give them inside information about the company, after which they would be given a chance to buy a piece of it on terms not available to the general public. It was just the kind of elitist process that had inspired Omidyar to create AuctionWeb in the first place.

Omidyar, accepting the road show as a necessary evil, put on a business suit and prepared to make the rounds. But he refused to capitulate completely. He insisted that Goldman, Sachs pick up the cost of the lavish travel—private jets, first-class hotels, and stretch limousines—that was standard road show fare. It was a rebellion against un-eBaysian extravagance, but Omidyar also had a more practical objection to footing the bill. He had always been proud to say that eBay had been profitable every month since it had started charging fees. Omidyar had no idea how expensive the road show would be, and he did not intend to let spendthrift New York bankers rob him of that distinction.

A road show presentation, like a business plan, is an upbeat story about a company's future. So it made perfect sense that Silicon Valley's reigning road show guru was Jerry Weissman, a sixtyish onetime Hollywood screenwriter who had reinvented himself as a high-priced "communications coach." Weissman had helped craft many of the most successful high-tech road shows of the past decade. One VC who had a stake in Cisco credited Weissman with adding two to three dollars to the networking giant's share price the day it went public. Weissman spent four days with Omidyar, Whitman, and Bengier, honing their presentations. He helped the eBay team with its slide presentation, and prepared them for what he warned was the most critical part of any road show: the Q & A. The general impression the managers made on their audience, Weissman told them, was as important as anything they said.

The heart of eBay's presentation was a twenty-minute overview, to be delivered by Whitman. Afterward, Bengier would run through eBay's finances in five minutes. Kicking it all off was a sixty-second introduction from Omidyar, focusing on his founding of the company and its early success. Whitman and Bengier, both seasoned presenters, had no qualms about their assignments. But Omidyar did not like public speaking, particularly in rooms full of wealthy men in suits. To avoid slipups, he decided to memorize his brief script, down to the last word. Omidyar repeated it over and over at practice sessions, like a novice actor painstakingly learning his lines. By the first day of the road show, Omidyar had his speech memorized—and so did Whitman and Bengier, who amused everyone by declaiming about how they had founded eBay and nurtured it through its early days.

The weeks leading up to the IPO were the first time that the gods who had smiled on eBay from the beginning withheld their favor. September 1998 was the worst IPO market in decades. In a stock market slide that had started in June, the Dow had fallen nearly 25 percent from its highs earlier in the year, and the Nasdaq had plummeted nearly 50 percent. Investment bankers were frantically advising clients to delay going public, and a number of high-profile offerings, including Pointcast, a push-technology Internet company, and CitySearch, an online entertainment guide, were pulled. After BankFirst, a Knoxville, Tennessee–based regional bank forged ahead with an IPO on August 27, no company dared go public, until eBay did on September 24. It was the longest IPO drought in nearly two decades.

But at a time when investment bankers were inventing new metrics daily to value money-losing Internet companies—market capitalization/users, market capitalization/page views, revenue per subscriber—eBay had something the others lacked: actual profits. It also had unheard-of gross profit margins—88 percent, compared to 22 percent for Amazon, 16 percent for CD Now, and 9 percent for Onsale. And its meteoric growth rate still showed no signs of slowing. From the first quarter of 1997 to the second quarter of 1998, registered users had shot up from 88,000 to 851,000. Listed items rose from 492,000 to 6,584,000. And gross merchandise sales had soared from $17.6 million to $139.6 million. Goldman, Sachs told eBay that given its numbers, there was no reason to put off the IPO, no matter how bad the market.

There were, however, some white-knuckle moments. On the first day of the road show, August 31, Whitman, Omidyar, and Bengier boarded a plane in San Francisco headed for Baltimore to present to the Alex.Brown sales force. When they took off, the Dow had already fallen 100 points. By the time they arrived in Baltimore, it had ended the day—a day that would be known as Bloody Monday—down 513. The Nasdaq, more relevant to eBay's IPO, had plunged 8.6 percent, the worst one-day decline in its history. Whitman and the rest of the team tried to remain upbeat. But when they made their pitch at 6:45 the next morning, says Bengier, the Alex.Brown team was "distracted."

On the second day, rumors started reaching the eBay team that Yahoo! was considering entering the online auction market. What no one realized was that Yahoo! intended to make its announcement during the road show. On September 14, Yahoo! told reporters it had entered into a deal with Onsale, which was discontinuing Onsale Exchange to run person-to-person auctions on Yahoo!'s site. It was eBay's worst nightmare realized: its bitterest rival had joined forces with one of the true powerhouses of the Internet, Yahoo!, a website with 20 million users. Worse still, Yahoo! would not charge fees—it intended to make its money entirely on advertising. Skoll, who had remained back in Campbell, scrutinized Yahoo!'s announcement looking for a silver lining, but the e-mail he sent the road show team was all cloud. "The offering is pretty nice, unfortunately, and seems to match us feature for feature," he wrote. "It is 'powered' by Onsale, branded by Yahoo!, and free."

Launching Yahoo! auctions just before eBay's IPO was not exactly a dirty trick—the two companies' talks were over, and they were competitors again—but it was a sharp competitive move. "They scrambled like crazy trying to derail the road show," says Whitman. "And we were scared." The road show team itself had to scramble to come up with an answer to the question investors would inevitably ask: didn't the Yahoo! announcement make eBay's business plan obsolete? Whitman, Omidyar, and Bengier sketched out a series of responses. Yahoo! had never been particularly successful at driving its traffic into specific applications, like Yahoo! classifieds. And Yahoo! could never match eBay's singular focus on the auction market, with only 10 employees working on auctions, compared to eBay's 138. The team also decided to emphasize its deal with AOL to reassure Wall Street that eBay had an Internet powerhouse of its own that could rival Yahoo! in traffic.

While the road show was under way, Omidyar, who could repeat his sixty-second spiel in his sleep, had the least to do. He decided to

use his free time to send a series of e-mails back home, to give the
eBay staff who could not come along a feel for what it was like. These
"Pierregrams," virtual postcards from the road, were filled with his
reflections on the absurdities of the process, and personal glimpses
of the management team in action. The road show really began,
Omidyar told the staff, not with the first sit-down meeting with investors, but when security at San Jose International Airport decided
that Whitman fit their terrorist profile and tried their new chemical
explosives tester on her. "Meg was kind of annoyed at being stopped
while none of us were," he wrote. "I thought it was especially amus-
ing given my dark beard and ponytail."

Omidyar told of the upscale restaurant in San Diego that
brought the raw meat out to the table to explain precisely how it
would be cooked. ("Never seen *that* before.") The stretch limo that delivered the eBay team to its destination, virtually across the street
from the hotel where they were staying, before he could even fasten
his seat belt. And the colorless fund manager who "could easily have
been replaced by [a] Borg drone." When Whitman was too nervous
to eat lunch before presenting to a large group of investors in San
Francisco, Omidyar suggested that she imagine the people in the
room in their underwear. "But since many of the participants are apparently semiretired high-net-worth types (read: crotchety old white
men)," he wrote back home, "that turns out to be a bad idea." At the
end of the second day, the team was being driven to San Jose in two
sedans, one for Whitman, Omidyar, and Bengier, and one, for complicated reasons, with only Omidyar's jacket. "Ordinarily, I would think
that was really weird," he wrote, "but somehow, now, it seems entirely normal."

Omidyar could afford to make fun—eBay was being well received at every stop. There were, however, a few puzzled questions
about strangers trading with strangers over the Internet. And some
investors had trouble understanding the importance of community,
since there was still no real community model of e-commerce. The
best presentations were the ones where someone in the audience was
an eBay user or knew an eBay user. At New York–based Alliance

Capital, a senior partner who was an eBay fanatic testified to the room about all the things he traded on eBay. At a large investment firm in Boston, a partner told the assembly that he had a neighbor who was an eBay addict. The only sour note in the road show was the continuing stock market free fall. While the team presented in San Francisco on the second day, the Dow plunged 300 points; a week later, when they were in Boston, it fell 200. It made it hard for eBay to read the investors, Bengier recalls, since they were being asked to "weigh our wonderful business story against the falling market going on outside."

After hitting more than a dozen cities—including regional financial centers like Chicago and Denver, and such unlikely spots as Shawnee Mission, Kansas ("some of the largest investors like to hang out in the strangest places," Omidyar observed in an e-mail)—the road show team ended up in New York on September 23 to watch the company go public. The formal offering was for 3,489,275 shares, which represented about 9 percent of eBay. The task fell to Goldman, Sachs to try to set a price range for the shares, and thereby decide what the company was worth. Goldman began at between $14 and $16, and then raised it to between $16 and $18. But the early indications were that the IPO was wildly oversubscribed. Goldman priced the IPO at the high end of the new range, $18. If that held when the markets opened, eBay would be valued at more than $715 million.

The morning of the IPO, Whitman, Omidyar, Bengier, and Skoll, who had traveled east for the occasion, gathered in the Goldman offices on the Nasdaq trading floor to await the verdict of the market. When the eBay team arrived, Lawton Fitt, who ran capital markets for Goldman, was at her computer trying to decide where to open the stock. The eBay team noticed that although the market was open, their stock-ticker symbol—EBAY—was not trading at all. It was good news. Fitt was having trouble finding a price at which owners of the stock, who had gotten in at $18 the night before, were willing to sell. Fitt was on the phone talking to large investors, trying to find out at what price they would be willing to divest some of their shares. The price was moving up—to $20, $25, and higher—but there still were no sellers. Looking out at the flashing lights and the manic commotion of the world's premier new economy stock exchange, Omidyar thought to himself that it was just like clunky old AuctionWeb in the early days: it still took both buyers and sellers to make a market.

Finally, the stock opened—at 53¼, up 197 percent. It was a wild moment, as Omidyar, Skoll, Whitman, and Bengier looked up at the Nasdaq ticker, and every stock symbol racing across it was EBAY. If the eBay team had stopped to do a quick mental calculation, they would have realized that their company was now valued at more than $2 billion. It would end the day at 47⅜, not far off the high. After the shouting and the hugs, the eBay team headed for telephones in the Goldman offices to share the good news with their families and friends. Only Whitman's husband was less than ecstatic. "As excited as he was," Whitman says, "he actually had someone he was about to do brain surgery on."

◆

When word reached San Jose that the IPO had opened with a pop, the celebration began. Song cried out, "Come on! Let's get on the party train!" and eBay employees formed a conga line, starting up on the top floor, and whooping and hollering as they wound their way down from the third floor, picking up eBay staff on each level. The revelers stopped at the engineering department on the first floor, where everyone settled in for a party, complete with high fives and bottles of champagne. The merriment came to an end when another tenant, not a participant in the day's financial windfall, called security.

EBay's entire staff had been given stock options, and some of the exuberance was simply youthful excitement over the large homes, fancy cars, and other material wants that were suddenly within reach. But for employees who had come to the company early, and endured the skepticism of family and friends, it was also vindication. No one was laughing at online auctions anymore—or confusing eBay, as Sonny Wagner's mother once had, with a porn site. At the end of the day, the party resumed outside, with a reggae band. Steve Westly, the most senior eBay executive in San Jose that day, gave a Silicon Valley version of Henry V's St. Crispin's Day speech, reminding the troops that they were not just doing a job, but making history.

EBay's top management had tried to prepare the staff for the IPO. Omidyar and Whitman did not want them to focus on the stock price, as employees at Silicon Valley start-ups so often did. Talking excessively about stock options was not eBaysian. It was also not good for the company, since morale could plummet if the stock took a sudden dive. In a company meeting before the IPO, Omidyar showed a chart of Yahoo!'s stock price. At the beginning of June 1998, the company was worth $4 billion, and a month later it was worth nearly $8 billion. Omidyar asked if anyone in the room really thought Yahoo! was worth twice as much at the end of June as it was at the beginning. No one did. It was important not to get caught up in the volatility, Omidyar advised. "In the long term," he said, "we are building the company to last."

But it was hard to be eBaysian with the stock shooting up as high as it did on the first day. Brad Handler had spent the night before the IPO at the printer's, and been dragged into a pool about where the stock would finish the day. Debbie Bailey, in billing, had Tom Adams help her set up an online stock portfolio, so she could check on her options. Despite the cautionary words from management, on the day of the IPO, when the staff wasn't celebrating, all eyes were on the stock price. "It was on every screen," recalls Kristie Reed. At the height, according to a quick traffic check by the engineers, the average staff member was checking every two minutes.

The big winners in the IPO, of course, were Omidyar and Skoll. When Skoll joined eBay back in 1996, he and Omidyar had been forced into an awkward discussion about how to allocate their shares. Skoll, naturally, had developed several complicated models valuing the company and measuring the two men's contributions. Omidyar was amused by Skoll's formulaic approach. "He had all sorts of analyses," Omidyar says with a chuckle. But in the end they used Omidyar's more intuitive approach. Omidyar assumed that his work for the company in the year before Skoll arrived was worth 15 percent of the total value; the remainder, he proposed, they should share equally. After Benchmark's equity stake was taken out, and with a few more variables thrown in, at the time of the IPO, Omidyar owned roughly 42 percent of the company, and Skoll 28 percent. Benchmark owned 21.5 percent, and Whitman had options, not yet vested, worth 6.6 percent.

The day of the IPO, Omidyar, Skoll, and Whitman all became instant multimillionaires. But the real rise in the stock came over the next nine months. In July 1999, *Forbes* put Omidyar at number thirty-six in its "billionaires club," with $10.1 billion; Skoll was eightieth with $4.8 billion. Whitman's net worth topped $1 billion. No one else at the company reached those lofty sums, but even lower-level staff had done well. About two-thirds of the pre-IPO staff, around seventy-five people, made multiple millions of dollars, and even the newest, lowest-level employees ended up with hundreds of thousands of dollars when their stock options vested.

It was an astonishing windfall, and it had landed in what many outside observers regarded as the unlikeliest of places. From Wall Street to Silicon Valley, people who had looked down on eBay as an online flea market were scratching their heads, wondering how it had produced three billionaires within months of going public. Omidyar's fortune struck many as the most incredible of all, both because of its sheer size and his low-key approach to entrepreneurship. "If there has ever been an age for accidental fortunes, this is the time," Matt Kursh, a former colleague of Omidyar's from eShop who went on to work at Microsoft, told the *Orange County Register*. "Pierre has always been very serious, very deliberate, and very good at finding the cutting edge. But of all the people at eShop, I never would have said Pierre was the one who would make the most money."

EBay's management tried to keep the IPO from changing the culture. When Whitman returned from New York, she laid down a new rule: employees could check eBay's stock price once in the morning, and once at the end of the day, but that was it. (The crackdown only drove stock-checking underground, with employees furtively whispering to each other for updates on the "s-word.") The founders led by example. Omidyar kept driving his beat-up Volkswagen Cabriolet. Skoll stuck with his ten-year-old Mazda RX-7, and continued to live in his rental group house. "Unless money is a fundamental value in your life," Skoll said, "it's not going to change you." Omidyar began making plans to create a family foundation to give away a substantial part of his newfound wealth. "What one person needs and what one family needs is a tiny, tiny fraction of this total number," he said as the extent of his net worth began to sink in. "That means that we now have, on a personal level, an awesome responsibility to see that the wealth is put to good use."

◆

For all its extraordinary success, the eBay IPO failed in one respect. Omidyar, Skoll, and Kagle had all hoped to include the community in the IPO. EBay had been built, in large part, on the unpaid efforts of eBay's early users. Before there was a customer-support department, there were people like Pongo, who spent countless hours helping sellers to list items, listings that produced fees for eBay. EBay had also derived significant value, as it acknowledged every time it wrote a business plan, from the community itself. Giving the community pre-IPO stock would have been a way to share the wealth with the people responsible for eBay's triumph.

Skoll made some initial inquiries into how it could be done, from handing out shares to eBay's biggest buyers and sellers, to creating a mechanism for the entire eBay community to buy pre-IPO stock. But the idea ran into resistance from the investment bankers and lawyers. The investment bankers had selfish reasons for opposing the plan. Pre-IPO shares were valuable commodities, particularly when they belonged to hot tech start-ups, and bankers generally reserved them for favored clients and friends. It was not in their interest to see IPO shares earmarked for ordinary people—or to set a precedent for other companies, who might have similar groups they wanted to reward. But there were also practical reasons not to offer shares to the community. Some had to do with the technicalities of how an IPO's price stabilizes, a critical part of the process that—at least in the view of investment bankers—is best accomplished if shares remain in the hands of a small number of large investors. Some members of the eBay management team were also worried that if the IPO did badly, community members could lose money, which could turn eBay's own users against it.

There was also a legal obstacle: federal securities laws restricting speculative investments, including IPOs, to "sophisticated investors." By the government's definition, most members of the eBay community did not qualify as sophisticated investors. An important factor in that determination, under the securities law, is whether the investor has a brokerage account. EBay included a question about brokerage accounts in a broad survey it did of its community shortly before the IPO, and found out that less than one-third of eBay users had one. EBay's management was worried that if it set aside pre-IPO shares for the community, and two-thirds of the people who applied were turned down, there would have been an uproar, even though eBay could have honestly said it was just complying with federal law. In fact, a year later, the open-source software company Red Hat ran into just this problem with its own IPO. It had invited a number of open-source programmers to sign up for shares, and was bitterly criticized when the broker handling the offering rejected some of them. "After I opened an account and moved my money, I was told that I'm ineligible for the IPO because I have no stock-trading experience," one programmer complained on Slashdot, an online forum for discussions of technology. "Isn't it ridiculous to 'invite' a bunch of Linux geeks to buy Red Hat if only experienced traders are eligible?" EBay briefly put a link on its site referring community members to the online stock broker E*Trade, which had a small number of IPO shares available, but the link came down quickly when E*Trade complained of being flooded by eBay users.

EBay looked for other ways to share the company's financial success with the community. Skoll proposed doing something no Silicon Valley company had ever done before: establishing a charitable foundation with a block of pre-IPO stock. EBay donated 107,250 shares to create the eBay Foundation, which was soon worth nearly $40 million. That fall, Omidyar, Skoll, Brad Handler, and Kristin Seuell, an early employee in the public-relations department, gathered for the foundation's first meeting. They also invited Karin Stahl, creator of the Powersellers program, because of her charitable work in Guatemala. Stahl showed up, and was immediately appointed chair of the governance committee, effectively making her head of the new foundation.

◆

In early October 1998, the entire staff piled into two buses and headed to Asilomar, a resort and nature preserve on the Pacific Coast, for a weekend retreat. It was their first chance to celebrate the IPO together, and to talk about eBay's future. Sunday was filled with team-building exercises and planning sessions, but Saturday was all fun at the beach. There was an eBay Olympics, in which the staff divided into twelve teams, one for each of eBay's major categories. Computers, Collectibles, Stamps, and the rest faced off in relay races and a tug-of-war.

The high point of the weekend was a surprise fashion show that management put on for the staff Saturday night. Skoll, Brian Swette, and a few of the other men got onstage in dresses and high heels, while Whitman came out in a rough semblance of a man's suit. The evening ended with a party in a big barnlike structure, featuring a live band. Westly took the microphone to announce that two of the staff were celebrating birthdays that day—Karin Stahl and Chris Downie, one of the Up4Sale founders who had flown in to represent eBay's Cincinnati outpost. Stahl and Downie had just met, but Westly called them up to do a long, slow birthday dance in front of the whole company. "We were so humiliated," Stahl recalls. Two years later they returned to Asilomar, and Stahl accepted Downie's marriage proposal.

chapter six

With the IPO behind it, eBay was ready to get back to business. Its first priority, overlooked for far too long, was a search for office space. The company had been snapping up offices in 2005 Hamilton Avenue as they became available. But even with five suites sprawled over three floors, space was tight for a staff that now numbered more than one hundred. In November, Omidyar, Whitman, and Bob Perales, eBay's new facilities czar, started office hunting.

EBay's real-estate agent had good news. A sleek new office building was going up in Cupertino, right next to Apple's main campus. The building was just a "cold shell," when the eBay team took a tour, but it was clear that it would be a marked improvement over the industrial architecture and endless blacktop of Greylands Office Park. The soaring lobby, the real-estate agent gushed, would have genuine marble floors when the building was completed. Many prospective tenants would have been impressed, but the eBay group was turned off. "It looked like the White House," Perales recalls. EBay decided to pass. The new building was missing, Omidyar declared, what mattered most — it was not eBaysian.

In the end, eBay remained in Greylands. As it happened, a large amount of new space was opening up on the other side of the complex, and eBay signed a contract for it over Christmas of 1998. The new Greylands deal called for eBay to add more than 100,000 square feet to its current 23,000, spread out over two additional buildings. The decision to stay put reflected, Whitman says, one of the core principles Omidyar had instilled in the company. "Low-key is far better than arrogance and extravagance," she says.

The expansion afforded eBay its first chance to design its own space. When the designers and architects were done, what emerged was a new headquarters that unmistakably reflected eBay's culture. With its large, spare rooms filled with simple cubicles, and its vending-machine-stocked kitchen areas, the new headquarters looked, at first glance, like the back office of a midwestern insurance company.

But on closer inspection, there were subtle eBaysian motifs built into the design. The floors had been laid out to resemble a marketplace, with long corridors suggestive of streets, and the cubicles were clustered to look like market stalls. In their space allocation, the new offices were actually more democratic than AuctionWeb's original suite. Everyone would work in a cubicle, even Whitman and Omidyar. That Whitman was willing to give up her office was a testament to how completely she had made the transition to dotcom culture. The new arrangement, she would later say, kept her in better contact with her staff. "People are far more likely to stop by your cube than they are to come into your office," she says. "I see ten people a day that I would never see if I was not in a cube." To allow for private meetings and phone calls, the design included conference rooms along the perimeters of the main rooms and in the large hallways. In another eBaysian gesture, this one a tribute to the company's status as a global marketplace, the small conference rooms were named after cities around the world, the larger ones after countries.

EBay started expanding into the new space the following year. In May 1999, the company moved into 51,529 square feet at 2125 Hamilton Avenue. The following December, eBay took over the rest of the new space, 51,529 square feet at 2145 Hamilton Avenue. Omidyar wanted eBay's new headquarters to retain the homespun feel of a start-up, and to a remarkable extent it did. Greyland Office Park was no plush corporate campus from back East, with geese-filled ponds and rolling lawns. EBay's expanses of greenery were limited to a few small lawns trapped between the complex's buildings and outdoor parking lots. Its recreational facilities were limited to a standard-issue Foosball table. And there was no employee cafeteria. Employees would have to keep dodging the lunchtime traffic on Hamilton Avenue on their way to Whole Foods, a health-food super-market in a nearby shopping mall. In keeping with eBay's low-key ethos, the decor hardly rose above the functional. To brighten up the space, eBay encouraged the staff to decorate their cubicles wih items purchased on eBay, and at one point held a cube-decorating contest. Kristie Reed turned her cubicle into a miniature golf course, complete with a sand trap and a water hazard. Westly's administrative assistant decorated hers in a "white-trash" theme, with paper flowers in fake pots, ugly furniture, and chicken figurines pecking on AstroTurf.

◆

The must-have toy of the 1998 holiday season was the Furby, a lovable ball of fuzz that started out speaking Furbish but could—through the expenditure of a truly colossal amount of time and energy—be taught to speak a few phrases of English. EBay quickly became the leading destination for parents desperate to acquire one of the scarce, gnomelike creatures, just as it had been a year earlier for Tickle Me Elmo dolls. By Christmas, twenty thousand Furbies had been sold on eBay. Wall Street, encouraged by the frenzy of holiday buying and the stronger-than-expected fourth quarter, bid eBay stock up to $262.25 in December, a new high.

But there was a Grinch at eBay's holidays—online auction

fraud. In the weeks leading up to Christmas, the press gave extensive coverage to Sonny Stemple, an Oklahoma man charged with selling $30,000 worth of items on eBay, cashing the money orders, and not delivering the goods. In Furbyland, the scam of the season was selling "rare," oddly colored Furbies, on the model of rare Beanie Babies, that went for as much as $1,000 on eBay. It turned out, however, that Furbies were all produced in equal quantities. Furby-maker Tiger Electronics came forward to warn that the sellers were dyeing the Furbies themselves, with everything from food coloring to Grecian Formula, and passing them off as limited editions. Most embarrassing, in December eBay participated in a charity auction for Toys for Tots that included a *Today Show* jacket autographed by Katie Couric and Matt Lauer. Bidding for the jacket, which was heavily promoted on the show, went as high as $200,000, but the top bids all turned out to be pranks. The highest legitimate bid was $11,400.

In addition to being embarrassing, the media reports helped awaken law enforcement to the growing problem of online auction fraud. Suddenly, government agencies from the Pennsylvania attorney general's office, which made Stemple deliver two Furbies to a buyer he had cheated and pay restitution to twenty-nine others, to New York City's Department of Consumer Affairs, which launched an investigation of fraudulent sports memorabilia, were taking a hard look at eBay. Private watchdogs were also speaking out. The National Consumers League told the *Wall Street Journal* that it was getting six hundred complaints a month about Internet fraud, two-thirds involving online auctions. The fraud stories also took a toll on eBay's reputation and its stock, which dropped below $200 for the first time since the fall.

Despite the media excitement, fraud on eBay was extremely rare. According to eBay's figures, less than .01 percent of its 40 million auctions had resulted in fraud complaints. Although these figures no doubt understated the problem—many incidents went unreported—eBay knew from its contacts with the community that fraud was less of a problem than the press was suggesting. Still, the scandals and investigations were making eBay rethink its casual approach. The Sonny Stemple case was a public-relations nightmare, but it was the false bids generated by the *Today Show* charity auction that made a deeper impression on the staff. "The jacket auction really opened our eyes and made us think that, you know, there are some bad people out there," says Sonny Wagner. "Looking back, we were probably very naive." EBay also had more practical concerns. The company was starting to worry about what government regulators might do if they decided to crack down on online fraud. EBay was also hearing rumors that another big competitor was preparing to enter the space, and it did not want to leave itself vulnerable to charges of laxness.

For all these reasons, in mid-January eBay unveiled a new anti-fraud campaign. The time had come, the company decided, to ease up on Omidyar's founding ethic of giving people the benefit of the doubt. Nonpaying bidders would receive only one warning before receiving a thirty-day suspension. Shill bidders would be barred for thirty days for the first offense and banned permanently after a second one. EBay also announced that it would be quicker to ban people from the site for frivolous bids. And for the first time eBay offered free insurance through Lloyd's of London, though it covered only the first two hundred dollars of an auction, and had a twenty-five dollar deductible. The critics were not assuaged. The insurance, they said, was paltry, and eBay's antifraud efforts were spotty. But Whitman insisted that eBay was doing its best. "What town has ever grown from a hundred thousand to two million in less than a year?" she asked. "We're trying to evolve and cope as best we can."

◆

In January 1999, in Crawfordsville, Indiana, Karen Young was not thinking about fraud or Furbies. She was still trying to figure out what mental lapse had led her to order a 26-foot rig to pull up to her home in a quiet, leafy historic district near the Wabash College campus and start unloading bubble wrap. Rolls of bubble wrap, 750 feet of wrap, now occupied every room and hallway of her house. They filled up her two-car garage, and they spilled off her front porch.

There were so many rolls of bubble wrap in the living room that her husband warned her they were going to lose the children in them.

When she discovered eBay, Young could not have foreseen the bubble wrap. A take-charge woman with an infectious laugh, Young had stopped working—as a photographer's assistant, among other small-town jobs—to raise her two young daughters. It seemed like the right decision at the time, especially since her husband's job investigating insurance claims kept him on the road so much. But Young eventually became bored with her domestic routine. To give herself something to do, she decided to sell the junk in the garage on eBay.

And it was junk. Old video games, and some boxes of her mother's knickknacks that had been packed away in boxes long ago. When Young started listing it on eBay, however, something unexpected happened—every last bit of it sold. She kept listing more items and, without ever making a conscious decision, found that she had taken on a full-time job. She went out to flea markets and tag sales around Crawfordsville and returned with carloads of antiques and collectibles. When she scored the right items, the rewards were handsome. At one estate sale, Young bought a bag of old Barbie junk for just a dollar. When she got it home, she discovered that it included a bed for Skipper, Barbie's lovable—and highly collectible—kid sister. She sold it on eBay for three hundred dollars.

The key to making a steady income, Young realized, was quantity. She steadily increased the number of auctions she listed at a time, from fifteen to twenty-five, to fifty. When she reached one hundred simultaneous auctions, and the listing and packing were too much for Young and her husband, she hired a retired neighbor to help part-time. Now that she had a real business, Young began looking for ways to cut costs and increase profit margins. When she reviewed her expenses, she noticed that she was spending a lot of money buying shipping supplies at Staples. Young did some investigating and found a manufacturer who was willing to sell her bubble wrap rolls, self-sealing bags made of bubble wrap, and Styrofoam peanuts, all at wholesale prices.

Young started just using the shipping supplies for herself. But then it occurred to her that other eBay sellers must be having the same problem with high-priced shipping supplies that she once had. She decided to list a few supplies on eBay to see if they sold. With product bought at wholesale and low overhead, she could charge less than retail, even when shipping costs were added. The first bubble-wrap auctions she listed did so well, she increased her order from the manufacturer a hundredfold. She made one other change in her business—she stopped selling antiques and collectibles.

Thus shippingsupply.com was born. At first, the eighteen-wheelers dropped the bubble wrap at Young's house. But as the business grew—and as her home became increasingly unlivable—Young rented a warehouse near her home. She expanded twice, until by early 2000 the business sprawled over seven thousand square feet. By then she had a staff of seven, including her father, who wrote the company's computer software; her mother, who helped process the orders; her husband, who had by now quit his insurance job; and six retirees from the neighborhood. By 2001, Young had 35,000 customers in her database, and shippingsupply.com was the biggest shipping-supplies seller on eBay, handling 150 orders a day, mainly for 50-foot and 250-foot rolls of bubble wrap.

Young had become one of thousands of Americans—the *New York Times* would later put the number at 75,000—running businesses entirely on eBay. EBay had empowered her in just the way Omidyar had hoped when he created AuctionWeb. It enabled her to start a business in her own small town, selling to customers around the country and the world. It also gave her more control over her life. She set her own schedule, taking weekends off to be with her daughters, and then staying up late most Sunday nights closing out her auctions and answering e-mail. And eBay allowed her to be her own boss. That meant she could keep a VCR running at work, listening to videotapes of musicals, her favorites. And she could set her own rules. "I come to work in sweatpants," she says. "And I don't wear shoes."

◆

On February 19, 1999, eBay banned guns and ammunition from the site. It was simply too difficult, eBay explained, to ensure that buyers on eBay met the legal requirements for purchasing a gun. By selling guns, eBay had stumbled into a thicket of federal and state laws—mandatory background checks, waiting periods, restrictions on sales to felons, and prohibitions on shipping guns through the mail to anyone other than a licensed dealer. EBay had no way of knowing if these laws were being followed by gun sellers on the eBay site, and it seemed certain that in at least some cases they were not. Just eight days before eBay announced the ban, a Brooklyn, New York, jury had ordered gun manufacturers to pay $3.3 million to a shooting victim. The suit introduced a novel legal theory, called negligent marketing, that eBay worried might be applied against it in future lawsuits.

Given the likelihood of a lawsuit at some time in the future and the fact that gun sales made up less than $100,000 of eBay's total 1998 revenues, the ban could have been justified purely on economic terms. But eBay went out of its way to say that the decision was not just about avoiding liability. "It's just the commonsense right thing to do," Westly insisted at the time. It was also good public relations. EBay was already being criticized in the media for some recent gun listings that had appeared on the site: a "pre-ban" Hungarian AK-47, six Uzi submachine guns, four lots of Talon flesh-shredding ammunition, and one Mas 49/56 sniper rifle. If a gun bought on eBay were ever used to kill someone, eBay management knew, the company would be pilloried in the media.

When the gun ban was announced, the response on the message boards and in e-mail to eBay staff was "volcanic," recalls Brian Burke, eBay's community support manager. Song alone received between four hundred and five hundred e-mails. Not all of the communications were critical of the ban, but both supporters and opponents objected bitterly to how eBay had reached its decision. The community had not been included in the process, and the ban was imposed without any warning. Burke felt worst for the gun dealers who had built small, perfectly legal businesses—and in some cases signed leases or ordered inventory—in reliance on their ability to sell their guns on eBay. "Then all of a sudden you come to them and say, 'You can't do it anymore,'" says Burke. "You've literally put them out of business." Song, who was hearing from many of these small businessmen, agreed. The gun ban was "the first time in eBay's history that we'd come off the mountaintop and ever said unilaterally how it's going to be," she says.

Ground zero for the explosion of anti–gun ban anger was eBay's Discuss New Features (DNF) message board. As eBay had added more boards, each one had developed its own personality, and the DNF board, where the community weighed in about changes eBay was making to the site, had a reputation for rebelliousness. When the gun ban was announced, posts on the DNF board came fast and furious. A group calling itself the "DNF Posse" emerged, composed of about forty DNF regulars who were outspoken critics of the gun ban, led by a poster with the eBay ID Pinkhamr. Pinkhamr was Randy Pinkham, a retired Air Force master sergeant from Altus, Oklahoma. "Pinkhamr" was simply a combination of his last name and first initial, but the ID gave him the added measure of respect on the board, where many posters believed he had chosen it to indicate that he liked to "hammer" the "pinks"—slang for both liberals and eBay staff.*

The DNF Posse was upset that eBay had sprung the change on the community, but many were also offended by the ban itself. Their posts claimed that eBay was depriving them of their Second Amendment rights—they were apparently unaware that even the National Rifle Association had said, when asked by a reporter, that as

---

*EBay staff were known as "pinkliners," or "pinks," because when they posted on the message boards, a pink line appeared at the top of their posts.

a private organization eBay was free to sell or not sell guns. Drawing on the imagery of the extremist wing of the gun lobby, members of the Posse portrayed eBay generally, and Whitman and Omidyar personally, as "jackbooted thugs." And they claimed to know that eBay had acted on orders from the Bureau of Alcohol, Tobacco and Firearms, an agency much hated by pro-gun forces, which had recently begun an investigation of online arms sales.

EBay responded in a way that stunned the DNF Posse. With a few keystrokes back at headquarters, Pinkhamr and thirty-six other members of the Posse were thrown off eBay. EBay's official reason for "NARUing" the Posse was feedback shilling—giving positive feedback ratings to each other in a collusive way. There was a kernel of truth to the charge. It was a tradition for DNF regulars to pump up the feedback ratings of new people who joined the DNF board when they said things the group liked. The Posse had set up one member of their group with ten positive feedbacks before he had even completed a single eBay transaction.

But the Posse insisted it had done nothing wrong. There was no rule that feedback had to be limited to transactions. In fact, in Omidyar's original conception, feedback was about reputation, and if someone made friends in the eBay community, the Posse argued, it was only right that it be reflected in his or her feedback rating. The user they rewarded with ten positive feedbacks "was a strong supporter of the boards," Pinkham says. "EBay used to say, 'Give people like that an atta boy!'" What's more, Jim Griffith himself had once led his own posse, the one with the motto "Only Do Good," that left feedback as a group. It seemed obvious to the DNF Posse that the feedback shilling charge was just a pretext, and that eBay's real intent was to clamp down on dissent over the gun ban.

When eBay reviewed the suspensions more closely, it found that three of the suspended users had been using false IDs to give shill feedback, and had been rightfully suspended. But the remaining thirty-four, the company had to admit, should not have had their privileges taken away. EBay restored Pinkhamr and thirty-three of his confederates. In explaining the situation to one of the wrongly suspended Posse members, an eBay staff member told him he had been a "dolphin caught in the net." From that offhand comment, the incident entered eBay lore as "the dolphins in the net." The incident was a small free-speech milestone that made eBay rethink its message-board policies and give posters more leeway in criticizing the company. EBay continued to have rules of conduct, as many on-line communities do, prohibiting threats, hate speech, and profanity. But since the dolphins incident, eBay says it has made a greater effort to respect the fact that, as Burke says, "sometimes our users have a right to scream at us."

The gun controversy was transformative in another way: it made eBay more respectful of the community's role in bringing change to the site. Management realized it was a mistake to announce the new policy and then say, "Oh, by the way, let's have a discussion on it," Burke says. But there was one part of the gun-ban blowup eBay never regretted: the decision itself. Just months after the ban took effect, the Columbine High School massacre occurred, resulting in the death of fourteen students and one teacher. Among Whitman's first thoughts on hearing the news was how glad she was that eBay had stopped selling guns. That feeling only grew over the next few days, as reports surfaced that one of the killers had an eBay account, and that the FBI was investigating whether the weapons used in the shootings had been bought on eBay. They hadn't been, but the attack left eBay management, which had been vilified for months, more convinced than ever it had done the right thing.

◆

Also that February, eBay shut down its live-support boards. The boards traced back to the original eBay Beta board, which had been created to talk people through the switchover from AuctionWeb to eBay. They had been, and still were, live, scrolling message boards— after two hundred people posted, the entire contents of the board turned over. EBay's official position was that scrolling boards no longer worked for answering support questions. There was now so much traffic on the site, and there were so many posts asking questions, that the staff simply could not keep up. The boards were replaced with an e-mail support system run by staff members.

To eBay staff and users looking for signs that the company's growth was coming at the cost of community, the closing of the live-support boards took on talismanic significance. "It was a very emotional issue for us," says Sonny Wagner, the longtime customer-support worker. "The support boards had always been our direct link to the community." The live-support boards were fast-paced and untamed—actual eBay staff used them to post responses in real time. In the glory days, Omidyar, Skoll, Song, and Skippy had all shown up on the live boards to speak to the community. Critics of the change suspected it was an attempt by eBay, now that it was a public company, to rein in its staff.

This unhappiness reflected a larger sense of loss. Since the IPO, eBay really *was* a different place. It was already attracting a different kind of employee. The old guard talked among themselves—as old-timers did in successful start-ups everywhere—about how the new recruits lacked their idealism, their pure commitment to the cause. The current crop of recruits actually asked openly about stock options when they came in for job interviews. In the old days, that sort of un-eBaysian talk would have ensured that a candidate was rejected. After they were hired, these new-style eBay employees talked in phrases picked up from their business school professors, and communicated with PowerPoint presentations. When Steve Westly, Tom Adams, and Rick Rock arrived in the fall of 1997, they had been an anomaly. Now the people who found their behavior strange were the exception.

EBay's senior management was also, necessarily, more guarded and more insular now, and they expected the staff to be the same way. Song was taken aback after the IPO when a top executive ran up to her while she was on the phone with a reporter, warning her to be careful what she said. But the fact was, now that eBay was a publicly traded company, a stray comment from a staff member could move the stock. The days when the entire company could gather in a circle and talk about the future were also in the past. The regular reports that Omidyar and Skoll had once shared were now inside information, which eBay had to protect carefully. And with hundreds of employees, there was no pretense that staff members at every level could have a say in company policy. "All of a sudden they were making decisions without everybody," says Song. "It started to be less egalitarian and more hierarchical, and there were more processes being put in place."

◆

On February 22, 1999, Randy Pinkham, Pinkhamr from the gunban blowup, decided to try something new on the Discuss New Features board. He carefully timed a post so it went up at 10:22 and 22 seconds P.M. eBay time. Since message board posts are date- and time-stamped, it appeared with the notation 22:22:22. Pinkham had chosen the date, of course, because it was 2-22. The only explanation he gave was that "it seemed kind of neat." In the days that followed, other DNF posters joined in posting at the same time, with a communal purpose: to see how many posts they could get up on the DNF board in that one-second window. An eBay tradition was born that day, pronounced "two's" and spelled TUZ.

The number of participants grew over time. Every night, as 10:22:22 P.M. approached, DNFers announced that it was almost time for TUZ, and postings on other topics stopped. It was a trick to time a posting just right: the X factor was the speed of the user's Internet connection. A post sent at exactly 22:22:22 would almost certainly be too late. But as with sniping, it was difficult to know just how much lead time to allow. For two years after the first TUZ, the record number of posts to arrive and be logged in as 22:22:22 was twenty-five. On February 22, 2001, the two-year anniversary of Pinkham's first TUZ post, a new record was set: thirty-eight. It was such an extraordinary performance that rumors spread through the TUZ community that eBay had delayed the clock for a second to let more posts in. One TUZer created an online homage to TUZ. The web page, at http://members.ebay.com/aboutme/tuzzled/#history, included a TUZ hall of fame, a TUZ history, and a list of birthdays of regular TUZ participants.

TUZ was one of the many little rituals that existed on eBay message boards. DNF also had regular Friday-night seventies sing-alongs, in which users posted, one after the next, lines from their favorite songs. The Elvis chat board had a virtual celebration of the King's birthday every January 8, complete with personal recollections of encounters with Elvis and digital photos of birthday cakes. These online amusements were mainly just about having fun. "We're being goofy, like kids," says Pinkham. "Hell, I'm fifty-two years old." But there was also a practical aspect. It was a way for hard-core eBay users, particularly sellers—some of whom had to spend twelve or more hours at their computers listing and responding to customer e-mail—to fend off boredom and loneliness. It was also evidence that even after the IPO, the increased emphasis on profits, and the dustups between management and users, the heart of eBay—the community—was still beating.

◆

Meg Whitman was on a rare vacation on the ski slopes of Colorado when the news hit: Amazon had launched an online auction site. Ever since eBay spurned Jeff Bezos's attempts to buy it, rumors had been reaching Hamilton Avenue that Amazon was considering moving into the online auction space. But the actual launch had come without warning. "That was the end of the vacation," Whitman says.

When Whitman arrived back in San Jose, she had a long list of calls to return. Wall Street analysts who followed eBay, institutional investors who owned the stock, and the company's own board of directors all wanted to be reassured that Amazon's move was no cause for alarm. On the phone, Whitman tried to be upbeat, using the same arguments she had made at the time of the Yahoo! launch: eBay had years of experience that could not be replicated overnight; the eBay community had consistently proven its loyalty, and eBay had a singular focus on online auctions that Amazon, with its emphasis on direct sales to consumers, could never match. "This is the only thing we do," Whitman told anyone who would listen. "We wake up every morning trying to figure out how to make it safer, more fun, with more features and a better user experience."

But talking to her staff, Whitman found it difficult to be as sanguine. EBay had always regarded Amazon as a more serious threat than Yahoo! because it was a pure e-commerce site, with extensive experience in selling things online. A Wall Street analyst Whitman trusted had called to say that Amazon's site looked remarkably good, and Whitman's own staff had reluctantly reached the same conclusion. EBay's management team began to hold meetings three times a week, Monday, Wednesday, and Friday at 5:00 P.M., to review the competitive landscape.

The more familiar the eBay management became with Amazon Auctions, however, the more reassured it was about eBay's chances. Whitman was pleased to see that almost all of the sellers on Amazon were big businesses with land-based operations and merchant credit-card accounts, not the mom-and-pop sellers who dominated eBay. Amazon had also, like so many eBay competitors before it, failed to appreciate the importance of community. The site had no message boards, and it was hard for users to contact each other. "It had a very clinical feel," Whitman says. A refrain emerged at eBay: Yahoo! Auctions had community without commerce, while Amazon Auctions had commerce without community.

EBay would later insist that it prevailed because it offered a better user experience than Amazon, with its traditional e-commerce focus, could provide. "The skills are very different," says Whitman. "I wouldn't know how to manage an Amazon warehouse." Ever the consumer marketer, Whitman also believed that a large part of eBay's advantage was that buyers and sellers thought of it as the place to go for online auctions. "Brands are quick-drying cement," she liked to say. Amazon had hardened in the public's mind as a fixed-price book, music, and video destination—not a place to go for auctions.

But there was a more basic reason Amazon did not take hold. Once again, eBay had been saved by Metcalfe's Law. EBay's network had so many buyers, it was difficult to lure sellers away, and so many sellers, it was difficult to lure away buyers. Before the launch, Amazon approached Jeff Fisher,* one of the biggest stamp sellers on eBay, and tried to persuade him to transfer some of his auctions to its site. Fisher's mailbox quickly filled with Post-it notes, pens, and personalized business cards, all gifts from Amazon. When those didn't work, a manager of the Amazon Auction stamps category called him personally and asked what it would take to get him to list on the site. Fisher said he had always wanted a poster of Buffy the Vampire Slayer. When a cardboard tube with a poster of Sarah Michelle Gellar showed up at his house, Fisher kept his word and listed some stamps, but he did it in the form of an experiment. He placed fifty identical stamps on each of the two sites. On Amazon, eight of them sold, two for more than the starting price. On eBay, thirty-seven sold, twenty above the starting price. "I got my answer right there," he says.

◆

Richard Rushton-Clem, of Lewisburg, Pennsylvania, listed an auction on eBay in March 1999 for what he described as an "Early Blown Glass Cathedral Pickle Bottle." He had bought the bottle the previous summer for three dollars at a tag sale in western Massachusetts. A onetime antiques dealer, Rushton-Clem knew it was an unusual pickle bottle. He listed it with a minimum bid of $9.99, and a secret reserve of $275.** As soon as the auction listing went up, the e-mail began pouring in. Pickle bottle collectors had detailed questions for Rushton-Clem about the shape and markings on

---

*Jeff Fisher is a pseudonym.
**In a reserve auction, the top bidder does not win the auction unless he or she bids at least the amount of the secret reserve.

his bottle. The collectors suspected what he had not: that this mid-sized, dark-amber Willington bottle was one of the rarest pickle bottles in the world.

Willington pickle bottles were manufactured in Willington, Connecticut, in the mid-1800s. They came in different colors, and amber was the rarest. There were three sizes—eight-, eleven-, and fourteen-inch—and the midsized bottles were the hardest to come by. The day after he listed his auction, Rushton-Clem amended the listing to say that he believed the jar to be a midsized, dark-amber Willington pickle jar, and that "sources have indicated to us that there may be fewer than five known to exist."

By the end of the second day, bidding on the pickle bottle had reached $2,500. Rushton-Clem, who had started the auction on a Wednesday, added another advisory to his listing the following Monday. "We are pleased to be able to add that over this past weekend, four separate bottle collectors from four different states visited our facility and viewed this fine bottle," he wrote. When the auction ended, the pickle bottle sold to an anonymous Pennsylvania doctor who collected antique pickle bottles. The final bid: $44,100.

Rushton-Clem's $44,100 pickle jar, which received considerable press attention, was a classic example of the power of a global marketplace to connect a seller with the ideal buyer. But it also raised a serious question: What, exactly, was eBay doing to prices? Collectors were by now complaining of an "eBay effect," which they believed was driving up the prices of rare collectibles. In pre-eBay times, collectors had usually been able to find a way to buy collectibles cheaply. Antiques collectors had their networks of pickers. Stamp collectors often knew of shows where they could find stamps at bargain prices. But now, it seemed, everything was ending up on eBay, where it sold, as the common complaint went, to the person in the world willing to pay the most for it.

The eBay effect was a hot topic of discussion wherever collectors gathered—coin shows, antique-toy conventions, Beanie Baby clubs—and it was a constant refrain on collecting websites of all kinds. On ghosttown.com, a poster warned ghost-town memorabilia collectors that eBay's prices for rare mining journals, maps, and diaries were excessive. On miscmedia.com, a popular-culture site, the creator bemoaned the fact that even though the "cocktail nation" fad had ended, bowling shirts and tiki statues on eBay were still overpriced.

Collectors liked to blame eBay, but their complaints were actually just a new version of a classic complaint about auctions—what economists call the "winner's curse." First described by three petroleum engineers who wrote about oil lease auctions in the *Journal of Petroleum Engineering* in 1971, it holds that the high bidder in an auction almost always pays too much. The petroleum engineers were writing about the dynamics of government auctions for the right to drill in an unexplored oil field. When the auction is announced, oil companies have their geologists study the area and estimate how much oil will be found. The geologists produce a range of estimates—some will likely be too high, others too low. But the auction will be won by the company whose geologist puts the highest value on the drilling rights, justifying the highest bid. The winner therefore finds himself in the unfortunate position of realizing that everyone he bid against thinks he has paid too much.

The winner's curse was certainly a factor in eBay auctions. But eBay's effect on prices was actually more complicated. Even as collectors were complaining that eBay was driving up the price of rare collectibles, sellers were complaining that it was driving down the price of everything else. EBay was causing people to clean out their attics and flood the market with "average" collectibles. Dealers who once competed only with other dealers were now competing with amateur sellers who had no overhead and who did not need much of a markup. In eBay's early days, sellers said it seemed almost anything they listed sold for a good price—their own versions of Omidyar's broken laser pointer. But as the supply increased, prices spiraled downward. A study by Auctionbytes.com, a website geared to online auction users, found that over one year the number of "consumer collectibles" sold on eBay climbed substantially, and the prices fell 25 percent. In one week at the beginning of the study, 1,314 auctions for Swarovski crystal closed with an average selling price of $51.61. A year later, 8,023 Swarovski crystal pieces sold at an average final price of $38.03.

If eBay seemed to be driving prices both up and down, it was because it was actually doing something else: bringing prices closer to their ideal. With millions of buyers and sellers able to participate in every transaction, market flaws that allowed goods to sell for more or less than they should have were being corrected. EBay was now a price-setting mechanism—a stock market for everyday goods. Buyers and sellers had actually begun using eBay's thirty-day search function, which let users search final prices in completed auctions going back thirty days, as an authoritative reference source. Dealers of all kinds were beginning to abandon price catalogs. The measure of what things were worth, increasingly, was what they were selling for on eBay. "People are always e-mailing me and saying, I'd like to buy X, but I don't want to pay eBay prices," says Fisher, the high-volume stamp seller. "I always say, 'I'm sorry, but those are the prices now.'"

EBay was moving prices closer to the ideal, but its prices still fell short of perfection. Jaron Lanier, a computer scientist best known for coining the term "virtual reality," was doing an informal study of the flaws in eBay's pricing mechanism. Lanier, a composer who was, among other projects, reconstructing the music of ancient Egypt under a grant from the BBC, used eBay to add to the extensive collection of rare, worldwide musical instruments that filled his loft in lower Manhattan. While Lanier bought his exotic Asian and African woodwinds and percussion instruments, he plotted the prices he observed in the instrument auctions. He wanted to test his theory that eBay prices would fall, in classic textbook fashion, in a bell curve clustered around the item's ideal price—the price that experts would say it was actually worth. But what Lanier found surprised him: the price curve looked more like a two-humped camel. One hump represented a group of items that sold above the ideal price; the other was items that sold below it.

The overpriced hump was due to what Lanier called smart sellers and dumb buyers. Smart sellers were the ones who worked the eBay system well, whether within the rules or not. One way smart sellers got high prices was by being creative about selecting the category they listed in. A sheet of Iwo Jima stamps from 1945 listed in eBay's stamp category sold for around its list price, less than ten dollars. But some sellers discovered that the same sheet listed in the Antiques & Art: Maritime category, where it would be seen by buyers who collected World War II memorabilia, could sell for five times as much. Dumb buyers, the other force driving prices above the ideal, often simply misjudged an item's worth. Another kind of dumb buyer fell prey to "auction fever." Caught up in the competition, they paid more for items on eBay than they would have in a fixed-price transaction.

The underpriced hump was primarily the result, Lanier found, of dumb sellers. EBay sellers often made mistakes that drove down the prices of their items. In some cases, the errors were as simple as poor spelling. Lanier saw a good bass clarinet that sold for well under its market price because the seller had listed it as a "base clarinet," which kept it from coming up when buyers searched for bass clarinets. Other dumb sellers failed to recognize the value of what they had. A Canon Hansa, a pre–World War II Japanese camera that is among the world's rarest, sold on eBay for $6,000, well below its $25,000 value. The seller, unaware of what he had, had listed it simply as "Old Japanese Camera."

◆

In late March 1999, eBay and AOL signed another deal, by far their biggest yet. According to the terms of this updated, new alliance, AOL would promote eBay to its 16 million members through prominent ad placement on a wide array of AOL services—AOL, CompuServe, Netscape, and ICQ. AOL also agreed to help with overseas expansion, an increasing priority for eBay. And AOL promised not to enter the online auction market for the next two years, the first such formal commitment on AOL's part. With Yahoo! Auctions and Amazon Auctions floundering, this commitment removed what eBay regarded as its most formidable potential rival. AOL, for its part, was to receive $75 million over four years, a remarkable price tag, given how much soul-searching eBay had done in late 1997 over paying AOL $750,000.

◆

In Rochester, New York, in April, Rick Gagliano was having career problems. Gagliano had been a respected journalist and the publisher of *Downtown*, a free newspaper covering Rochester's politics, entertainment, and local news. *Downtown*'s iconoclastic city reporting had once caused it to be banned from Rochester's City Hall, a prohibition Gagliano had overturned on free-speech grounds. But his scrappy weekly faced tough competition from a paper owned by the well-funded, hard-driving Gannett chain and *Downtown* eventually went under. Gagliano spent the next few years looking for a way to make a living. He worked as a bartender in a Maryland seafood restaurant and later returned to Rochester, moving into an apartment owned by his sister and brother-in-law.

The apartment was a mess when Gagliano moved in. The previous tenants, who had cleared out in a hurry, had left boxes of junk strewn about. When Gagliano started going through them, he found that a few of the boxes contained old toys, including about twenty-five Barbies and some Barbie accessories. A friend suggested he put them up for sale on eBay. Gagliano did not know much about the Barbie market, and he was amazed at how much his dolls ended up selling for. Still between jobs, he decided to try to support himself by selling on eBay. Gagliano headed to Art's Used Furniture, a thrift store in downtown Rochester, and looked for things he could sell. More Barbies would have been great, but he was willing to take anything underpriced and easy to ship.

That was when Gagliano spotted the wall. In a dark corner of the store, he came across shelf after shelf of old magazines—classic porn magazines. There were roughly twelve hundred, ranging from *Playboy, Penthouse,* and *Hustler* to more obscure titles like *Jugs, Gents, Wild Honey, Erotic X Films, Gallery, Cavalier,* and *Cover Girls.* Gagliano bought about two dozen *Playboy*s for a dollar each, and decided to test them on eBay. They sold for between four dollars and ten dollars, a rate of return he was quite pleased with. Gagliano had found a new career.

Art's Used Furniture was happy to unload the whole wall. Gagliano bought all twelve hundred magazines for $120, or ten cents each. He started listing forty to sixty of them on eBay each month, scanning the covers and writing up a description of each magazine. These sold even better than his test-run. Gagliano had not realized it, but the more offbeat magazines were especially collectible. *Hustler*s and *Penthouse*s sold well, but he got the highest prices for *Adam Film World,* a guide to adult movies, and a specialty title called *Big Tits.* Gagliano sold a copy of *Big Tits* number 1, the magazine's premier issue, for $86. An issue of *Erotic X Films,* featuring famed porn star Traci Lords, sold for $46. *Wild Honey,* volume 1, number 1, went for $43. In the end, Gagliano sold his $120 of magazines for more than $15,000.

When his pile of pornography ran out, Gagliano decided to focus on *Playboy*s. He had long been a fan—he liked to point out that the first issue of *Playboy* appeared in November 1953, and he was born just a month later. Gagliano also felt better selling *Playboy,* which he considered "sophisticated," than the more hard-core titles. New stock wasn't hard to come by. Rochester's garage sales were filled with stacks of old *Playboy*s, cast off by older men who collected them in the 1960s and 1970s and were now retiring, dying, or just emptying out their closets. Gagliano also found he could make good money buying large lots of *Playboy* magazines in bulk on eBay, and then reselling them as single issues.

The secret of Gagliano's success was changing how adult magazines were sold on eBay. Most sellers typed in the name of the magazine and the issue date, and left it at that. These listings appealed to collectors and to people who just wanted an old dirty magazine, but there was no salesmanship to it. Gagliano got top dollar for his magazines because he made an eloquent sales pitch for each magazine he listed. When he sold a *Playboy,* he described the major pictorials and included the name of the cover girl and the Playmate, the title and author of the fiction, and the subject of the "Playboy Interview." The same issue that another seller listed as simply "January 1975," Gagliano turned into an homage to mid-1970s cool. He noted that the issue had a pictorial featuring hipsters like Rat Pack crooner Sammy Davis Jr., New York Jets celebrity quarterback Joe Namath, and Ralph Nader, known then as the author of *Unsafe at Any Speed.* He mentioned the Vargas Girl, a classic bit of erotic art by Alberto Vargas, whose work appeared monthly in *Playboy* from 1960 to 1975, and the feature "Brigitte Bardot au Naturelle."

Preparing these *Playboy* listings led Gagliano to his next business idea. In January 2000, he started publishing an online *Playboy* guide, which gave sellers detailed information about the contents of each issue, and an idea of how much they could expect to get for it. For anyone selling *Playboys* on eBay, the guide—which cost $14.95 the first year and $7 to renew—was a bargain. It took a seller about a half-hour to scan in a cover and prepare a detailed description of a magazine on his own. Gagliano's subscribers could just copy and paste his entries, a process that could be completed in minutes. The guide sold well enough that Gagliano gradually began putting out guides to other magazines, including *Life, Rolling Stone,* and *Sports Illustrated.*

Gagliano was grateful to eBay for creating a marketplace for him to sell his magazines, but he was troubled by some of the specialized rules for sellers of adult items. The one that bothered him most was that adult magazines published after 1980 had to be listed in a separate adult section of the eBay site, which required a credit card to enter. Magazines published before 1980 were regarded as collectibles, and could be listed on the main site. It struck him as an illogical line to draw, since *Playboy* introduced full-frontal nudity in the mid-1970s. It also cost him a considerable amount of money. The same magazine that sold for ten dollars on the adult section of the site could go for forty dollars on the more heavily trafficked main site.

Gagliano's larger problem with eBay came down to respect. The adult material was not only segregated from the main site—it was hidden. EBay never mentioned the adult site in its advertising and didn't promote it on the eBay home page. And when eBay's public-relations department suggested stories to the media, it never tried to interest them in pornography. Adult listings on eBay were less than 1 percent of overall sales, which indicated to Gagliano that eBay simply wasn't trying, since pornography sold so well everywhere else on the Internet. Gagliano was also upset that eBay's adult site did not include a search engine, which meant that buyers were forced to scroll through the entire site manually to find what they wanted. "We pay the same fees but we don't get the same service," Gagliano complained. "They treat us like the crazy aunt in the attic."

◆

In April, Tom Bowen, a gun collector and avowed eBay-hater showed up at eBay headquarters looking for Meg Whitman. He was there to participate in Voices, a new program eBay was launching to take the pulse of the community and so to avoid another blowup like the one over guns. Bowen had first attracted eBay's attention when he packed up an eBay T-shirt he had received as a promotion and sent it back to Whitman. He was protesting what he called the "great gun massacre" and the fact that eBay had excluded Civil War era guns, like those he collected, from the site along with modern-day guns. "It's not like someone is going to buy a Confederate musket to knock off a liquor store," he complained. He was also offended by what he calls eBay's " 'it's our company' mind-set."

Bowen had expected that returning the T-shirt would end his relationship with eBay. But instead he got a call from Matt Bannick, eBay's vice president for product and community. The two men talked for two hours about the gun ban and what eBay was doing wrong in its relations with the community. When the conversation was over, Bannick decided to invite eight buyers and sellers to visit eBay and talk with management about what was on their minds. Bannick wanted a mix of fans and foes for Voices 1, as the group would later be called. He talked to customer service, and found someone who complained that eBay was not doing enough about fraud.

At the other extreme, he chose Dottie Sucara, a Powerseller from Florida, who sold art and jewelry from her husband's homeland of Thailand and who spent a couple of hours a day on the Q & A Board helping other users.

In a full day of meetings with eBay management from Whitman on down, the Voices members sounded off about eBay's policy on guns, and problems ranging from winning bidders who didn't pay, to Feedback Forum abuse. Back in the days of AuctionWeb, none of it would have been necessary—Omidyar and Song knew from their e-mail exactly what everyone was thinking. But now eBay was too large to rely on that kind of informal barometer. Bannick decided to continue the Voices program, inviting a different group of eight to ten eBay community members to headquarters each quarter and continuing to solicit their views afterward by conference calls and e-mails.

Voices groups weighed in on matters as large as the upcoming alcohol and tobacco ban, and as small as the text of Whitman's "Millennium Letter to the Community," which Voices 1 members read and edited. The Voices program also allowed eBay to get its own message out to the community. Randy Pinkham, leader of the DNF Posse, was invited to be a member of Voices 3. After visiting eBay headquarters and talking with management, Pinkham said he came to understand eBay's decision to suspend him and the rest of the DNF Posse. "If I had been in their position," he said later, "I could see myself doing the same thing."

◆

EBay opened a customer-service office that June in Draper, Utah, twenty miles south of Salt Lake City. As towns go, Draper did not seem particularly eBaysian. Settled by Mormons in 1849, Draper was best known as the home of Draper State Prison, where Gary Gilmore was put to death by firing squad in 1977. But the economic rationale for the move was obvious: it made no sense to employ hundreds of customer-support workers in Silicon Valley, one of the highest-priced labor markets in the world, when the work could just as easily be done in Utah.

EBay invited several of its remote employees—including Uncle Griff, Aunt Patti, and Sonny Wagner—to move to Draper and become supervisors. The remotes appreciated the chance to join the eBay fold, but they were not excited about the location. "I was thinking, Utah?" Wagner recalls. "There's a lake and a desert. No way am I going there." But Wagner moved from Cleveland, Patti Ruby left Indianapolis, and Jim Griffith abandoned Vermont. In the first month, the Utah eBay veterans trained a class of thirty new hires, and the customer-service center was up and running.

In time the eBay transplants came to appreciate Draper's relaxed pace and the natural beauty of northern Utah. Griffith was concerned at first about how he and his life partner would be received in such culturally conservative terrain, but they managed just fine. "The big question in Utah, when you go into a store or to get a haircut, is whether you're married," Griffith says. He always responded that he was, but his marriage was only recognized in Vermont. "Of course, that shuts them up right away."

chapter seven

When eBay's site went down just before 7:00 P.M. on Thursday, June 10, 1999, no one at headquarters was alarmed. Outages had always been a fact of life, going back to the AuctionWeb days, when the site seemed to be down as much as it was up. Despite Mike Wilson's new architecture, and the roomful of engineers who were now working for him, crashes were still common. On May 5, the site had been down for five hours, and on May 20, seven. Just a day earlier, on June 9, eBay had launched a site redesign, and the system had crashed for six hours. EBay had always taken site instability in stride—it was, after all, a company that had managed to extract $5 million from one of Silicon Valley's top VC firms even though the site was down during the sales pitch.

But this time the site refused to come back up. Whitman, who had left the office for the evening, began worrying around five hours into the outage. After six hours, when she spoke to the engineers, it became clear how serious it was. "There was a little panic in their voices," she says. "They weren't sure they could actually bring the site back up again." The timing could hardly have been worse. Wilson had just taken off for a week's vacation on Bonaire, a sun-splashed former Dutch colony off the Venezuelan coast that, Whitman was not happy to learn, only had commercial air transportation three days a week. In a matter of hours, she would tell Wilson to charter a plane and get back to Campbell.

If the engineering department had been more conventionally organized, Wilson's absence might not have been calamitous. But critics said that Wilson had always resisted installing a strong second-in-command. It was, his colleagues had come to suspect, a way of keeping himself indispensable. "Mike was very protective of his group and would never let anyone see what was going on under the hood," says Skoll. "Without Mike there, the only one with any authority to deal with the engineers was Meg." The trouble was, Whitman had been hired six months earlier knowing almost nothing about technology.

Few companies depended on technology in as direct a way as eBay. If Coca-Cola's or Ford's computers went down, there would still be products in the stores and dealerships, and in the delivery pipeline. But the minute eBay's technology went down, the company ground to a halt. EBay's site was vital not only for eBay to operate, but for millions of sellers, some of whom relied on eBay as their main source of income. When eBay's computers went down for any length of time, it was a serious problem. When it seemed like they might not come up again, it was a crisis.

That was precisely what it was beginning to look like by 4:00 A.M., when Whitman, who had been anxiously monitoring the situation from home, came back to headquarters to take charge. Whitman's assistant, Anita Gaeta, sister of office manager Sandra Gaeta, turned a conference room into a makeshift hotel, complete with cots and a table covered with soap, towels, razors, shaving cream, toothbrushes, and toothpaste. It was a new kind of eBay war room, for a new kind of war. Over the next few days, the engineers and senior staff dropped in for short naps, but the room got less use than anyone expected. "The adrenaline was running so high nobody thought of sleeping," says Westly.

In the dead of night, Whitman called Sun Microsystems, which manufactured the eBay servers that had crashed, and got the company to wake its engineers and rush them to Hamilton Avenue. As fifty eBay and Sun engineers tried desperately to identify what had brought the system down, Whitman was the unlikely Winston Churchill in the middle of it all, issuing orders and deploying troops as the blitzkrieg raged around her. The engineers were impressed to see that just a few hours into the crisis, through sheer determination, she had made herself an expert on the intricacies of eBay's technology, talking with them at a rapid clip about the site's kernel and its busy buffer rates. "It was the most remarkable thing I've ever seen," says Skoll. "Meg became the leader of our technology team." She knew almost nothing about technology, he says, but "she managed to create order from that chaos."

On Friday morning, with eBay's site still comatose, Whitman called an emergency meeting of the management team. She was bleary-eyed and visibly shaken as she announced that the engineers still had not located the problem, and could not say when the site would be back up. In this group, Whitman was the consumer marketer once again, looking desperately for a way to stop the technology meltdown from turning into a business meltdown. The reports from eBay's customer-service department were as grim as the ones from engineering. In a flood of e-mails and on clogged message boards, the community was attacking eBay for technological incompetence, and for not appreciating the plight of the small sellers who depended on it. "Just so you all know, there are some people whose only income is that generated by auctions," one poster wrote on AuctionWatch's eBay board. "My business provides income to two single mothers," the poster continued. "I can't afford to pay them if I don't have auctions closing."

Even at the height of the outage, however, other community members were rallying around eBay. EBay staff were receiving e-mail pep talks from users, some of which they began to circulate among themselves to keep up morale. One came from a user who asked eBay to charge $100 to his credit card, which the company had on file, and use the money to treat the beleaguered engineers and customer-support staff to "donuts, or bagels or something." EBay staff who were reading the internal and external message boards were also encouraged to see that many community members were at least keeping their sense of humor. One posted a "Joke for Meg & Pierre" on AuctionWatch. "Knock knock," it went. "Who's there? . . . Anita . . . Anita who? . . . Anita new auction site." Another volunteered: "Guess I COULD talk to my husband."

Whitman had a simple question, which she repeated constantly throughout the Friday morning staff meeting: "How are we going to make it up to them?" It was not rhetorical. She and Omidyar were about to write an open letter of apology to the community, and she wanted ideas. Whitman decided on the spot that eBay would auto- matically refund the fees for any items listed during the outage— even if the auction had been completed, and even if the item had sold for a good price. Bengier told her the offer would cost about $4 million, a significant amount of money to eBay at the time. But Whitman decided that not doing it would ultimately cost the com- pany more.

The grimmest moment of the meeting came when Whitman had to tell her management team she feared the worst—that the engi- neers might never get the site up. It would, of course, be possible to reconstruct it and relaunch eBay. But if all the data were gone—user registrations, feedback, live auctions that had been under way at the time of the crash—it could be a loss from which eBay would never recover. That same morning, Whitman and Omidyar were sitting alone in a conference room when Wilson came by to report, yet again, that the engineers still did not know what had caused the crash. When he was gone, Whitman turned to Omidyar and admit- ted what was on her mind. "Pierre, what if they can't fix it?" she asked. "Don't worry," Omidyar replied. "Usually when the engineers are at their lowest is when they figure out what's wrong."

At this low moment, the last thing anyone at eBay wanted to do was face the media. But eBay spokesman Kevin Pursglove told Whitman he was being deluged by reporters, and did not know what to say. The parking lot had by now filled with TV trucks, and crews were pointing their cameras through the building's first-floor windows, trying to capture the chaos. Yielding to the inevitable, Whitman and Westly took turns staring into the lights. But all they could say was that they did not know when the site would be back up.

Throughout the outage, customer-support representatives, both in-house and remote, were communicating with the community through eBay message boards, which still remained operable. Every fifteen minutes, they posted an update, and reiterated that eBay was doing everything it could to fix the problem. "After three hours of this, we couldn't think of any other way to say 'we're still down,'" says Sonny Wagner, who manned the message boards all night from home. "So we started posting about every hour."

On Friday, Whitman and Omidyar posted their letter on the announcement board. EBay understood that users reasonably expected uninterrupted service, it said, and "we haven't lived up to your expectations." Whitman and Omidyar explained that they now believed eBay had isolated the problem and set out what they intended to do—install a "hot backup" system to avoid future outages, refund fees, and offer a free listing day in July "as a token of appreciation for your continued support and understanding." EBay also instituted a "call-a-thon," in which staff members from Whitman on down phoned users at home to apologize and to explain the steps the company was taking.

The outage ended at 4:25 P.M. Friday, twenty-two hours after it had begun. But the site was not at full strength; it crashed several more times over the next few days. As eBay limped back, it began an investigation of what had gone wrong. There was considerable debate about whether the fault lay with Sun, whose servers went down, or with eBay's engineers, for not maintaining them correctly. In the end, eBay decided not to assign blame publicly.

EBay was more focused on winning back trust. The *Wall Street Journal* put it bluntly in its Monday edition: "Will eBay Inc.'s customers stay loyal?" CNET News, which covered the crisis closely, declared that eBay outages "have upset users before, but the latest may be the last straw for many of them." It was certainly the last straw for many investors. On Friday, June 11, the first trading day after the start of the crash, eBay's stock plunged 9 percent. When the market opened on Monday, it was down another 18 percent. The outage ultimately sliced more than $6 billion from eBay's market capitalization.

One reason Wall Street was rattled was that eBay's users had begun to flee to other sites. On Friday, bidding on Auction Universe was 45 percent higher than normal. And Yahoo! Auctions' usage rates on Saturday were double what they had been on Thursday. But eBay's users did not stay away long. On Sunday, eBay registered almost 25,000 new users, a 12 percent increase over the Sunday before the outage. Bids were up 13 percent in the same period. The upswing was partly due to pent-up demand, but it also seemed to be a new economy confirmation of the old public-relations adage—that there is no such thing as bad publicity.

◆

Twenty-two hours of computer hell demonstrated that eBay had made a grave mistake by not building "redundancy" into its computer system. Onsale, its usual graciousness on display, had been boasting to reporters that its own system would never have gone down as eBay's had, because any one of its four backups would have sprung into action first. But the fact was, eBay had blundered badly. Given how much money the company had in the bank, and how high its gross operating margins were, there was no excuse for not having spent more money on technology. Failing to do so, Whitman would later concede, was perhaps the biggest mistake of her eBay career—and one that could have led to the company's demise.

The June outage was a rite of passage for eBay. It revealed just how inadequate and disorganized eBay's technology operations were. Whitman vowed to begin spending considerably more money on technology, even if it meant that the company's famously large operating margins would suffer. And she decided that eBay needed to put a recovery system in place that was "more like the military, with policy, procedures, and disciplines for how to bring the site back up."

Whitman took away one more thing from the outage—that it was time to replace Mike Wilson. The theme of Whitman's first eighteen months had been professionalization, but the last few weeks had exposed her to just how much of a backwater Wilson's technology operations still were. EBay's technology was now too complex a system, she decided, to leave in the hands of a brilliant programmer who was averse to corporate structure. Whitman launched a search for a new chief of technology, perhaps the most important personnel decision she would make at eBay. She hired three new high-ranking engineers, and as she watched them work, she settled on Maynard Webb, who had been chief of technology at Gateway Computers.

Webb, like Whitman, had worked his way up through several large corporations, including Bay Networks and IBM. A soft-spoken man with the look of a midwestern insurance salesman, Webb was never the most dazzling personality at eBay's management meetings. But he projected the quiet confidence Whitman was looking for, and he had a genius for running sprawling technology systems like eBay's. In a move that was equal parts symbolism and pragmatism, Whitman installed Webb in a cubicle adjoining her own. Webb had never worked in such physical proximity to a CEO before, but then he had never had a job where he had been as mission-critical as he would be at eBay. "Maynard in many ways saved the company," Whitman would say later.

Site stability would be Webb's highest priority, but Whitman also wanted him to focus on providing better engineering support for new features. In eBay lingo, every change in the site that required the engineering department's involvement was a "train seat." With the growth of the site, the new categories that were being added weekly, and the international expansion that was under way, there was a severe shortage of seats. EBay's departments were fighting bitterly for room on the train—Westly wanted his development deal to go first,

Song wanted her new message board. When Wilson was in charge, through some mysterious process—Whitman called it the "black box"—he would decide what happened when. Webb established a more formal system for taking requests, and in his first year he increased the number of train seats from 125 to 524.

Webb also made strides in stabilizing the site. Whitman opened the purse strings, and Webb brought in a new infusion of engineers. The outages did not stop right away—the site was down several times in August, including once for fourteen hours, and again in November and December. But 2000 was the first year in eBay's history when there were no major outages. The issue of site stability had not been put to rest, however. In January 2001, eBay crashed for eleven hours, bringing a new round of charges that the company was insufficiently concerned about technology, and was relying on its market dominance to make up for the site's weaknesses.

The odd man out in eBay's technological transformation was Wilson. Whitman gave him the title of chief scientist, and he would continue to undertake discrete projects, primarily involving system architecture, the work that had first brought him to AuctionWeb. But the computer genius with the unruly red hair who had once saved eBay—and who, as Skippy, had embodied its quirky early culture better than anyone—would no longer be given any role in the company's day-to-day operations. In a more carefree time, Skippy used to joke on the message boards that he did not work at eBay, because they moved the headquarters whenever he found out where they were. It was an oddly self-fulfilling prophecy: in his new role, Wilson would be doing almost all of his work from home.

◆

In late June 1999, eBay bought Alando.de, Germany's largest online auction site. EBay had long had a global reach; its registered users were drawn from ninety countries. But on the main site, they felt like foreigners—official announcements and message boards were exclusively in English; auctions were conducted in U.S. dollars; and the cultural feel, from the categories to the rules governing the auctions, was distinctly American. EBay's management liked to tell Wall Street analysts that it had still barely begun to tap the domestic market: less than 2 percent of U.S. coin and stamp sales, for example, were currently being transacted on the site. But when the company sat down to do its growth projections, it was clear that moving into overseas markets would be critical. A period of cyberempire-building was under way, with American Internet companies starting to carve up the globe, and eBay wanted to move into key markets before Yahoo!, Amazon, or local companies locked them up. EBay's strategy was to expand aggressively into new countries in the order of their Internet population, which meant that after the United States, whose nearly 100 million users made it the world's leading Internet market, it wanted to move into Japan, the United Kingdom, Canada, and Germany.

Of these, the expansion into Germany was the most easily accomplished. EBay had been hearing reports about a start-up called Alando.de, a homegrown online auction site that was well on its way to becoming the eBay of Germany. Alando had been started in March 1999 by the Samwers—three young brothers from Cologne—and three of their friends. One Samwer had spent time in Silicon Valley researching a book on successful start-ups, and had been particularly taken by eBay's business model. When he returned home, he began rounding up seed money, recruited his cofounders, and found offices in Kreuzberg, a low-rent neighborhood of Berlin.

Alando had done an impressive job of replicating the eBay experience. Its one-room offices looked a lot like AuctionWeb's first suite in 2005 Hamilton Avenue. The furniture was from Ikea, and new Alando hires even assembled their own desks. There were biweekly companywide meetings, at which the whole staff was encouraged to participate. And the ties between the staff and the Alando community were so close that many users knew individual employees by name. Alando even had its own Onsale-like rival, Ricardo.de, which was better funded, but had an unfriendly black website and was less focused on community.

Alando was off to a fast start. In its first two months it had sold more than 250,000 items, and it had fifty thousand users. Knowing what they did about network effects, eBay's senior managers knew they had to act fast—either by buying Alando or Ricardo, or by getting into the German market themselves. Omidyar decided to travel to Berlin to investigate, much as he had paid a visit to Up4Sale a year earlier. Alando's founders were nervous when the time came to pick him up at the airport. They knew he was a billionaire, and thought he might expect to have a limousine waiting. But instead, one of the founders showed up in a beat-up Volkswagen Golf. It was an eBaysian move, Omidyar told him, explaining that he drove a beat-up VW himself. Omidyar and the founders talked for more than four hours that day about Alando and its approach to online auctions. It was a test, and Alando had passed. A few weeks later, Omidyar returned with Gary Bengier, and they offered to buy the company for more than $42 million in eBay stock.

Alando did not feel the change in ownership right away. "The only difference was we wore eBay shirts instead of Alando shirts," says cofounder Joerg Rheinboldt. But eight months later, eBay installed Philipp Justus as the new director of the German office. In keeping with eBay's commitment to local staffing of its foreign sites, Justus was German. But he had graduated from Northwestern University's Kellogg School of Management, had worked for the Boston Consulting Group, and spoke flawless English. Justus, a thin, square-jawed man who spoke with clipped precision, had the same task before him that Whitman had taken on—professionalizing a somewhat unruly start-up. He realized he had his work cut out for him during the interview process, when he saw something that deeply offended his management-consultant sensibility: he asked each of the six founders to draw him an organizational chart for the company, and each of the six drawings was different.

Once Justus was in place, eBay began to impose itself more on the Alando culture. Within a few months of his arrival, all three Samwers and two of the other founders—all but Rheinboldt—were gone. Justus drew up an organizational chart, with six clearly defined units reporting to him, and began hiring the same kind of corporate professionals—a finance director, a head of human resources—that eBay had in the months leading up to its IPO. Justus had weekly conference calls with Steve Westly, who was now heading up international, and eBay instituted a "Get to Know Your Colleagues in the U.S." program, in which Alando staff had regular phone conversations with the staff in Campbell.

The month Justus started, Alando instituted its first listing fees. Since its founding, Alando had—like Yahoo! Auctions—charged only final value fees on auctions that ended in a sale. The German staff warned there would be an uproar in the community, and there was. Alando received three thousand e-mails a day protesting the new fees, and listings plunged from 1.2 million to 200,000. EBay's position was the one Omidyar had come to back in 1996 with AuctionWeb: that listing fees actually strengthened the site, by removing listings that were not worth paying a fee to list. In fact, even though the listings on Alando plunged nearly 85 percent, gross merchandise sales remained virtually unchanged.

That summer, Alando.de changed its domain to eBay.de, and the transition was complete. "Der Weltweite Online Marktplatz" looked and felt a great deal like the original eBay, the World's Online Marketplace. But at the same time, it was unmistakably German. The listings were weighted toward practical items—computers, electronics, and mobile phones. Many of the collectibles that showed up on the site would have struck Americans as odd—notably *Kinder uberraschings Eider*, chocolate eggs with a surprise toy inside, one of the most hotly traded items on eBay.de. EBay-Germany also had its own standards for what was acceptable: wine was permitted, and was one of the site's best selling items; pornography was prohibited; and Nazi items were banned even before eBay removed them from its U.S. site, because they were illegal in Germany.

But the biggest difference between eBay.de and eBay was in their users. Consistent with the stereotype of Germany as a nation inordinately devoted to rules, eBay.de's buyers and sellers took features like the Feedback Forum far more seriously than their American counterparts. When Germans got a single negative—or even a neutral rating—from another user, they often called eBay.de to lodge a formal complaint, and demanded the right to submit detailed documentation for use in adjudicating the dispute. It fell to Renate Maifarth, an anthropologist who had studied West African tribal culture before becoming eBay.de's head of community, to try to convince callers that a stray feedback comment was not important, and that they should just accept the fact that the system was imperfect. But Maifarth found she was getting complaints from users even when the other party to their transaction had left no feedback. It was a common enough occurrence on eBay.com and lightly shrugged off by American users, but the Germans were outraged. "They say, 'I have done my best, I paid the next day, why didn't I get my feedback?'" says Maifarth.

◆

In July 1999, David Lucking-Reiley sent a bot—a piece of software designed to mine for data—to eBay's site. The bot, written in PERL programming language by a University of Michigan computer science graduate student, was designed to harvest information from twenty thousand auctions of mint-condition Indian head pennies. EBay discovered Lucking-Reiley's digital intruder and blocked access—eBay's user agreement barred the use of bots—but not before the bot had collected a month's worth of data.

This particular bot did not come from a competitor—it was no repeat of Onsale's Halloween-night sneak attack. Lucking-Reiley was an assistant professor of economics at Vanderbilt University, collecting data for his latest project, a scholarly treatise on the economic effect of the Feedback Forum. Lucking-Reiley had been hearing for years about how Omidyar's invention built community and instilled trust among strangers. But he did not believe it had a demonstrable effect on how buyers and sellers acted. "I really felt the Feedback Forum was mostly cheap talk," he says. He was convinced rigorous mathematical analysis of eBay auctions would prove that point.

Lucking-Reiley was part of a small but growing subspecialty: academics who studied eBay. A tall man with a mop of curly brown hair, Lucking-Reiley, thirty, became interested in online auctions as a graduate student at the Massachusetts Institute of Technology in 1993. He had been slogging away on a thankless dissertation on price competition in the ulcer-drug market when a friend told him primitive auctions were starting to appear on the Internet. Lucking-Reiley went to the Usenet newsgroup his friend mentioned, for a science-fiction card game called Magic: The Gathering, and was immediately taken in.

Lucking-Reiley had always regarded auction theory as a sleepy backwater of economics. When he got to the Magic: The Gathering newsgroup, however, he discovered a remarkable little online economic world. MTG, as it was known, had been invented in the early 1990s by Wizards of the Coast, the same group of role-playing game (RPG) entrepreneurs who went on to create Pokémon. MTG attracted more than a million players, who bought hundreds of millions of dollars' worth of sixty-card starter decks, fifteen-card booster decks, and assorted MTG paraphernalia. The game is set in the "Multiverse of Dominaria," where dueling wizards cast spells on each other, and otherwise do battle, using five colors of magic and assorted creatures represented by more than three thousand game cards. The MTG newsgroup that Lucking-Reiley discovered, rec.games.deckmaster.marketplace, was originally a place for players to meet to discuss strategy, but it was soon overrun by players seeking to trade cards.

The exchange of cards on the site started out casually. Players offered one-for-one trades—a Dragon card for a Doppelgänger—so they could fill gaps in their arsenals. But trading soon gave way to selling, which was done through crude auctions. Users typically posted lists of several dozen cards they were selling and, in one common auction format, buyers then e-mailed the sellers their bids. At the end of each day, the seller updated the high bid. If a card went one day without a new bid, that was "going once." Two days was "going twice." On the third day without a bid, it was sold. The MTG site had hundreds of auctions running at any time, with some cards selling for under a dollar, and rarer ones—particularly the powerful Black Lotus—going for hundreds of dollars.

Lucking-Reiley dropped the ulcer-drug pricing research. He went out and bought several thousand dollars' worth of MTG cards, and put together a field experiment. He auctioned the cards off in various carefully arranged ways on the MTG newsgroup to test the theories of William Vickery, winner of the 1996 Nobel Prize for his pioneering work on the economics of auctions. Lucking-Reiley's work on Vickery's theories became the basis for his dissertation, published in the *American Economic Review* under the title "Using Field Experiments to Test Equivalence between Auction Formats: Magic on the Internet."

In early 1996, Lucking-Reiley stumbled on eBay. A student in a class he was teaching at MIT's Sloan School of Management, a single mother, had created a personal web page—a rare thing back then—and when Lucking-Reiley looked at it, he noticed that she was auctioning off a date with herself. Her date auction was being held on eBay, and when he clicked on the link on her page it brought him to the eBay site. Lucking-Reiley began exploring eBay, and he could see right away that it was a far richer economic world than the MTG auctions he had been studying. One day, it occurred to him, researchers would use eBay to investigate broad economic questions, like the impact of recessions on buying patterns, and how trade occurs across national borders. But Lucking-Reiley, focused as he was on auction theory, was more interested in exploring the economics of eBay itself.

EBay was, economically speaking, uncharted territory. Its fees had been established by Omidyar almost at random. It had hard closes simply because Omidyar thought auctions should last a predetermined number of days and no more. And it had a Feedback Forum because Omidyar thought it would free him of the obligation of policing the community. Lucking-Reiley quickly realized that he could be among the first economists to investigate whether any of Omidyar's intuitive decisions made economic sense.

In his first study, Lucking-Reiley examined an issue that had long divided the eBay community—reserve auctions. EBay provided sellers with two ways of setting a minimum price for their auctions. They could set a minimum bid, which was stated openly in the auction listing. If a buyer tried to make a lower bid, eBay's computer would reject it. The alternative was a reserve price. In a reserve auction, bidders were told there was a reserve price, but not what that price was. EBay's computers accepted bids below the reserve, but until a bid came in that was above the reserve price, the auction listing stated that the reserve had not been met. Buyers had long complained about reserve auctions: many said they did not like bidding on an item without knowing where they really stood. Many sellers liked minimum pricing—they saw it as the only way of ensuring they were not forced to sell an expensive item at too low a price. And of the two methods of setting a minimum price, conventional wisdom among sellers was that reserve auctions were better than minimum prices, because when a seller plainly stated a minimum bid in the auction listing, it scared away potential buyers. "A high minimum bid is a turnoff even to bidders willing to pay full market price," the *Official eBay Guide to Buying, Selling, and Collecting Just About Anything* advises. The better course, the authors say, is to set a reserve price and start the bidding low. "Bidders are likely to bid early or track your item," the book says. "Such auctions can generate a lot of curiosity, which can translate into bids."

Lucking-Reiley's research found that this conventional wisdom had it completely backwards. In a study later published as "Public versus Secret Reserve Prices in eBay Auctions: Results from a Pokémon Field Experiment," Lucking-Reiley auctioned off fifty pairs of identical Pokémon cards on eBay. He put one card from each of the pairs up for auction with a secret reserve price of 30 percent of its value and no minimum bid. He put the other card up with a minimum bid of 30 percent of its value and no reserve. When the auctions ended, 72 percent of the cards with minimum bids ended up selling, but only 52 percent of the cards with reserves did. The fifty cards with minimum bids sold, on average, for sixty-two cents more than the fifty cards with reserves. What the conventional wisdom did not recognize was that buyers were so put off by secret reserve prices that many simply refused to participate in auctions that used them. Despite the popularity of reserve auctions in the seller community, Lucking-Reiley concluded that they "represented a clear loss for the seller."

It was after his minimum-bid research that Lucking-Reiley moved on to the Feedback Forum, and launched his bot. In constructing a study to test the influence of feedback, he decided it made sense to look at a large number of auctions in which the value of the items was as predetermined as possible. Mint coins were ideal. It would be relatively easy to isolate the effect of feedback in these auctions, because the actual value of the coins, which could be found in a catalog, was virtually a constant. And there were enough Indian head pennies up for auction on eBay that the sample size could be large. If the Feedback Forum did what eBay claimed, buyers should be paying more for mint Indian head pennies from sellers with high feedback ratings than from sellers with low ratings.

Defying his expectations going in, Lucking-Reiley found that the Feedback Forum worked. In "Pennies from eBay: The Determinants of Price in Online Auctions," he performed a regression analysis of a subset of the auctions, 461 auctions of pennies made between 1859 and 1909, with a mint state of between 60 and 66 on a 70-point scale. The feedback ratings, it turned out, had a measurable effect on the price a buyer was willing to pay. Not all feedback counted equally. Positive ratings had only a slight, statistically insignificant, impact. A 1 percent increase in a seller's positive feedback rating raised the selling price of a coin 0.03 percent. But the effect of negative feedback was substantial. A 1 percent decrease in a seller's negative feedback rating lowered the price by 0.11 percent.

In fact, Lucking-Reiley's findings gave support to two distinct Omidyar doctrines. The negative feedback results showed that the Feedback Forum really did affect how members of the community regarded each other—it was not, as Lucking-Reiley had originally thought, just "cheap talk." Positive feedback, by contrast, had less of an impact, because eBay users had adopted Omidyar's presumption that the people they were dealing with were honest. In the absence of evidence to the contrary, a positive rating simply encouraged buyers and sellers to do what they were already doing—trusting other members of the eBay community.

◆

On July 4, eBay launched its eBay-U.K. site, eBay.co.uk. The date, which had been pushed back several times, was not the most auspicious one for an American corporation to begin its assault on the British market, and it produced the expected round of jokes. In England, eBay took the opposite of its approach in Germany—it decided to build its own site, rather than acquire an existing one. An all-British staff, working in inexpensive space on the outskirts of London, put together a site that looked like eBay.com, but with a British sensibility. It had a variety of British-interest categories, like royal commemoratives and rugby collectibles, prices were in pounds, the spelling was British, and there were U.K.-specific chat areas.

It took eBay-U.K. some time to find its footing. Internet use in the United Kingdom was well behind that in the United States, in large part because web surfers had to pay British Telecom for their telephone connection by the minute. The site also had to iron out some cultural differences. When eBay-U.K. sent out eBay's standard responses to customer e-mail, which had been written in Campbell, British users complained that the exclamation point–filled messages were insincere. In England, it seemed, people were not used to being thanked profusely for making a complaint. The eBay-U.K. staff had to draft new versions, written with typical British reserve. Another problem was that the message boards were not building community in the United Kingdom the way they had in the United States. British users, it turned out, did not feel comfortable nattering on to strangers the way Americans did about how they had cleaned out their garage that morning or had seen Elvis Presley perform before he became famous.

The U.K. site also had a significant legal obstacle eBay.com did not. England had no First Amendment, and its defamation laws were far stricter than in the United States. EBay-U.K. found that when its users received negative feedback, they often called up and threatened to sue both the writer of the feedback and eBay. In many cases, the criticism was what American users would regard as trivial. But in England, sellers who received feedback saying they charged buyers too much for postage had no hesitation about notifying eBay that they were contacting their solicitors. These incidents were so common that eBay-U.K. developed a form for users to fill out when they believed they had been defamed by feedback. When the form was completed and signed by a solicitor, eBay launched an investigation into the merits of the offending feedback.

For all of their cultural miscues and idiosyncracies eBay.de and eBay.co.uk were both clear successes. By the first quarter of 2000, eBay had pushed aside the two biggest homegrown European sites—British QXL and German Ricardo.de—bringing in $87 million in sales, compared to the European sites' combined $38 million. By the fall of 2000, eBay.de's listings had soared to 500,000, fully one-tenth the listings on eBay.com, and by 2001, the volume of sales on the site surpassed what eBay itself achieved in 1998. Within a year of its launch, eBay-U.K. had passed its bitter rival, QXL. In early 2001, eBay continued its march across Europe, acquiring Paris-based iBazar, which had 2.4 million registered users and was the leading site in France, Italy, Spain, Belgium, Portugal, and the Netherlands. By the fall of 2001, eBay was the leading online auction site in sixteen of the seventeen markets it competed in.

The seventeenth, unfortunately, was Japan, the second-biggest Internet market in the world. EBay was hardly the only foreign company to find the Japanese market hard to penetrate. But eBay had been handed a rare opportunity: Softbank's Masayoshi Son, who had tried to get Yahoo! to buy eBay in 1998, wanted Yahoo! to partner with eBay on a Japanese auction site. The catch was that the deal gave Softbank more than half of the ownership in the site, more than eBay's management considered fair. "We didn't see how it made sense for us to relinquish majority control given that it was going to be our mechanism and our brand," says Kagle. Another concern for eBay was the prospect of collaborating with Yahoo! in Japan while the two companies remained fierce competitors in the U.S. market. It was inevitable, eBay's leadership believed, that Yahoo! would take what it learned from the collaboration and use it against eBay at home. Yahoo! had far more users and daily traffic, and eBay was afraid that if it ever got auctions right, it could seize control of the online auction space. In the end, eBay decided the risk was too great.

In February 2000, five months after Yahoo! Japan launched its online auction site, eBay entered the Japanese online auction market. The site got off to a grim start. Sticking to company policy, eBay charged fees, even though Yahoo! Japan was both highly popular and free. It also required credit cards, even though many Japanese didn't have one. The site itself was regarded as culturally remote, lacking horoscopes, newsletters, and other features that Japanese users expected. And while Yahoo! Japan advertised heavily, eBay did little promotion. A year later, eBay-Japan was a poor fourth in the Japan market, with just four thousand listings, compared to Yahoo! Japan's 2 million. EBay's failure to break into Japan had the management team ruing its decision not to partner with Yahoo! "Right now we would own close to half of an unassailable position in Japan," Kagle said, his voice tinged with regret, in the fall of 2000. Whitman did not disagree that eBay had paid a high price for rejecting Son's offer. But at the time, she said, Yahoo!'s threat to eBay in the U.S. market seemed far greater than it later turned out to be.

EBay was not completely shut out of Asia. It was number one in Australia, where it had launched in October 1999, giving it a strong presence in a country with close ties to Asia's major economies. And in early 2001, eBay bought a majority stake in Internet Auction Ltd., South Korea's largest online auction site, putting eBay in a dominant position in Asia's second-largest Internet economy. EBay planned to use those two countries as beachheads from which to expand across the continent. Every step of the way, however, it would run into Yahoo!, which was a powerful presence in nearly every Asian country. The stakes were high: if there was a single weakness in eBay's plan for becoming a truly global market, it was its inability to claim a dominant position in the fast-growing, Internet-heavy Asian market. And eBay's poor standing there traced directly back to its decision not to partner with Softbank. "With twenty-twenty hindsight," says Whitman, "it was probably one of the bigger strategic mistakes we've made."

◆

Back in the United States in July 1999, twenty-nine-year-old high-tech entrepreneur Josh Kopelman was setting up a dot-com in a cramped office in the suburbs of Philadelphia. Kopelman, a graduate of the University of Pennsylvania's Wharton School of Business, had already helped found one Internet start-up, Infonautics, that had gone on to a successful IPO. He left Infonautics with $300,000 in seed money, a computer-engineer colleague named Sunny Balijepalli, who had agreed to be his new chief technical officer, and a plan for beating eBay at its own game.

The idea had come to Kopelman one day when he was at home on his computer, trying to buy his wife the latest John Grisham novel. Kopelman had gone to Amazon, and was about to pay twenty-eight dollars for a new copy. On a whim, he decided to look on eBay. He found twelve copies there, at prices starting as low as a dollar. And no one was bidding on any of them.

Kopelman had stumbled on a basic fact about eBay: that, like all auctions, it worked best for items whose value was uncertain. Buyers on the site did not think it was worth participating in an auction for a mass-produced item whose value was well established—like a John Grisham novel. Kopelman decided to exploit this weakness in eBay's model. He wanted to create a company that combined the best aspects of eBay and Amazon. Like eBay, it would be a network of buyers and sellers. Anyone on it could buy or sell with anyone else, allowing the company to benefit from network effects. The company would also, like eBay, be virtual: it would never come in contact with the items that were traded. This virtualness would allow it to take full advantage of the Internet's power, and potentially give it the same kind of off-the-charts profit margins eBay had. But like Amazon, the site would offer fixed prices, and buying and selling on it would be fast and easy. Kopelman originally intended to sell only books, but he realized the model made just as much sense for CDs, videos, and computer games. He registered the domain name "ebazon.com," a tribute to the two companies that had inspired him. But when his lawyers raised trademark concerns, he changed the name to Half.com after a rule, since abandoned, that no item on his new site could sell for more than half list price.

In many ways, Half was actually better than eBay. Listing was far easier on Half. The site dealt only in mass-produced items, which came with ISBN or UPC numbers, long strings of digits that are part of the bar code. Once sellers registered with Half, they could list an item simply by typing in its ISBN or UPC number. Drawing on existing databases, Half's software then converted the number into a professional-quality listing. For books, it produced an image of the dust jacket and blurbs. For CDs, it showed the CD cover and song lists. Kopelman liked to say his goal was to make it easier to sell an item than to throw it away. He was not there yet: items that sold still had to be packed up and taken to the post office. But listing on Half required only a fraction of the keystrokes needed to list on eBay.

The transactions themselves were also considerably more efficient on Half. A buyer could make a purchase with just a few mouse clicks. When an order was placed, Half removed the item from its listings, notified the seller that the buyer's credit card had been charged, and provided the address to which the item should be shipped. There was no delay and, for the buyer, no risk of losing out to a rival. "There are people who love the thrill of bidding and winning," says Kopelman. "But there are other people who don't want to win an auction, they just want the CD."

Kopelman's model also confronted fraud more directly than eBay's. Buyers paid Half directly, and Half in turn paid the seller, so sellers did not need to worry about bounced checks. Half also accepted credit card payments, an attractive feature in the days before online payment services were widely available. And it offered a buyer-protection plan for all transactions up to fifty dollars, the vast majority of sales on the site. "You might be buying it from Bob in Des Moines," Kopelman liked to say. "But you're also buying it from Half." Half could afford the expense, because Kopelman had improved on the eBay model in one final way: Half took 15 percent of every transaction, far more than eBay.

Kopelman and Balijepalli spent the rest of the year building the site. They wanted to take Half live on January 19, 2000, but to launch it they needed items to sell. It was a problem, because sellers had no way of finding out about Half. Even when they were told about the concept, sellers were reluctant to take the time to list items on a website that was not even operating yet. Half's marketers spent months making personal visits to used book, video, and CD stores, explaining the site and trying to talk managers into listing inventory. In some cases, they literally had to help their would-be sellers set up AOL accounts to get them on the Internet.

In its first months, Half used an old eBay tactic: flying under the radar. Half employees were barred from discussing the company or its business model, except in their pitches to potential sellers. Kopelman demonstrated the lengths to which he was willing to go to protect his idea when he sent representatives to a career fair at Wharton. Half's booth had a big Half.com banner, but when prospective applicants came over, the recruiters said they could not discuss what the company did. No one ended up being hired that day.

As the January 19 launch date drew near, Half.com was ready to swing wildly in the other direction. Kopelman made it known that he was looking for a publicity stunt outrageous enough to elevate Half above the horde of new dot-coms that were showing up in cyberspace each day and competing for consumers' attention. At an early December brainstorming meeting, someone threw out the idea of persuading a town somewhere in the United States to rename itself Half.com. It struck everyone in the room as interesting but improbable, particularly with the launch only weeks away. But Mark Hughes,

Half's head marketer, started looking on Yahoo! and MapQuest for towns with names suitably close to Half. After rejecting Halfa, Iowa, he decided that Halfway, Oregon (population 345), was the best prospect.

Three days later, Hughes was in Boise, Idaho, behind the wheel of a rented car, driving through the snow toward Halfway. On the day he arrived, as it happened, the city council was holding a regularly scheduled meeting. Hughes made his pitch, and the council voted to enter into negotiations. The two sides worked out a deal: in exchange for $75,000 and twenty-two computers for the town's schools, Halfway was prepared to become Half.com. With dot-com frenzy near its peak, the story proved irresistible to the media. When the *Today Show* was tipped off, bookers called to invite Kopelman and the mayor of Half.com to appear together on the morning of January 19.

◆

Also in July 1999, Connie Bacon, a Charleston, South Carolina, antiques dealer, put five Rolex watches up on eBay. Bacon knew eBay well, and she sometimes ran auctions on consignment for other sellers—in this case it was an estate jeweler in town. As soon as the watches went up, Bacon got e-mails asking for the serial numbers and inquiring about their condition. One e-mail was from a Kelvin Johanis, who was interested in the priciest one, a gold Rolex that had been listed with a minimum bid of $13,500. He needed it right away—to wear that weekend, he said—and offered $13,500 to end the auction. The e-mail was a little sloppy. "I was kind of thinking, here's this guy who's going to pay thirteen thousand five hundred dollars for a watch, and he can't spell," Bacon says. But she checked with the seller, and they agreed to accept the offer.

Johanis wanted to use the online escrow service iEscrow. That was common for sales of this size, Bacon knew. If the watch was broken or a fake, the buyer could get his money back from the escrow company, which would hold it until both parties agreed to clear the transaction. Johanis drew up a contract for the sale, as iEscrow required, and had Bacon approve it by e-mail. The next morning,

Bacon got an e-mail with an official notice from iEscrow that it had received Johanis's $13,500 payment. Bacon called the estate jewelry seller and told him to go ahead and ship the watch.

About an hour later, Bacon got a panicked call from iEscrow. The company's investigators had just closed in on Johanis—an alias, it turned out, for a nineteen-year-old Washington State man—after determining that he had already used stolen credit cards to buy almost $20,000 in goods through iEscrow, including watches and laptop computers. But his con on Bacon was more resourceful than just using a stolen credit card. The e-mail telling her to send the watch had not come from iEscrow at all. He had registered the e-mail address I_Escrow@Hotmail.com with Hotmail, Microsoft's free e-mail service. To a seller who was not paying attention, it looked like it was coming from iEscrow. The "official" notice Bacon received, telling her to go ahead and send the watch, had been copied and pasted from a real iEscrow notice. Bacon ran to the phone to call the seller to tell him not to send the watch. But he told her he had already mailed it from a post office in suburban Charleston. Bacon tracked it down there. "The woman who answered the phone said, 'Oh, it's right here,'" says Bacon. "I said, 'Thank you, Jesus.'" The watch was never mailed out, but Bacon was fuming.

Johanis was not much of a crook. The police were already after him, focusing on the obvious weakness in his scam: at the end, he had to take delivery of the goods. He had recently gotten a seller to ship him a laptop computer, giving an abandoned house in Lynwood, Washington, as his shipping address. This time, the police wanted to stake out the address he provided to Bacon, and arrest him when the watch arrived.

The iEscrow investigators who called Bacon to tip her off asked if she would agree to play along, and she did. Johanis, who was apparently refining his technique, had instructed her to send the Rolex to a post office box. Bacon e-mailed him and said that FedEx was telling her it would only deliver to a physical address. Johanis wrote back, giving her the address of the abandoned house. Bacon wrapped up a box containing chipped glass in a soap dish, and sent it off.

While the police staked out the abandoned house, Johanis went to the FedEx office and intercepted the delivery. He signed for Bacon's package and sped off on a red-and-white motorcycle. But the police got a description of him and the bike from the FedEx clerk, and they arrested young Johanis—who had pleaded guilty to a different computer theft days earlier—at his mother's house.

Bacon's story got wide press attention. It joined a long list of other eBay fraud stories, which reporters delighted in. In the Christmas season of 1998, Sonny Stemple had been the poster boy for online auction fraud. More recently, *USA Today* had given prominent coverage to Robert Guest, a former pizza delivery manager with a video poker addiction, who took $36,193 from thirty-one eBay buyers for electronic equipment he did not deliver. Now the press seemed to be suggesting that any eBay buyer could be a Kelvin Johanis, with a bad credit card and an abandoned house to take deliveries in.

EBay, as always, bristled at the reports. Despite the site's explosive growth, eBay insisted, fraud remained extremely rare—a small fraction of a percent of all transactions. But the same media that had largely ignored eBay during its rise were now fascinated with this one aspect of the company's story. The national press, eBay staff grumbled, would never write an article about an off-line theft of $30,000.

EBay always said that fraud was more of a concern for reporters than it was for users of the site, and it was true. Most regular users reported that they had never experienced a dishonest trade, and didn't know anyone who had. Many other eBay policies had produced uproars in the community, but fraud never had. Bacon, for her part, said her sale to Johanis was the only case of fraud she had encountered on eBay, and she had listed up to sixty auctions a week for years. And eBay compared favorably to her experience selling in the bricks-and-mortar antiques store she once ran. "I've never even had a bounced check on eBay," she says. "I got a bad check at my store for five hundred dollars, and I still haven't collected on it."

◆

In August 1999 eBay announced that, for the first time, it would charge an additional one-dollar fee for listing a reserve auction. EBay insisted it was not trying to generate more fees, but rather to discourage reserve auctions, which were now 15 to 20 percent of all auctions on the site. EBay had noticed that reserve auctions often did not end in successful bids. In fact, in many cases the seller did not want them to: eBay was increasingly hearing about sellers who listed items with unreasonably high reserves just to get an appraisal of what they were worth. These unwinnable reserve auctions were frustrating to bidders, who blamed eBay for their wasted time and effort.

That was eBay's official explanation for the one-dollar reserve auction fee. But a driving force for the new rule was something that was hurting eBay more than user dissatisfaction: fee avoidance. A growing number of eBay sellers were listing items with enormous reserves, knowing that the auction would end without a winner. The seller then had a list of e-mail addresses of every losing bidder, and could contact them directly to negotiate a price. The result: buyer and seller were meeting through eBay, but eBay was not ending up with a final value fee.

When eBay announced the one-dollar charge, the message boards erupted. Boards that usually got fifty posts in a day were getting ten times that, with subject headings like "Greedy eBay." Sellers, particularly those who specialized in low-priced items, complained that the extra dollar on every reserve auction could drive them out of business. They charged eBay with failing to see the importance of reserve auctions to sellers. It was their only way, they insisted, of protecting themselves from having to sell an expensive item for less than its value. (They were, of course, unaware of David Lucking-Reiley's finding that setting a minimum bid, which was still free, would have earned them more money.) When a poster on one particularly heated message board asked if, amid all the eBay bashing, anyone had anything positive to say, another seller wrote: "I'm positive that eBay will no longer have ninety-nine point nine percent of my auction business."

In response to the complaints, Omidyar posted a letter on the Announcement Board defending the new fee, ending it by saying: "And finally, it's only a dollar." The remark enraged opponents, particularly volume sellers, who saw nothing "only" about it. "For me, I will probably use about four thousand to five thousand reserves this year," one poster wrote on OTWA's eBay message board. "So that's $4,000 to $5,000, not just a buck." The phrase "It's only a dollar" quickly became a rallying cry. It did not help that the words came from a multibillionaire. "For him to tell us 'it's only a dollar' is just the latest insult that eBay has piled upon our injury," the OTWA poster wrote. "That's a bit like me telling a hungry homeless guy 'it's only a sandwich' as I eat it in front of him."

That was not, of course, Omidyar's intent when he used what he would later call "those famous words I wish I could retract." But eBay had lost the battle for the hearts and minds of the community. It backed down and modified the fee: for reserve auctions of twenty-five dollars or less, it would be only fifty cents, and whenever an item actually sold, it would be refunded. The reserve auction flap was more than a public-relations setback, although it certainly was that. It was also a reminder—the latest reminder—of the importance of including the community in proposed changes to the site. Skoll, who was out having back surgery during the reserve auction controversy, says the people who made the change were too focused on eBay's interests to consider the fee from the community's perspective. The lesson, he says, is that "you can hire people to do deals," but it doesn't mean they "understand this community."

chapter eight

Simon Rothman, who worked on strategic planning for eBay, noticed something odd when he went on the site to add to his die-cast car collection. He typed Ferrari 355 in the search engine, trying to find a 1:18-scale metal replica of the classic Italian sports car, which sells for about thirty dollars. But it brought up a real Ferrari 355. EBay currently had no official car category, so sellers were at a loss about where to list them. Most cars ended up in the general section of the Miscellaneous category, eBay's traditional dumping ground. Some, like Rothman's Ferrari, were being listed with toy and model cars.

Cars had been showing up since AuctionWeb's first month, when Omidyar had been shocked to see a listing for a 1952 Silver Dawn Rolls Royce. But eBay had never actively pursued them. The conventional wisdom at the company was that cars would never sell in large numbers on the Internet. They were the most expensive purchase Americans made after their homes, and the skeptics said buyers would insist on kicking the tires in person. Cars were also large and heavy, so even if eBay could bring prices down, it seemed that any saving would be more than offset by shipping costs. Still, Rothman could see that even without eBay's help, cars were selling on the site every day. He started calling some of the sellers, asking them how their auctions turned out. The conversations convinced him that eBay should pull cars out from the shadows, creating an Automotive category and actively promoting it.

Rothman was a natural for the role of in-house car advocate. Growing up in Cincinnati, the son of a onetime auto mechanic, he spent his childhood taking things apart and putting them back together. "I was the guy you made fun of in high school," he says. Rothman and his father used to spend summers fixing up old cars, selling them at the end. The two men bonded over the slow, painstaking work.

After college, Rothman left manual labor behind, getting an MBA at Harvard and then signing on as a consultant for McKinsey & Company. He had gotten to know Skoll when they worked for the same consulting firm one summer, Rothman in New York, Skoll in San Francisco. They kept in touch, and in 1998 Skoll began trying to recruit Rothman for eBay. Rothman had been following the company's progress, and he could not help being impressed by the IPO. In early 1999, he took a job working with Skoll on strategic planning, mergers and acquisitions, and identifying companies for eBay to invest in. In May 1999, Rothman got to use his knowledge of automobiles when eBay bought Kruse International, the world's largest off-line car-auction company, and he was assigned to help integrate it into the company.

Rothman's arrival coincided with a shift in strategic thinking at eBay. It had been a year since the off-site at which Whitman and the senior management team had decided to emphasize collectibles. That made sense at the time, when eBay's highest priority was attracting more buyers and sellers. But now that eBay was a public company, Wall Street was doing what it always did: demanding higher quarterly earnings. Financial analysts were pointing out that one way to increase revenues was to raise the average selling price of items on the site, which would produce higher final value fees for eBay. The management team considered trying to attract higher-priced collectibles to the site—$400 items rather than $40 ones. But Whitman was coming around to the view that the best way to raise average sales prices was to increase the number of "practical" items sold on eBay.

EBay was not sure what kind of practical items to emphasize. Some of the staff were pushing consumer electronics. But Rothman made a formal pitch to the senior managers in which he urged them to "strip down to the core of what we do." The early success of collectibles showed, he argued, that eBay was most effective in selling items buyers were passionate about, which certainly applied to cars. EBay was also particularly successful in markets where existing methods of selling were flawed, and the used-car business was notoriously just that. Rothman's pitch worked. "It was a bold move," he says. "They decided to go into the deep end of practicals."

EBay launched its Automotive category in August 1999. All the cars listed were used—new car sales were governed by a thicket of laws that made it almost impossible for anyone but a dealership to sell to the public. As soon as the category went up, it was flooded with cars, car parts, motorcycles, and ancillary items like automotive memorabilia. Rothman expected the new category to attract mainly collector cars, but everyday vehicles—used Honda sedans, Chevy station wagons—made up the vast majority of the listings.

Once the category proved itself, Rothman argued that the next step was establishing a separate Automotive site. It was an audacious request: eBay had never created the kind of separate site Rothman was asking for, with its own home page and domain name. But he argued that cars were different from other items sold on eBay. Car buyers were asking for a more refined search function, enabling them to look for cars by make. They also needed special services, including inspections and financing, that a separate site could display prominently. But most of all, Rothman believed eBay's Automotive category needed its own look and feel. "The main eBay site is simple, folksy in all the right ways, with a lot of white space and simplistic charm," he says. He wanted the car site to have a serious look, one more suitable for items selling for thousands of dollars. EBay's senior management once again backed Rothman. Starting in late 1999 he began working with Maynard Webb's engineers on designing the new site.

◆

The famous listing, which went up on August 26, 1999, was brief and to the point. "Fully functional kidney for sale," it said. "You can choose either kidney. Buyer pays all transplant and medical costs. Of course, only one for sale, as I need the other one to live. Serious bids only." The seller, identified only as "hchero" of Sunrise, Florida, started the bidding at $25,000. The auction went on for eight days, and bidding reached $5.7 million before eBay declared it a hoax and shut it down. Hoax or not, it violated eBay's prohibition on selling body parts, as well as federal law, which made selling one's own organs a felony, punishable by up to five years in prison.

The kidney auction set off a media frenzy. From National Public Radio's *Morning Edition* to the syndicated entertainment-gossip television show *Extra*, journalists—and experts of all stripes—offered up kidney-sale punditry. The president of the American Medical Association told the Associated Press he doubted "the ethics of any doctor who would participate in that kind of transaction." The head of the Transplant Donor Network fretted on the *Today Show* that people would now think there was a free market in body parts. A Boston University public health professor argued on the network news that it was ethically less defensible to sell kidneys than blood or sperm, because body parts are not renewable. And in San Francisco, the Libertarian Party's national director declared on morning drive-time radio that organ selling was every American's right. EBay, for its part, did its best to minimize the auction's significance. "We get items we have to take down on a fairly frequent basis," spokesman Kevin Pursglove said. "From time to time, we'll get a kidney or a liver."*

The kidney was eBay's most famous prank auction, but hardly the first. In July, under the category Miscellaneous: Services: General, a seller with the ID "f.cornworth" had listed an auction, slightly misspelled, for a "Young Man's Virginty." The description included a picture of a geeky kid with large glasses, and stated that Francis D. Cornworth was seventeen years old, a virgin, in the top 5 percent of his class, and president of his high school's computer and A/V clubs. "I live in Miami, Florida," the listing said. "If you live in Florida, I could probably meet you halfway up to Orlando in my 1990 Civic Hatchback." The bidding reached a high of $10 million, from one "ferris41," before eBay pulled the auction. In April, when a group of engineers auctioned themselves off as "high-priced, professionally trained cybergeeks," the bidding hit $3.14 million. And in February, a seller purporting to be from Osaka listed "24 Small Children," and included a photo of what appeared to be a Japanese elementary-school class. Shipping costs would vary, the seller said, because he and his friend Jerry had to prepare specialized wooden boxes with airholes.

There were more pranks to come, and they often hit in waves. An auction of "Pure, Uncut Cocaine," was followed by one for five hundred pounds of marijuana. Going into the 2000 presidential election, there was a brief flurry of voters auctioning off their votes. "Why should the American citizen be left out?" a Maryland voter using the ID "apragmatic" asked. "Congressmen and senators regularly sell their votes to the highest bidder." At the height of the dot-com collapse, a former employee of a dot-com called Quokka Sports got back at his old employer by listing the company on eBay. The

---

*The media did not linger on the kidney listing for long. In a few days, they had moved on to a new eBay auction story: that three babies had been offered for sale on the site. One of the three auctions was for a boy to be born later in the month, whose parents were both University of Chicago law school students. That auction may have been an inside joke: the school's most famous professor, Richard Posner, had coauthored an article entitled "The Economics of the Baby Shortage," which made an economic argument for the sale of parental rights.

description offered "the twelve employees left after three rounds of cost-trimming layoffs" and "e-mail archives, ninety-eight percent of it being taken up by pointless, long-winded, chest thumping ramblings" from management. Not included, according to the write-up: "A revenue model."

Kembrew McLeod, a University of Iowa communications professor, elevated the prank auction to performance art when he sold his soul on eBay in March 2000. McLeod had a history of media activism, much of it tweaking restrictions on free speech. He registered a trademark on the phrase "freedom of expression," for use as a magazine title, with the U.S. Patent and Trademark Office, and then loudly threatened to sue anyone who used it without his permission. ("If the ACLU wanted to put out a magazine with the title *Freedom of Expression*, they would have to pay me royalties," he insisted.) McLeod's scholarly writing included a study of "Happy Birthday," a song rarely heard in movies or on television because it remains copyrighted and the copyright owners charge for every use. The title of his paper was " 'Happy Birthday, Screw You': The Collision of Copyright Law, the Folk Song Tradition, and the World's Most Popular Birthday Song."

McLeod's soul, which came with a jar labeled "Kembrew's Soul" and a deed of ownership, sold for $1,325—he claims—to an anonymous New York real-estate dealer and art collector. McLeod enlisted a friend in public relations to help him pitch the story, which was picked up by the *Boston Globe,* Fox television, and the *London Guardian.* McLeod's performance art continued when the reporters called. He conducted interviews about the auction in character, as a corporate drone whose only concern was how much money he made from his soul. It was, he says, a critique of materialism. "Everyone sells their soul metaphorically," he explained to the Springfield, Massachusetts, *Union-News.* "I wanted to be the first to sell it materially—and profit from it." The *Union-News* appeared to have accepted his story at face value, responding to McLeod with, of course, an expert's opinion. "Asked about the consequences of selling one's soul," the news story stated, "retired *Union-News* Associate

Publisher Richard Garvey, a local historian and lifelong Catholic, replied simply, 'You go to hell.' "

EBay did not come off particularly well in these accounts. The staff never seemed to know about the auction until a reporter tipped them off, and even then they usually could not say who the seller was, or even whether it was intended as a prank. But what the media invariably missed was just how good all of this bad publicity was for eBay. The widespread media coverage of the kidney auction was how many Americans first heard of eBay and learned what it did, and each prank drove a wave of new traffic to the site. At eBay, senior managers talked quietly among themselves about how, for all the press's disapproval, the stories invariably hit the company's main promotional themes: that millions of people were buying and selling on eBay; that the site was a fun place to trade; and that, clearly, listing items was not hard to do.

◆

On September 6, 1999, eBay pulled down Ross Wright's auction of a crayon drawing entitled *JEFF BUCKLEY'S Soul Dances With Shiva.* EBay acted after a user named "JeffDefender" filed a Verified Rights Owner (VERO) complaint charging that the auction infringed on her intellectual property rights. Wright, who had done the crayon drawing himself, had fully expected the auction to be pulled when he put it up, and he was relishing the upcoming battle.

The subject of Wright's primitive artwork was a broodingly handsome rock-folk balladeer who drowned in 1997, at the age of thirty, after walking into the Mississippi River fully clothed. Buckley's death had tragic echoes of the death of his father, Tim Buckley, a musician who had been compared to Jackson Browne and Neil Young when he died in 1975, at the age of twenty-eight, of a heroin overdose. Jeff Buckley had long been popular on the Greenwich Village bohemian music circuit, and his one CD, *Grace,* had been warmly received by critics. But after his well-publicized drowning, and the posthumous release of two acclaimed CDs, *Sketches (For My Sweetheart, the Drunk),* and *Mystery White Boy,* Buckley developed a cult following.

JeffDefender, who had the art auction pulled, was the eBay ID of Jeff Buckley's mother, Mary Guibert. Guibert was known in the music world for zealously protecting her son's reputation, and for campaigning aggressively against piracy of his work. Guibert was also one of the most aggressive users of VERO—the successor to Brad Handler's Legal Buddy program—to end auctions. No one objected when she pulled bootleg concert tapes, but JeffDefender was rankling buyers and sellers alike by objecting to any auction even tangentially related to her son.

This unhappiness came to a head when Marie's CD, a well-known seller of music on eBay, complained on the AuctionWatch boards that JeffDefender had gotten eBay to pull her auction of a CD by a group called Arid because the listing—which was simply quoting from the album's own liner notes—compared Arid to Jeff Buckley. JeffDefender had objected that the auction was using Jeff's name to "peddle a product that is not Jeff and cannot even begin to equal Jeff's artistry." AuctionWatch, in a news report on the events, accused "the estate (a.k.a., Mom) of the late singer Jeff Buckley" of going "on a search-and-destroy rampage of any auctions that offered Buckley recordings or even made mention of the deceased musician."

JeffDefender became a flash point for the eBay community's ambivalent feelings about VERO. When the Legal Buddy program was first established, rights holders were upset with eBay for not doing more to keep infringing items off the site. But as both VERO and Internet law evolved, it became clear that eBay was fully complying with its obligations under the Digital Millennium Copyright Act.*

---

*A federal district court held just that in a September 2001 decision ruling that eBay was not liable for the sale of pirated goods when the rights holder did not comply with the VERO program's requirements. EBay had received a complaint from an alleged rights holder that bootleg copies of his Charles Manson documentary were being sold. But when eBay asked him to submit a sworn written statement, as the VERO program mandated, he refused, and instead sued eBay for not removing the items based on his unsworn complaint. The court held that under the Digital Millennium Copyright Act, eBay had a "safe harbor" against legal claims, because without appropriate notice from the rights holder, it did not have "the right and ability to control such activity."

The community's more recent complaints were that eBay had gone too far in the other direction. Sellers, who had taken to calling the Legal Buddy program the "Legal Bully" program, were complaining that eBay almost invariably pulled any auction a rights holder objected to. Sellers had the right to appeal eBay's decision, but in many cases—including Marie's CD's Arid auction—they decided it was not worth the trouble. The worst abusers of VERO, sellers complained, were not concerned about intellectual property rights at all. They were just trying to prevent eBay from becoming a secondary market for used items that competed with their merchandise. There had been a few notorious incidents, like the time a charity called First Response Search and Rescue Team tried to sell Mary Kay cosmetics that had been donated to it, and ended up receiving a threatening letter from Mary Kay's lawyers and being pursued through VERO.

After the Marie's CD dustup, critics of the VERO program decided to make an example of JeffDefender. They began inserting Jeff Buckley references into their auctions, just to get them pulled. One listing became legendary: a lamp that the seller said he got from his friend "Jeff," that worked well but was a little "buckley." A seller from the Midwest auctioned off an oversized book of American folk art, promising that the proceeds would go to the ACLU to protest JeffDefender's incursions on free speech. Among the most cold-blooded listings were one billed as the chemical that killed Jeff Buckley—a bottle of water—and another that blamed Guibert for not teaching her son how to swim.

But no one made more of a sport of going after JeffDefender than Ross Wright. A onetime punk rocker from Thousand Oaks, California, who supported himself in part by selling autographed drumsticks on eBay, Wright was a self-declared eBay rogue. He was proud that he had been suspended repeatedly from auction message boards for his outrageous and contentious posts. And he often listed items for sale in private auctions—a rarely used eBay option in which the identities of bidders were kept secret—because, he said, he was tired of "do-gooders" e-mailing his bidders and telling them that his items were overpriced. To protest JeffDefender's aggressive use of VERO, Wright made a series of crude drawings of other-worldly Jeff Buckley art—Buckley's soul ascending to heaven, Buckley's soul dancing with Vishnu, Buckley's soul encountering Buddha and the Tree of Knowledge—and put them up on eBay. Wright expected all the auctions to be canceled, and they were. He appealed the cancellations, taking his case directly to Jay Monahan, eBay's senior intellectual property lawyer. Wright argued that "fan art" was protected expression and did not infringe on the intellectual property rights of the person depicted. Monahan agreed and ordered the auctions restored. All of the paintings ultimately sold, Wright says, for between five dollars and thirty dollars, and he took pride in having struck a blow against eBay's policy of "pretty much taking the word of VERO rights holders."

Guibert says the mockery of her son's death, by Wright and others, was "cruel and heinous." And she insists that her critics misunderstood her. She joined VERO, she says, after a fan e-mailed her to say that eBay was rife with pirated Jeff Buckley items. When she looked on the site, she found not only bootleg tapes of her son's concerts made by fans, but recordings of his music taken off the radio by professional music pirates, who resold them without paying royalties. She even found watches with Buckley's likeness, made by a watchmaker that did not bother to ask for the family's permission or to obtain a license. Guibert denies pulling down everything that mentioned her son—it was more like five or six items, she says, out of about sixty on the site at any given time. Wright may have believed he won the battle with JeffDefender, but Guibert was just as convinced her own crusade was a success. When she started, pirated Jeff Buckley items were "rampant" on the site. After a year of aggressive enforcement, she says, most of the pirates had been driven away, and it was rare that she had to ask eBay to pull an auction.

◆

On September 13, 1999, six months after the firearms ban, eBay announced it was prohibiting the sale of alcohol and cigarettes. As with guns, the laws governing the sale of both substances varied widely from state to state. EBay had no system in place for informing sellers of the law that applied in a buyer's home state, and no means of ensuring that a buyer was of age. Sellers who were not careful about these "complex and contradictory" rules could, eBay explained, inadvertently commit a felony. Alcohol and cigarettes also raised the kind of legal liability issues for eBay that guns had. It was easy to imagine scenarios—drunk-driving accidents caused by alcohol purchased on eBay, children using eBay to buy cigarettes in bulk—that would be both legal and public-relations disasters.

EBay braced for a repeat of the guns blowup. Drawing on what they had learned the last time, eBay's management announced the ban a month in advance, rather than a mere week, to give the community more time to assimilate it. EBay also hosted a Q & A with the community to discuss the new rules, and presented a draft of the new policy to Voices members for their input. When the proposal was first shown to Voices 1, eBay was considering a complete ban on alcohol and tobacco products. But Voices 1 urged eBay to soften the ban by carving out an exception for certain tobacco and alcohol collectibles. The suggestion was accepted, which led to some Talmudic line drawing in the final policy. One rule eBay came up with was that sales of alcohol in a container would be allowed if the buyer was purchasing it for the container rather than for the alcohol. Bottles of Château Lafite Rothschild would be prohibited, even though wine aficionados collect them, because the "value is based on the wine in the bottle, not the bottle itself." But a can of Billy Beer would be permitted, since no one who bought it would ever think of drinking it.

The angry reaction eBay had steeled itself for never came. There were some mild objections, notably from fine wine sellers, who argued that their elite buyers did not raise the sort of liability issues eBay was concerned about when it implemented the policy. But overall, the wine community was considerably more restrained than gun collectors had been. Tobacco users, perhaps because they were already used to having their freedoms reined in, were equally uncomplaining. EBay's attempt to include the community in the process at an early stage may also have had its intended effect. Whatever the reason, the message boards were remarkably calm. One of the few posts that tried to generate sparks, entitled "More categories bite the Dust . . . is yours next?," drew only a handful of responses.

◆

In early September 1999, a cloud of disenchantment hung over the eBay seller community. At the height of the June outage, Whitman and Omidyar had promised the community a free listing day in July. But the summer had come to an end without eBay making good on its commitment. What had started out as mild grumbling on the AuctionWatch and OTWA message boards was by now taking on a distinctly bitter tone: uncommunicative eBay, uncaring eBay, greedy eBay. The delay was frustrating, but there was a further indignity to it. Since eBay sellers were convinced that eBay would announce the free listing day on short notice, they felt they had to keep coming back to the Announcement Board every day to be sure of not missing out.

It was during these discordant times that Rosalinda Baldwin, a message board regular, became a force to be reckoned with in eBay. Baldwin went on the eBay message boards and made an open offer to the community: she would check the Announcement Board on a regular basis, and when the free listing day was announced she would send an e-mail to anyone who sent her their address. Baldwin collected a long list of addresses, and true to her word sent out daily updates in the form of an e-mail newsletter she called *TAG Notes*. *TAG Notes* monitored the free listing day situation, but it also had a lot more to say about eBay.

The "TAG" in *TAG Notes* stood for The Auction Guild, an organization Baldwin had been quietly, and single-handedly, laying the groundwork for. She intended The Auction Guild to be, in part, an old-fashioned trade guild, a voice for eBay's smallest and weakest users. "It was about making a level playing field," she says. "I didn't care if people were selling something for a dollar or a million dollars." But unlike most trade guilds, The Auction Guild was going to be a for-profit business, an online auction portal that offered auction-related products and services. The Auction Guild would be "user-centric" and "semisocialistic," Baldwin promised, with the profits distributed back to the participants. She had been working since the spring to line up funding and computer servers. The launch was still months away, but the dissatisfaction over free listing day was too good an opportunity to pass up. *TAG Notes* was The Auction Guild's debut before the eBay community.

TAG Notes' nominal reason for existing ended quickly. Just a few days after the first issue, eBay came through with the free listing day it had promised. Baldwin, however, was just getting started. In the first issue of *TAG Notes,* she explained why she had undertaken to watch out for the free listing day. "Lots of folks don't have time for this foolishness," she wrote. That comment set the tone for what *TAG Notes* would become—Baldwin's impassioned, near-daily screed about eBay, filled with outrage at virtually everything it had done, large or small, since the last issue.

Baldwin spent up to fifteen hours a day at her computer, much of it researching and writing *TAG Notes.* She sent a dragnet out across the Internet, culling information from the eBay message boards, OTWA and AuctionWatch, and news and finance websites, and she had a network of people who e-mailed her news nuggets. Whether it was the eBay search engine acting glitchy, or Meg Whitman filing to sell 6 million shares of her own stock, Baldwin knew about it—and she was indignant. In one edition of *TAG Notes,* she told her readers that Jim Griffith, Uncle Griff, was scheduled to host an informal chat entitled "History of eBay" on The Park, one of the eBay discussion boards. After dutifully giving the date and time, she added an editorial aside: "*TAG* thinks it will be interesting to see which version of eBay history is presented—and hope[s] long-time ebaY members will be there with the 'real' rather than the PR fantasy version."

A maternal-looking woman in her late forties, with long brown hair that fell over the shoulders of her 1960s-style dashiki, Baldwin was seated on a couch in her sister's tidy Staten Island town house, struggling to explain her love-hate relationship with eBay. Baldwin grew up in Brooklyn, one of six children in a middle-class, Orthodox

Jewish family. Even as a child she was, she says, a "born rebel." As a student at Abraham Lincoln High School, she and her friends marched on City Hall to demand an end to the Vietnam War, and shut down the U.S. Army recruitment office in their Sheepshead Bay neighborhood. The war eventually ended, but Baldwin's personal rebellions continued. She left her parents' religious orthodoxy behind, and after high school she abandoned New York City to attend agricultural college upstate, where she studied animal husbandry. Eventually, she moved to a hundred-acre subsistence farm in upstate Varick, New York, a town of fifteen hundred.

Baldwin was at a loss to explain her eclectic political beliefs. Starting on the left, she said, she was pro-choice, pro-environment, a strong supporter of the ACLU, and had what she called "democratic socialist tendencies." But she was also militantly pro-gun—"you can have my gun," she said, "when you remove my cold dead finger from the trigger." And she had spent the past twenty-two years in the Army Reserves where, as a combat engineer officer, she trained soldiers to blow up bridges. Baldwin had recently adopted a new cause. "I'm becoming anti-corporation," she said. "The older I get, the more I see that they are destroying the world."

In 1997, Baldwin was dabbling in antiques when she stumbled across eBay. She started out buying pineapple-themed items, which she had been collecting since she met her second husband on a blind date and he brought a pineapple to help her recognize him. Baldwin also used eBay to sell some of her antiques, deriving a small but steady income. But the individual transactions hardly seemed to matter. It was eBay itself that won her over. "I was absolutely, totally, and completely in love with eBay," she said. "I still am."

Baldwin understood right away what Omidyar had been trying to create, and she shared his dream. "It's putting power in the hands of people who up until now have been powerless," she said. Baldwin saw eBay as a great leveler—one of the most powerful democratizing forces she had ever encountered. It permitted a seller with multiple sclerosis, she said, to compete on an equal basis with an able-bodied seller. Third-world sellers could compete with first-world sellers on an even playing field. The more Baldwin observed eBay in action, the more convinced she became that it was, simply, "the most amazing thing in the world."

But as Baldwin saw it, eBay had fallen from grace. The fall came when Omidyar stepped aside in favor of Whitman—"Miss MBA," Baldwin sometimes called her—who had spent her entire career in corporate America. "You hand it over to a CEO and you can't control it any more," Baldwin said. "And Meg's focus was not Pierre's focus." For Baldwin, the first clear indication that eBay had lost its way came when it failed to follow through on the plan to issue pre-IPO stock to the community. Baldwin blamed Whitman for the betrayal, scoffing at the idea that eBay was constrained by the SEC's sophisticated-investor rule, or that it was concerned small investors would lose money. Whitman's real interest, Baldwin insisted, was enriching the large institutional investors who came from the same rarefied world she did. If the shares had been distributed, she said, the world—or, at least, the world of eBay—would have been completely different. "It would have been a more social and socialistic and community-based wealth-building organization," she insisted. "Not a corporation that cares only about profits."

Other moments of disillusionment came in quick succession. Baldwin was upset at how eBay handled the gun ban. The "dolphins in the net" was an even sharper blow—"I went ballistic," she said—and Baldwin went on to become one of the DNF Posse's biggest champions. "A pattern started to emerge," she said. "It exposed a sort of sleazy underbelly that I, in love, didn't see." After beginning her reminiscences sweetly, Baldwin was now barely able to control her anger at what eBay had become. "Meg changed us from a community into a commodity," she said. "And you know, like sheep, if she has to slaughter a few million of us for profit, it was for our own good, she will say."

Baldwin argued that buyers and sellers needed The Auction Guild to counter eBay's tremendous power. But challenging eBay would be difficult, she said. The company had many ways of crushing dissent. EBay's staff monitored the message boards, she said, and when they came across a popular dissident like Randy Pinkham, of gun-ban fame, they either threw him out of the community or co-opted him, or, in Pinkham's case, did both. Baldwin was horrified to see Pinkham go from being one of eBay's most fearless critics to being a Voices member, hobnobbing with eBay's staff at headquarters. "What better way to silence the opposition than to make them part of your little group?" Baldwin asked.

Really, it was to be expected. "Unfortunately, people are easily corruptible," she said. Baldwin, however, was not. EBay staff had approached her, over the years, to say they were sorry she was upset, and to ask if there was anything they could do to address her concerns. "They tried two different times to give me someone at eBay to be my 'buddy,'" Baldwin said, wincing at the word as she straightened her dashiki. "But it's been an absolute and total failure—I see right through it."

◆

In October 1999, eBay launched Great Collections, its first foray into high-end art and antiques and other premium offerings. Among the first items listed: a collection of balls, bats, and memorabilia that once belonged to Joe DiMaggio. Most of the new site's inventory would come from Butterfield & Butterfield, the venerable San Francisco auction house that eBay had purchased in April for $260 million. At first Great Collections appeared to be an obvious extension of the platform. It would advance eBay's goal of raising the average selling price of items on the site, and it fit in neatly with Omidyar's original vision. Great Collections would "democratize" the world of high-end auctions, Westly said, by making "world-class items available to people who never had access to these auction houses before."

The launch of Great Collections came at the height of dot-com mania, when it looked as if all commerce—including high-end auctions—was about to uproot itself from the land and migrate to the Internet. Sotheby's, the prestigious Manhattan auction house, had announced in January it would spend $25 million to start

Sothebys.com, challenging eBay directly in the online auction space. More disturbing for eBay, a few months later Sotheby's unveiled Sothebys.Amazon.com, a collaboration with eBay's archrival. Cyberspace was also filling up with an array of fine-art-and-antique Internet companies, with names like ArtNet.com and NextMonet.com. If eBay wanted to stake out part of the market, it seemed, the time to act was now. EBay's stock surged more than 5 percent on the Great Collections announcement, hitting a new high. "There are only so many Beanie Babies and old records you can sell," one Wall Street analyst gushed.

It turned out that there were only so many expensive paintings and silver candelabras eBay could sell—and the number was not large. Great Collections was unable to attract upscale buyers in significant numbers. In part, it was a matter of cultural fit between eBay's users and the upscale auction world. Before it bought Butterfield & Butterfield, eBay had briefly considered entering into an alliance with Sotheby's, but the management team decided the Sotheby's name would be a turnoff for the average eBay user. "It's tuxedos and white gloves," Kagle objected. But to many eBay users, Butterfield & Butterfield seemed to be just as evocative of formal wear.

Fear of fraud was also a bigger hurdle than eBay had anticipated. EBay promised buyers that anything they bought on the Great Collections site would come with "the same guarantees auction houses traditionally provide in the off-line world," including a five-year guarantee of authenticity, and a thirty-day money-back guarantee that the item was as described. It was far more protection than buyers got on eBay's main site, but, given the high selling prices on Great Collections, buyers were still hesitant. As it turned out, there was one thing the land-based high-end auction houses provided that online auction sites never could: staff whose very presence reassured buyers they were not making a terrible mistake.

Attracting sellers proved just as difficult. EBay marketed Great Collections to dealers, who they hoped would sell items in quantity on the site. But the company made a decision at the outset not to charge a 10 percent buyer's premium, which was standard in the off-line auction world—and on Sothebys.com. It made sense as a matter of principle: eBay was opposed to unnecessary fees. But it also meant that Great Collections could not offer sellers top price for merchandise. As a result, the site was hampered by a shortage of good inventory. A year later, Great Collections relented and added the buyer's premium, but by then the site was floundering. A week later, eBay announced that Butterfield & Butterfield had laid off 15 percent of its staff.

Great Collections was also plagued by execution problems. Butterfield & Butterfield was new to the Internet, and its staff was not used to dealing with online customers. Buyers complained to eBay that they were having trouble getting responses to simple e-mail questions, and high bidders were waiting weeks, even months, for deliveries—an eternity in Internet time. Feedback Forum ratings on Butterfield's sales were running as high as 9 percent negatives and 9 percent neutrals. It was well below the general eBay average, and a distinct embarrassment, since Great Collections was supposed to be a premium site.

But in the end, a significant reason for eBay's problems in high-end auctions was simply that what eBay offers—economic efficiency—is less valued in this market than in most. When rich people make purchases at exclusive auction houses, it is an experience as much as an economic decision. The auction house is filled with fine antiques, Oriental rugs—and other rich people. Potential buyers are plied with expensive champagne by a charming and ingratiating staff. And the auction itself is a social ritual, in which delivering the high bid bestows prestige on the winner. It is an experience far different from buying a Beanie Baby or a set of golf clubs, and one that cannot be duplicated online.

EBay continued to tinker with Great Collections, trying to find a formula that worked. In January 2001, the site was relaunched as eBay Premier. EBay tried to address buyers' insecurities about fraud by assembling a database of millions of pieces of art, and putting in place a system of online appraisals and an improved authenticity guarantee. But even with these upgrades, the high-end market proved elusive. In April, eBay announced a promotion in which all winning bidders would be eligible for a drawing for a five-day museum trip to a European city. Rosalinda Baldwin, announcing the contest in *TAG Notes*, was gleeful. It was, she said, eBay's latest "desperate effort to boost their dying ebaY Premier" site.

The best thing that could be said about eBay's efforts with Great Collections and eBay Premier might have been that no one else was doing any better in the high-end space. Whitman tried to put a positive gloss on the Butterfield & Butterfield purchase by saying that it had helped defensively, since eBay had been worried that Sothebys.com would succeed and that Sotheby's would then move down into eBay's lower-end market. "It seems laughable now, but it seemed real at the time," she says. "We had to be sure we had a buffer zone."

◆

In November 1999, Justin Jorgensen put together an online conceptual art gallery dedicated to eBay. Jorgensen, who lived in Burbank, California, was a designer and art director who had spent years working on Disney theme parks. He helped design *Leave a Legacy*, a sculpture at Epcot Center that allowed visitors to take a photo of themselves that became a permanent part of the site. Less successfully, he contributed to the agricultural area of California Adventure, a new Disney theme park adjacent to Disneyland. Most of the agricultural area was dropped to make room for *It's Tough to Be a Bug*, a 3-D tribute to the world's "Ten quintillion bugs."

Jorgensen created a personal website, Justinspace.com, to express his unique aesthetic sensibility. He did not own a scanner, so he was limited to artwork and photos that were already on the Internet. The first conceptual art gallery Jorgensen posted on Justinspace.com, *Obscene Interiors*, caused a minor stir. Jorgensen collected photos from amateur porn sites on the Internet and blacked out the naked people. What was left was the bad interior decorating that was generally found in Internet porn: the ugly couches that the naked bodies were sprawled on, the shag carpets underfoot, and the cheesy knickknacks crammed onto hideous bookshelves. Or, as the gallery's slogan put it, "bad porn, worse drapes."

Jorgensen's next gallery was devoted to eBay. EBay had long been a topic of fascination in the arty circles Jorgensen traveled in. "My friends were always e-mailing each other and saying, 'Look at this crazy thing on eBay,'" he says. "'Someone's selling the state of Alaska!'" There were already several websites, with names like whowouldbuythat.com and disturbingauctions.com, that provided lists of odd items sold on eBay—the mounted rear end of a deer, a dead reptile dressed in a miniature wedding gown, a black velvet painting of Jesus hovering over an eighteen-wheeler, entitled "God Bless Our Truckers." What intrigued Jorgensen, however, was not the items themselves but the bizarre pictures people included in the listings.

Jorgensen's *eBay Conceptual Art Gallery* was composed of photos culled from actual auction listings. *Diet Croc* was a picture of a croc-odile head on a kitchen counter beside a can of Diet Coke, apparently the seller's way of showing how large the crocodile head was. The gallery also contained a picture of a naked female mannequin in a wooded field, and another of tiny dolls disturbingly laid out on a tiny bed. Captions were an integral part of the gallery. One photo showed an obese woman in a vest, bra, and panties standing next to a cat. (It was the vest that was being auctioned.) Jorgensen was particularly proud of the caption he added: "Eight lives." He coined the phrase for the gallery, he says, but he noticed it entering the lingo in southern California for something horrific enough to kill a cat.

Jorgensen, who graduated from the California Institute of the Arts, considered the gallery an exhibit of found art, sometimes called inadvertent art. "If you're paying attention, you can see accidental works of art wherever you go," he says. "I happened to focus on eBay, but it could be a weird way your laundry falls on the floor, with the lighting just so, and you realize it's just perfect." Jorgensen's gallery was also an homage to kitsch, the artistic style Columbia University classics professor Gilbert Highet once defined as "everything that took a lot of trouble to make and is quite hideous."

Jorgensen received hundreds of e-mails from fans of the gallery, including one from clothing designer Todd Oldham. He also got a steady stream of recommendations from people who saw photos on eBay they thought should be added. But Jorgensen was continually struck by how few of them understood the point of the gallery. "They don't realize it's not about weird items," he says. "It's about great photographs."

◆

In November 1999, a small website called PayPal appeared in cyberspace. Its origins dated back to the previous summer, when Max Levchin introduced himself to Peter Thiel in a lecture room at Stanford University's Department of Engineering-Economic Systems and Operations Research.

Thiel, a blond California native who was running a hedge fund, had returned to his alma mater to give a talk on international finance. Levchin, dark-haired and intense, had an idea for his fourth start-up, and was looking for funding. The twenty-three-year-old Levchin, who had emigrated from Kiev in 1991, came from a family of intellectuals—all four of his grandparents had Ph.D.'s. He had recently graduated from the University of Illinois at Champaign-Urbana—the same campus at which, a few years earlier, Marc Andreessen had developed the first web browser with graphics. The two men talked after the lecture, and Thiel was intrigued enough to schedule breakfast with Levchin for a few weeks later.

Levchin's idea was an encrypted payment system that would allow people to transfer money securely from one Palm Pilot to another. Thiel liked it, and in July he and Levchin formed a company called Confinity, a combination of "confidence" and "infinity." Thiel rounded up $3 million in financing from Nokia Ventures and, in the kind of only-a-geek-could-love-it publicity stunt common in the dot-com world at the time, executives from the Finnish cellular telephone giant "beamed" the investment to Thiel's Palm Pilot at Buck's Restaurant, a famed venture capitalist watering hole in Woodside, California.

But it was not long before Thiel and Levchin decided that the market for secure person-to-person fund transfers was far bigger off Palm Pilots than on them. That fall they relaunched Confinity as PayPal, a new service that would allow people to transfer money from computer to computer, using e-mail. Individuals who wanted to make a payment gave PayPal their credit card or bank account information, and the e-mail address of the person they wanted to send money to. The payee received an e-mail from PayPal telling them they had been sent money, and a hyperlink that took them to www.paypal.com, where they could indicate how they wanted to receive their funds.

PayPal's fee structure was hard to resist. In keeping with the dot-com ethos of "get big fast," the company offered the service for free to both buyers and sellers, and used millions of dollars in VC funds to hand out bounties of five dollars to everyone who signed up, and five dollars for anyone they referred. To build up the network at the beginning, Thiel had his twenty employees, who were working out of a crowded office in Palo Alto, send five- or ten-dollar payments to everyone in their e-mail address books. To get the money, the recipients had to sign up for PayPal. Handing out free money was costly, but fairly effective: by the end of 1999, PayPal had signed up twelve thousand registered users.

In early 2000, PayPal began receiving a flood of e-mail and phone calls from eBay sellers asking if they could include a PayPal link in their auction listings. Thiel and Levchin had not given any thought to online auctions when they launched the service. But eBay turned out to be PayPal's killer application. Payment was the most inefficient link in eBay's transaction chain. Item listings, bids, and communications between buyers and sellers all occurred online and instantaneously. But when an auction ended, unless the seller was a high-volume merchant with the ability to process credit card charges, the process slowed to a crawl as the high bidder sent a check or money order through regular mail. Buyers had to wait several extra days before receiving their items; sellers had to deal with cashing checks or money orders and storing merchandise until the payments cleared.

PayPal and eBay combined with nuclear force. Powersellers were e-mailing their fellow Powersellers, telling them there was a revolutionary new way of handling end-of-auction payments. The eBay and off-eBay message boards overflowed with posts explaining the service, complete with links to the PayPal site. PayPal was also benefiting from a specific kind of viral growth: since both parties to a fund transfer had to be registered, sellers were constantly urging buyers to sign up, and buyers were prodding sellers. At the same time, PayPal continued to hand out its VC money in five-dollar increments, which provided a powerful incentive of its own. Whatever the reasons, PayPal was soon growing at a rate with few precedents in the history of commerce—7 percent to 10 percent a day. The twelve thousand users PayPal ended 1999 with skyrocketed to more than a million over the next four months.

PayPal's small staff was overwhelmed. By mid-March, the company had a backlog of 100,000 unanswered e-mails. Thiel wanted to hire more staff, but there was no space in PayPal's headquarters, where as many as eight people were already crammed into each ten-foot-by-ten-foot office. He rushed to open a new two-hundred-person customer-service center in Omaha, Nebraska, to handle the flood. PayPal interviewed applicants at a Holiday Inn near the new headquarters, and hired everyone who showed up.

In Campbell, eBay was watching PayPal's success with concern and frustration. EBay had been trying for over a year to develop its own online payment system, but it had run into a series of roadblocks. Whitman and the management team had decided it was not a business they wanted to enter on their own. Online payments were outside eBay's core competency of running Internet auctions, and the substantial risk of fraud involved in wiring money over the Internet made it a dangerous field for amateurs. EBay had made overtures to large financial services companies, including Citibank and Bank of America, to handle eBay payments, but got turned down everywhere. EBay then entered into negotiations with Accept, an online payment company that had been incubated at Benchmark, eBay's own VC firm. But Amazon swooped in and paid $175 million in stock for Accept, which it intended to use in its own newly launched online auction site.

In April 1999, eBay acquired Billpoint, another online payment service. Billpoint was "a very nascent company" at the time, Whitman says. In fact, it was a serious disappointment. While rivals were moving in and claiming the space, Billpoint was having trouble getting a workable payment product up and on the Internet. In late 1999, when PayPal was sending out e-mails inviting users to sign up, Billpoint was still tentatively beta testing its own service. In March 2000, eBay announced that Billpoint was ready to launch, and that Wells Fargo Bank had agreed to do the back-end work for the site in exchange for a 35 percent interest. But while Billpoint was now ready to start registering users, PayPal was already well on its way to signing its millionth customer.

EBay had some legitimate excuses for falling behind. The concerns about fraud were real: in 2000, PayPal was targeted by Russian and Nigerian Internet crime rings, and ended up being hit with $8.9 million in charge-backs for unauthorized credit card use. If eBay had stumbled into the payments space and been similarly victimized, the media and Wall Street would have been unrelenting. Nor was eBay about to go head-to-head with incentives for new users and referrals. PayPal was in spendthrift dot-com mode, handing out millions of dollars in VC money just to grab market share. But eBay, which had proudly put its own VC money in the bank untouched, expected Billpoint to turn a profit. So while PayPal was free, eBay announced that Billpoint would charge thirty-five to fifty-five cents per transaction, plus a commission of between 3.5 percent and 5.5 percent. EBay had seen in Japan how hard it was to compete against a popular, free source with an untested one that charged a fee. To give Billpoint some chance of succeeding, eBay entered into a joint promotion with Visa, in which Billpoint would initially be free for any charges made on a Visa card. Still, Billpoint had the disadvantage of being nominally a fee-charging site, and it was not matching PayPal's sign-up bonuses.

PayPal's momentum, meanwhile, showed no sign of slowing. The day after eBay's Wells Fargo announcement, PayPal merged with X.com, another leader in the space. Days later the combined company secured another $100 million in VC funding. In May, PayPal was the most heavily trafficked financial site on the Internet. By year's end it had reached 5 million users, and was listed on nearly one-third of all eBay auctions. Billpoint could not match PayPal's growth, but eBay consoled itself that its rival was only succeeding because it was exploiting a money-losing business model. On the eBay message boards, PayPal users were boasting that they had made more than $10,000 registering people. It was a lot of money to hand out to get people to sign up for a free service.

With the bursting of the dot-com bubble, PayPal was forced to get serious about its revenue model. It cut back on its incentive payments, and began pushing users into Business and Premier accounts, for which it charged fees. As PayPal raised its fees, Billpoint lowered its own. By mid-2001, the two companies were charging users roughly the same amount for similar services. PayPal had the advantage of a larger installed-user base, which made it the beneficiary of network effects. Billpoint was smaller, but it had the eBay imprimatur, and it was increasingly being integrated into the eBay site. When sellers listed an item on eBay, they were offered a one-click option to use Billpoint, but not PayPal, to close the sale. EBay was convinced that Billpoint's early stumbles were behind it, and that it would increasingly take market share away from PayPal. "This isn't a sprint," Whitman said, "it's a marathon."

◆

Just before Christmas, in central Florida, John Hannon was awakened by a phone call. It was one of his regular customers, shouting, "You did it!" Hannon, who sold on eBay using the ID name Parrothead88, had no idea what he had done; but he had made eBay history. He was the first user ever to hit the $10,000 feedback level and earn a shooting star. Much to his astonishment, Hannon's mailbox was quickly flooded with e-mailed congratulations from customers and strangers.

Hannon was a laid-back superachiever. He had fashioned his eBay ID from the word that fans of beach-bum rocker Jimmy Buffet use to describe themselves, and he was living a Parrothead life. Hannon and his wife—the "88" in his ID was a reference to the year they met—had been selling odd items at flea markets near their home, thirty miles west of Tampa. But when he discovered eBay, he found that his mix of laser pointers, knickknacks, and shipping supplies sold better online than off. Selling on eBay also allowed Hannon and his wife to set their own work hours, rather than having to wake up every weekend morning while it was still dark and drag themselves to the flea markets.

Hannon had no particular affection for eBay. He did not hang out on the message boards, had only vaguely heard of Skippy and Uncle Griff, and had never disagreed with eBay about any of its policies. To Hannon, eBay was just business. "I'm just trying to support myself and enjoy my life," he says. Hannon assumed having a high feedback rating helped him as a seller, but he never gave it a lot of thought.

Not everyone in the eBay community was as indifferent to feedback as Hannon. On the AuctionWatch and OTWA boards, feedback-related topics were a sure conversation starter. Sellers and buyers endlessly debated the fine points of giving feedback, and told richly detailed stories about particular feedback ratings and comments they had received. Before David Lucking-Reiley did his regression analysis, the eBay community had already concluded that feedback made a difference. Jeff Fisher, the stamp seller, went so far as to say that "the feedback rating is the most essential thing on the entire site." When he advanced to a shooting star, Fisher found that his sales shot up, particularly among buyers new to eBay. Buyers often made reference to Fisher's shooting star in their e-mail to him. A high-bidder from France once sent him a twenty-dollar bill for six dollars in stamps and said he trusted him to send back the change because he had a shooting star.

As a company, eBay certainly believed in the importance of feedback. It had gone to great lengths in recent months to keep the Feedback Forum exclusive to eBay. Early in 1999, Yahoo! Auctions had imported eBay's feedback ratings onto its own site, but eBay registered a protest that got Yahoo! to stop. And it would fight others, including the Toronto-based online auction site eDeal, that tried to use Feedback Forum ratings on their own sites. To eBay's critics, its insistence that the ratings were proprietary was yet another example of eBay's attempting to build walls in cyberspace, fencing off information for its own economic benefit. But eBay considered the Feedback Forum ratings its intellectual property, and argued that the sites that were trying to take them were just as mercenary in their motives.

EBay was far more excited about Hannon's shooting star than he was. It was, after all, not all that long ago that Song had been pilloried by the community for even creating the rating system. Hannon had vindicated her decision, and eBay's staff was pleased to see that several other users were drawing close to the 10,000 mark. Song was one of four eBay employees who jointly called Hannon at home to congratulate him on being eBay's first shooting star. Hannon was surprised to get the call, he says, and never quite caught the names of anyone.

chapter nine

Half.com launched as scheduled on January 19, 2000. Kopelman and the mayor of Half.com, Oregon, got their *Today Show* gig, and the story of the website that took over a town grabbed headlines as far away as the *London Telegraph* and the *South China Post*. Back in Campbell, eBay's management team were following the new site with particular interest. Kopelman had been saying that he created it because he had found a weakness in eBay's model, and Whitman and her staff knew he was right.

EBay had already been considering extending its platform to fixed prices. In addition to Kopelman's point that some items did not lend themselves to auctions, eBay's internal market research showed that some people had a visceral dislike for buying by auction. These auction-haters were of both sexes and all incomes, and lived in all parts of the country—the factors that set them apart were what marketers called "psychographic." According to eBay's research, auction-avoiders were more time-pressed than the average person, and had a greater psychological need for certainty. EBay wanted to attract this sizable cohort by introducing a fixed-price option, but with all the other projects under way, no one had even drawn up a Marketing Requirements Document, the first step at eBay for getting a project off the ground.

Now Kopelman had forced their hand. EBay's management had to admit that Half.com was a brilliantly executed site, and they could see it was attracting users at a rate that rivaled the early AuctionWeb. Knowing a little about network effects, they realized that if they did not act quickly, Half might become too big to stop. EBay's market strategists rushed out a "build or buy" analysis, which concluded that eBay could create its own version of Half in six to nine months. That was not good enough, Whitman decided. By then, Half would have a full year's head start. Building would also entail significant opportunity costs, taking eBay's limited staff resources away from areas like international expansion, where the competitive pressures were just as intense. And eBay was, of course, experiencing an attack of its usual big-competitor phobia. "I was having nightmares," Kagle says. "I thought, 'My God, if Amazon bought Half, I just couldn't stand it.'"

The negotiations took three months. In the end, Half extracted roughly 5 million shares of eBay stock, worth about $340 million. It was a rich price, but it was only, fittingly, about half of what Half.com had started out asking. Fortunately for eBay, while the talks were under way the Internet bubble burst, causing dot-com valuations to plunge. EBay's investment bought it a site that already had 250,000 registered users and that was, between February and April of 2000, the fastest-growing e-commerce site in cyberspace.

The Half.com scare got eBay thinking more seriously about fixed prices on the main site. In time for Christmas 2000, eBay experimented with a "Buy It Now" feature, which allowed sellers the option of including in their listings prices at which they would be willing to end their auctions and finalize the sales. In addition to appealing to auction-averse buyers, Buy It Now significantly increased "auction velocity," the speed with which items moved off the site. It also made it easier for buyers to do their holiday shopping on eBay, because they could be sure of getting an item right away, rather than having to wait up to ten days for an auction to end. The company's internal research found that Buy It Now extended eBay's Christmas season—which had historically hit a wall in mid-December—by more than a week. When the holidays ended, eBay announced that Buy It Now would be extended indefinitely. By early 2001, fully 30 percent of eBay's listings offered it.

EBay had installed new management teams at Alando and Billpoint, but it kept Kopelman in place, and it allowed Half.com to remain in suburban Philadelphia. Half was a "gifted little brother," says Kagle. "I thought we could learn at least as much from Half as they could learn from us." Helped along by promotions and hyperlinks on the main eBay site, in December Half became the third-largest e-commerce site on the Internet, trailing only Amazon and eBay. By the fall of 2001, Half—with its easy-listing technology and absence of listing fees—had more than 50 million items for sale on the site at any given time, more than eight times as many as the main eBay site.

But Half still faced significant obstacles. Average sales prices in its core areas of books, music, and videos were low. To raise that average, and to increase overall listings, in April 2001 Half added categories for consumer electronics, computers, and sporting goods. But these items could not take full advantage of Half's model, since many came without ISBN and UPC numbers. Nor was it clear that buyers would be as willing to purchase expensive, fragile items like Palm Pilots and CD players secondhand and from strangers, as they were doing with books and CDs.

Still, analysts who scrutinized Half.com's business model came away impressed. In the second quarter of 2001, according to a Deutsche Banc Alex. Brown estimate, Half was contributing from $9 million to $11 million to eBay's bottom line, about 5 or 6 percent of the company's total revenues. An Internet analyst at Robertson Stephens concluded in the spring of 2001 that Half.com was "eBay's silver bullet," and one of its most powerful engines for growth. Whitman stated publicly a few months later that "if you scroll way into the future" Half.com might even surpass eBay's core site.

But Half never got the chance. In October 2001, eBay announced it would begin integrating Half into the main site. Listings from eBay and Half would be combined, users' accounts would be merged, and feedback ratings would be cumulated. ("How many of you guys would even WANT your whacked-out Half.com feedback 'merged' with your eBay feedback?" a poster named StormThinker grumbled on the OTWA eBay board.) Eventually, the name Half.com would be dropped entirely. The move was widely seen as a swipe at Amazon, and an indication that eBay would compete aggressively for the books, music, and videos that were the core of Amazon's business. But more significant, it was eBay's clearest indication yet of just how important fixed-price sales would be to its future. EBay did not want to be a global auction site; it wanted to be what it had long called itself—a global marketplace. Wall Street hailed the merger as shrewd strategy, but longtime eBay sellers were, as usual, wary of where eBay was headed. "Well, for those folks out there who have refused to see the shift away from collectibles and antiques, maybe this is a wake-up call!!," a poster named Blanche wrote on OTWA. "However, I already think it's too late to do anything about it."

◆

Yahoo! made another run at eBay in March 2000. With a market capitalization that had soared to $90 billion—more than three times eBay's—Yahoo! was in a financial position to make the acquisition. And its management liked the strategic fit now more than ever. As the Internet's leading portal, Yahoo! could steer its 39 million unique monthly visitors to eBay, quickly ramping up the auction site's metrics. And its strong overseas presence could speed eBay's movement into foreign markets. An acquisition would also allow Yahoo! to dominate online auctions, something its own fledgling auction site was nowhere near doing.

But eBay was more ambivalent. With a successful IPO behind them, Whitman and the rest of the management team were more open to being acquired than the last time around, but they wanted assurances that eBay would be allowed autonomy within the Yahoo! empire. Going into the negotiations, eBay's management believed such an understanding was possible. From the outside, Yahoo!— with its goofy name, brightly colored website, and TV commercials with hollering cowboys—looked fun and eBaysian. And Omidyar and Jerry Yang, who had known each other for years, seemed to have similar approaches to management. But Yahoo!'s looks were deceiving. Up close, "Yellow," eBay's code name for Yahoo! during the talks, struck the eBay team as arrogant and controlling. "You would assume based on the nature of the companies and the age of the officers the cultures would be similar," says Whitman, "but the cultures were not similar at all."

The negotiations foundered on a most un-eBaysian point: Yahoo!'s insistence that Whitman report to president Jeff Mallet, rather than directly to CEO Tim Koogle. In such a structure, eBay would inevitably relinquish its independence, says Whitman, and "that was not going to be acceptable." The loss, as it turned out, was entirely Yahoo!'s. Just weeks after the talks broke down, Yahoo! was crushed by the dot-com collapse, which hit advertising-based revenue models like Yahoo!'s especially hard. Within a year, CEO Tim Koogle was out of a job, and Yahoo!, whose market cap had plunged 92 percent from its high, was worth $2 billion less than eBay.

◆

Also in March, eBay switched to "transactional feedback," the biggest change to the Feedback Forum in its four-year history. As Omidyar originally conceived feedback, it was supposed to be an aggregation of all the good and bad opinions community members formed of each other. Most feedback was generated by the parties to a sale—the buyer rating the seller, and the seller rating the buyer—but some arose from more random encounters. Users left positive feedback for people who answered their questions on a message board, and negative feedback for users who were abusive to other members of the community. In Omidyar's conception, eBay was to be a community as well as a place of commerce, so it made sense that members were being evaluated on everything they did, not just on how they carried out a trade.

A noble sentiment, but it was not working in practice. Because anyone could leave feedback for anyone at any time, fraud and gimmickry were rampant. Groups of online friends were forming shill feedback rings—as the "dolphins in the net" had been accused of doing—to pump up each others' ratings. Individual users were signing up for multiple accounts and using one to leave positive feedback for another. And there were scattered reports of "feedback solicitation," people offering to pay, or to be paid, in exchange for positive feedback. A year earlier, eBay had made negative feedback transactional—limited to buyers and sellers rating each other—because of complaints that people who got into fights on the message boards were sabotaging one another's ratings. But the latest move was far bigger, since the vast majority of ratings in the Feedback Forum were positive.

EBay approached this policy change with particular caution, since it saw feedback as going to the core of what the community was about. In the months leading up to the decision, Brian Burke and Mary Lou Song presided over the Feedback Revision Project, which Song calls "one of the longest and most painstaking" attempts eBay has ever made to get into the minds of the community. EBay staff hosted open forums about feedback on the Discuss New Features board, and they called on Voices groups to weigh the fine points of transactional feedback. EBay asked users to send in their thoughts about feedback, and nearly a thousand e-mails came in. The vast majority, it turned out, agreed with eBay's staff that a switch to transactional feedback was needed to protect the integrity of the Feedback Forum.

At the same time, eBay made a few smaller changes involving feedback. Most significant was the addition of a new line to users' feedback profiles indicating how many bid retractions they had engaged in. Bid retraction—canceling a bid while an auction was still under way—was a sore point with eBay sellers. But despite pressure from the selling community, eBay had never prohibited it. As eBay saw it, there were circumstances under which bid retraction was understandable, such as when a buyer entered the wrong bid by accident, or the seller changed the item description in mid-auction. But too often, sellers charged, buyers retracted bids without justification. In the worst cases, the retractions were a deliberate attempt to game the system. In a practice known as "bid shielding," prohibited under eBay's rules, buyers placed a low bid on an item, and then quickly used another account to place a second, unreasonably high bid. The high bid discouraged other buyers from putting in bids of their own. At the last minute, the buyer retracted the high bid, leaving his low-ball bid as the winner. Even when bid retraction was innocent, the false high bid hurt sellers by discouraging other bidders. The switch to transactional negative feedback meant that victims of bid retraction could not even alert the community through the Feedback Forum, since, by definition, a bid retractor was not part of the final transaction. The new line in users' feedback profiles for bid retractions closed the loophole.

There were other problems with the Feedback Forum that had no easy solutions. Chief among them was "retaliatory feedback." Many eBay users complained that the feedback system underreported bad behavior, because victims hesitated to leave negative feedback out of fear of getting hit with negative feedback in return. "Absolutely people are afraid to neg," one AuctionWatch poster wrote. "The thinking goes thusly: bidder has already stiffed me over a fifteen-dollar auction; it would be stupid for me to neg him/her and then end up with a retaliatory neg on top of the no pay."

Some of these critics believed eBay should investigate complaints of retaliatory feedback and, when they were found to have merit, remove the challenged feedback. But the whole reason Omidyar created the Feedback Forum was to stay out of disputes between users. EBay had no desire to inject itself into them now. Besides, even with the threat of retaliation, plenty of users were still willing to leave negative feedback when they were treated poorly. On the message boards, old-timers encouraged users not to be intimidated, and not to worry about a stray negative feedback. "Sure, when I was new I was afraid," a poster named looselips wrote on AuctionWatch. "Now I neg 'em all and let God sort 'em out."

◆

On April 14, 2000, the dot-com bubble burst. In a trading day that National Public Radio described as "like watching the film of a crash test in slow motion," the Nasdaq dived 355 and the Dow fell 617, the largest point losses those indexes had ever seen. The immediate cause of the meltdown was a troubling report about consumer prices released that day. But the market jitters had begun to set in three weeks earlier, when *Barron's* published a hard-hitting cover story arguing that Internet stocks were wildly overvalued. The piece, "Burning Up," listed 207 Internet start-ups in order of their burn rate—the amount of money they lost every year—and predicted that fifty-one, including household names like Drkoop.com and CDNow, would run out of cash in the next twelve months.

Silicon Valley's boom times were officially over. A few weeks later, over Memorial Day weekend, a twenty-four-year-old aspiring journalist from New York launched a website called Fucked Company. F*cked Company, as the mainstream media usually called it, was conceived as a "deadpool"—a game in which competitors get points for correctly predicting who will die within a given time period—for companies. But it would become better known for its Recent News and Happy Fun Slander Corner features, where anonymous posters gleefully exchanged rumors about tech companies slashing staff or closing up shop. In the next few months, Fucked Company reported the demise of some of the Internet's most celebrated names: European high-fashion site Boo.com in May, discount retailer Value America in August, and Pets.com in November. Even Internet companies that survived the downturn were hard hit, including onetime superstars like Amazon. In June, the company announced second-quarter revenues significantly below what Wall Street was expecting, and Lehman Brothers blasted Amazon's corporate bonds as "extremely weak and deteriorating."

EBay's stock was not immune from the dot-com collapse—by midsummer, it was down 50 percent from its pre-crash highs. But eBay itself was doing better than ever. When eBay announced its own second-quarter results in July, its highly profitable business model and viral growth once again powered it to an array of upside surprises. Quarterly earnings were five cents a share, well ahead of the two-cents-a-share estimates. Registered users now numbered nearly 16 million, an increase of 183 percent in a year. Item listings, gross merchandise sales, and online revenues had all doubled from the second quarter of 1999. "EBay is positioned to thrive, not just survive this shakeout," Whitman declared. Even as investors were fleeing the Internet sector, twenty-eight of the thirty-one Wall Street analysts who followed eBay rated it a buy or a strong buy.

◆

On April 24, eBay Motors launched as a separate site within eBay. There were five major categories—Cars, Motorcycles, Other Vehicles, Parts and Accessories, and Related Collectibles—and more than four hundred subcategories. Simon Rothman had been working with Maynard Webb's engineers for months, and he got the site he was hoping for. EBay Motors' site had a more professional, even somber, look and feel than the rest of eBay. The shading was black and dark gray—not the bright primary colors of the main site— and the images of cars were real photographs. The site also played up a critical strategic alliance eBay had made with AutoTrader.com, an online auto site owned by Atlanta-based Cox Communications. AutoTrader listed 1.5 million cars on its site, and through its relationship with automotive distribution channel Manheim—also owned by Cox—it had relationships with more than 90 percent of the nation's car dealerships.

No one was looking forward to the launch more than Scott Wellhausen, known on eBay as oldmc. Wellhausen, a parts manager for a trucking firm in Columbus, Ohio, was a fanatical collector of motorcycle memorabilia. He had a vast collection of motorcycle magazines, including his prized possession, a rare 1903 bound volume of the first twelve issues of *MotorCycle*, America's oldest motorcycle periodical. His home, which resembled a motorcycle memorabilia museum, was packed with ephemera, including a wide array of programs, ribbons, and photographs from Laconia, the huge motorcycle rally that attracts twenty-five thousand bikers to central New Hampshire every June. Wellhausen also had one of the world's leading collections of memorabilia associated with the Motor Maids, the nation's oldest women's motorcycling organization.

Wellhausen first heard of eBay while making the rounds of the motorcycle-memorabilia tables at an Ohio flea market. He had an assortment of motorcycle collectibles to sell, and a dealer suggested he try eBay. Wellhausen began listing items, but he ended up buying even more. Before long, he had spent more than $10,000. "I fell in love," he says. "I went hungry for the first five or six months, I was so busy buying stuff on eBay."

Wellhausen wanted to like eBay Motors, but he hated it. Separating automobiles and motorcycles from the main eBay site struck him as an enormous mistake. If he wanted to sell a motorcycle postcard now, he had to choose between putting it on the main site or on eBay Motors. If he chose eBay Motors, eBay buyers who stuck to the main site — and used the categories there as a guide — would not see it. If he put it on the main site, buyers who searched eBay Motors would not see his item in their results. The new categories also struck Wellhausen as having been designed by someone who knew nothing about motorcycles. He could tell just by looking at the motorcycle subcategories, which included brands like the Ural, a cheap Russian BMW knock-off, that he thought clearly belonged in Miscellaneous.

Wellhausen was upset enough to take action. He founded Bikers Against Motors, and created a BAM website to agitate for his new cause: a boycott of eBay Motors. The Soapbox, one of the eBay discussion boards, became the center of the BAM movement. "I drove eBay crazy on Soapbox," Wellhausen says with a biker's rebellious pride. "No matter what the topic was, I would stick in a reason why eBay Motors sucks." Wellhausen also posted on other boards and sent e-mails to hundreds of eBay Motors sellers, informing them of the boycott and urging them to rabble-rouse on the Soapbox. The response was enthusiastic: he got more than a hundred e-mails a day supporting the boycott. In a sign of solidarity, sellers began writing "Boycott eBay Motors" at the bottom of their auction site.

It was not just bikers who objected to eBay Motors. Caryl Coleman, a seller of classic auto parts from Long Island, New York, was also seething. "April 24 was Black Monday," she says. "The site was the most poorly constructed technical abomination possible." Coleman was a businesswoman, and she was convinced the site was so confusing it would drive her customers away. The auto parts categories were excessively specific, she says, asking sellers to search by exact makes and years. If the site's designers knew anything about auto parts, she argued, they would have known that many classic parts fall into more than one such category. "There's one transmission gasket for 1934 to 1937 Plymouths, Dodges, and DeSotos," she says. "Do you want to tell me where I should put it?" Coleman became another outspoken critic of eBay Motors, attacking it in AuctionWatch news articles and to anyone who would listen.

Rothman was overcome by the same feelings Song experienced years earlier, when the community attacked the stars she chose for the Feedback Forum: surprise, remorse, and more than a little panic. "At the time it all seemed very scary," he says. "They talk to you the way you talk to family members." EBay took the boycotters' complaints seriously, and addressed many of them. The eBay Motors search engine was redesigned so it would be capable of bringing up items from the main site. The categories were also modified, in many cases along the lines suggested by critics in the eBay community. Some were merged with others, some were expanded, and a few — like Collectibles: Transportation: Automobiliana, and Collectibles: Transportation: License Plates — were moved from eBay Motors back to the main site. Coleman approved of the changes, but believed they did not go far enough. A year later, when eBay invited her to Campbell to talk to the eBay Motors group, Coleman brought along a

1972 Buick dealer brochure. "I told them there were six categories where it could be listed," she says.

When the eBay Motors boycott died down, which it did just a few months after it started, it was hard to see what all the fuss had been about. It was, in part, a reflection of a lesson eBay kept having to relearn: that the community almost always rebelled against major changes made without its input. But Rothman also believes that the boycott was never as big as it appeared. Just seven individuals were responsible, he says, for two-thirds of the message board posts attacking eBay Motors. Some of the people who were most upset, according to Rothman, were car dealers and other sellers who had been doing well under the old system and were afraid that eBay Motors' higher profile would subject them to greater competition. "They felt we were putting their special marketplace out in the open," Rothman says.

After its choppy launch, eBay Motors succeeded beyond anyone's expectations—even Rothman's. The conventional wisdom that consumers were afraid to buy used cars online was completely wrong. Rothman and his staff started out e-mailing one another excitedly every time an expensive car sold. But within months there were so many large sales—a $200,000 Ferrari, the Jeep John F. Kennedy Jr. drove on the night of his fatal plane crash—that no one bothered sending e-mails anymore. The economics of selling cars online turned out to be far more favorable than anyone expected. In many cases, cars were selling on eBay Motors for thousands of dollars less than they would have at a used-car dealership, which had to earn back a sizeable commission on the sale. The savings were more than enough to pay for shipping the car, even long-distance. EBay had expected that most of the car sales would be local, but it turned out that more than three-quarters of the cars bought on the site were shipped out of state,

By the first quarter of 2001, eBay Motors was on track to sell $1 billion in cars a year, making it the largest car seller on the Internet. It also meant that out of every nine dollars that sold on eBay, one dollar was from one of Rothman's cars. EBay Motors did not contribute as high a percentage of its sales to the bottom line as other eBay categories: it had an unusual fee structure for cars that limited eBay's take to a twenty-five-dollar listing fee, and another twenty-five dollars if the car sold. But eBay Motors was still wildly profitable. Remarkably, it operated with a staff of just five, making it one of the most stunning examples of the efficiency of eBay's virtual model. "Our profit margins are so high it's almost impossible to have higher margins," Rothman says.

In addition to being a business success, eBay Motors was, in its way, a force for reform. It changed the power dynamic in used-car sales. In eBay Motors focus groups, the participants often compared buying a used car to going through an Internal Revenue Service audit, or having a root canal. They cringed when they recalled haggling with dealers who lied about how low they could go, pretending to need authorization from a nonexistent manager; who covered up defects in the car; and who refused to discuss problems that turned up after the sale was complete.

But dealers who sold on eBay Motors—and more than half of the listings were from professional dealers—could not treat their consumers so callously. It was difficult to overcharge, because dealers were now competing directly with individuals selling cars at prices that did not include a dealer markup. And the Feedback Forum kept dealers honest about flaws in their cars, because a disgruntled customer on eBay could affect the dealer's ability to make future sales. Rothman was even hearing anecdotal evidence that dealers were improving their sales practices off-line. Used-car salesmen now knew, Rothman said, that unhappy customers could cut the dealership out entirely and buy their cars on eBay.

◆

On April 28, Kenneth Walton listed a painting he called *RD-52* for sale in a ten-day featured auction. Walton, who used the eBay ID golfpoorly, described it as "GREAT BIG Wild Abstract Art Painting" and set a twenty-five-cent minimum bid. The listing contained three photos, including one that showed a hole in the right-hand corner, near the initials *RD*. In the description, golfpoorly said he had purchased the painting at a Berkeley, California, garage sale before he was married, and that his child had poked a hole in the canvas with a Big Wheel.

From the initials in the name and the look of the painting, it appeared *RD-52* might be a rare work of the California abstract artist Richard Diebenkorn (1922–1993). Diebenkorns were highly prized, and their prices had been rising steeply since his death. In November 1998, Sotheby's had sold his *Horizon-Ocean View* for $3.9 million. Even with the punched-out hole, *RD-52* looked like it could be a very valuable painting.

Based on the looks of the auction listing, which did not mention Diebenkorn, it appeared golfpoorly did not know what he had. A bidder who did a little investigating to determine if golfpoorly was in fact an art rube would have learned from his personal description that he was not a regular art trader on eBay, and that his other auctions had included a deflated basketball, a Mexican voodoo mask, and a roll of twine.

The first bid on the *RD-52* auction came from someone with the eBay ID big-fat-mamba-jambas, for thirty cents. When the bidding hit $7, someone with the ID artpro jumped in and bid $3,000. The bids rose steadily, until a bidder named howdyhi bumped it up to $7,000. Two other bidders, astheworldturns and birdaroo, also pushed the price upward. In a final flurry, howdyhi went up to $135,505, but lost out to a buyer from Houten, the Netherlands, who bid $135,805.

The sale was a scam. Golfpoorly was actually Kenneth Walton, a Sacramento, California, man who did not buy the painting before he was married—he was not married. His child did not damage the painting with a Big Wheel—he had no children. Walton had actually purchased the painting at a thrift store in the southern California desert town of Little Rock earlier in the month. It was not, of course, a Diebenkorn. The IDs howdyhi, artpro, and big-fat-mamba-jambas were all registered to one Kenneth Fetterman, of

Placerville, California, a confederate of Walton's. The IDs asthe-worldturns and birdaroo belonged to Scott Beach, of Lakewood, Colorado, a third member of the group. When eBay was tipped off about what had happened, it voided the sale, saying it had been tainted by shill bidding.

The phony Diebenkorn was part of the biggest shill-bidder ring ever uncovered on eBay. EBay eventually learned that Walton, Fetterman, and Beach had engaged in shill bidding in more than half of the eleven hundred art auctions they put up on eBay from October 1998 to May 2000. The men shopped for art together in antiques stores and thrift shops, and then bid on them on eBay using false IDs. In addition to the IDs he used in the *RD-52* auction, Fetterman also went by thriftstorebob, estate-queen, show-boy, and mr. underbid, among others; Walton and Beach went by cool-arturo, pigroast, and pickinlickingood. Their fraudulent auctions produced more than $450,000 in winning bids.

The three men went to great lengths to make it appear that their thrift-store art was valuable. In an auction that Beach listed of a work that he purported to be by the noted French painter Maurice Utrillo (1883–1955), Fetterman used the name utrillo@monocourrier.com to bid, suggesting that a relative of the artist wanted to buy it. At the end of an auction for a painting with the forged signature "C. Still 1955," which appeared to be the work of the American painter Clyfford Still (1904–1980), Fetterman e-mailed the winning bidder claiming to be one Gerald Stone, who was writing a book on the New York school of abstract expressionism. Fetterman, as Stone, said he had watched the auction and thought the bidding might not go as high as it did because the painting was signed "C. Still," not the artist's usual signature. "Not a lot of people know that he used the 'C. Still' signature for a while in the 1950s, so I thought there might be some skepticism," Fetterman wrote. "But you obviously knew better!" The e-mail failed to reassure the high bidder, who backed out of the purchase. But when it was forwarded to the second-highest bidder, he happily bought the C. Still for $30,500.

Shill bidding was hardly limited to eBay. In real-world auctions, there was a long tradition of both shill bids and "phantom" bids, bids the auctioneer placed himself to drive up prices. But shill bidding was far easier to pull off online, where bidders could hide behind multiple false identities. EBay had installed proprietary software called Shill Bidder that detected shill bidding by looking for unlikely correlations between buyers and sellers, and it insisted it was doing all it could. But critics argued that eBay either used Shill Bidder too little, or that the software was ineffective. EBay would not say how many shill bidders it caught, but it did not detect the Diebenkorn ring—an eBay user turned them in. EBay's detractors charged it was not in the company's interest to detect shill bidding, since it drove up fees at the same time it drove up prices. As long as eBay did not develop a reputation as a rigged venue, they argued, it had no incentive to hunt down shill bidders aggressively.

Fetterman, Walton, and Beach were charged with sixteen counts of wire and mail fraud, and, in Fetterman's case, money laundering. Walton and Beach pled guilty, agreeing to pay $100,000 in restitution and to refrain from online auctions for three years. Walton, a lawyer, was disbarred. Fetterman disappeared, and was a fugitive at the time the other two men submitted their pleas. After his client's arrest, Walton's lawyer tried to minimize the crime. "This is a dumb, juvenile thing that got out of hand," Walton's lawyer said of his client. "It makes me want to hit him over the head."

◆

In May 2000, a simple toaster advertisement appeared on eBay with a small image of a toaster burning a piece of toast and copy reading: "Is your old toaster crummy? Save $15 on appliances and more." It had a link to Ourhouse.com, an online site that sold appliances for Ace Hardware. The ad appeared on eBay's search page, and it appeared only when prompted by specific search terms. If a user typed in a search for "toaster"—but not, say, "pottery"—the ad would show up along with the search results.

When eBay's small sellers saw the toaster ad, the message boards exploded, and eBay was flooded with angry e-mail. This time, eBay had gone too far, the sellers fumed. Now it was actually trying to steal customers away from its own sellers and direct them to a company that sold on another website. EBay had sold out the community that built it, they said, for ad revenue.

EBay had a complicated relationship with advertising. There was much less of it on eBay than on many other commercial websites, and some members of the eBay community, even some of the staff, thought there should not be any ads at all. But eBay did not have a tradition of being ad-free. As far back as 1996, when it was still AuctionWeb, Omidyar had experimented with banner ads from OnSale, which had not yet become a competitor in person-to-person auctions. "I don't think anyone clicked on them," Omidyar says. "That was the end of the experiment." Omidyar also briefly enrolled in the Interlink Exchange program, in which websites put up ads for one another. Still, advertising at eBay had always been low-key, and it had never competed with the site's own sellers.

But in May 2000, eBay's thinking about advertising changed. With the pressure from Wall Street to steadily increase earnings, eBay was starting to look for revenue wherever it could find it. In a filing with the Securities and Exchange Commission, the company advised that although "to date online advertising on the eBay Web site" had not made a "significant contribution to net revenues," it now expected ad revenue to increase. Kevin Pursglove, in a press interview, confirmed that users would begin to see more banner ads on the site, particularly for what he called "complementary services," like ISPs and shipping companies, for which eBay's user base was a natural market.

At the same time eBay was pushing for more ad revenue, it was starting to crack down on the informal, cost-free ways that community members had been using the site to promote their own businesses. There was a long tradition of eBay sellers', in describing one auction item, including descriptions of other items for sale as well as links to other websites where they were available. But this was precisely the kind of marketing eBay charged a fee for when it sold an ad. In March, eBay had implemented a new policy sharply restricting these promotions. It was all intended to increase ad revenues. But it seemed to some sellers that eBay was intentionally trying to hurt their businesses at the same time it was helping non-eBay sellers.

EBay tried to soften the blow by saying that most of the ads it accepted would be for ancillary services, not for goods that competed directly with items listed for sale. But since eBay billed itself as a market where people could trade nearly anything, it was not clear what it hoped to advertise that would not take business away from eBay sellers. Pursglove had suggested shipping services, but that would compete directly with Karen Young and other sellers who specialized in shipping supplies.

To critics of the ads, they represented not just competition for small sellers, but a fundamental change in eBay's philosophy. EBay was abandoning Omidyar's original conception of a level playing field, in which buyers and sellers came to the site as equals, they said. It was becoming just another commercial realm where sellers who had a lot of money could grab buyers away from sellers who did not.

The message boards quickly filled with outraged posts. One, titled "ebaY SELLING US DOWN THE RIVER WITH BANNER ADS!!!" warned that eBay was "JUST GETTING STARTED WITH THIS!!!" and that "If we let them keep it up without a peep, you will find YOUR CUSTOMERS that YOU pay for them to bring you through FINAL VALUE FEES redirected to other off-ebaY sites when they do searches." It drew sixty-five replies, overwhelmingly critical of eBay. "This is really really sickening," wrote a poster with the ID Kailin. "I can't imagine a more blatant message from eBay that they don't want us anymore."

The Online Auction Users Association, a nonprofit group that represented small sellers and buyers, also lambasted eBay. "The ability of big business to target and effectively market their product creates a playing field that is no longer level," it declared in a formal position paper on the toaster-ad controversy. "Where once users competed equally with their hard work, ingenuity, knowledge, and skill, now big businesses are welcomed to eBay and use their marketing savvy and deep pockets to take larger and larger numbers of bidder dollars away from the person-to-person sales that have built eBay."

During the toaster-ad blowup, an eBay executive called Young to ask what impact it would have on her business if eBay accepted ads from Staples and E-Stamp.com, which was considering expanding into shipping supplies. It would most likely put her out of business, Young replied, adding that eBay's new ad policy was disloyal to the community of sellers who had built eBay into what it now was. If eBay was going to have an official "eBay source for shipping supplies," she asked, why not make it her own shippingsupply.com? "The executive responded by asking if I had four to five million dollars a year to spend on advertising," Young says. "It was all about the money."

In the end, though, it wasn't all about the money. Faced with open rebellion from the seller community, eBay backed down. On June 3, it put up a message on the Announcement Board saying there would be no more ads tied to specific search terms. There were also published reports, which eBay would not confirm, that the company had canceled several large contracts with corporate advertisers. According to Whitman, the toaster-ad incident permanently changed the company's thinking about advertising. "We cannot compete with our customers," she says.

◆

In late May, Ronald Whyte, a federal judge in San Jose, ordered Bidder's Edge to keep its bots off the eBay site. Bidder's Edge, a Burlington, Massachusetts–based auction aggregator, compiled listings from several different auction sites and presented them on a single website. Bidder's Edge simplified life for auction buyers. Rather than conduct separate searches on eBay, Yahoo!, Amazon, and other auction sites, one global search on Bidder's Edge would locate items from seventy different sites.

EBay had raised its first objections to the Bidder's Edge bots back in September 1999. Around the same time, eBay posted a revised user agreement barring bots from its site. Bidder's Edge insisted it was not bound by the user agreement, but it voluntarily stopped sending bots for a while. "We're a nine-million-dollar company, they're a multibillion-dollar company," Bidder's Edge vice president of marketing George Reinhart said. "We think we would ultimately win a court battle, but in the meantime they would probably do all sorts of nasty legal things and we don't have the resources to fight them." But in late October, the bots were back, and Bidder's Edge was once again including eBay's listings on its site. EBay tried unsuccessfully to block the bots from collecting data. Then it tried to negotiate with Bidder's Edge about how its listings could be used. When Bidder's Edge refused, eBay went to court.

EBay charged that Bidder's Edge was stealing its intellectual property and profiting from it unfairly, since it sold advertising on the pages listing eBay's auctions. Bidder's Edge argued that it was merely roaming through cyberspace, where all information is free, and collecting data that belonged to no one. But eBay responded that because the Bidder's Edge bots had to use eBay's servers to harvest the data, Bidder's Edge was engaged in "trespass to chattel," a legal doctrine that prohibits interference with the physical property of others. EBay was not able to show that Bidder's Edge had ever crashed the eBay site, but eBay's lawyers argued that it raised the likelihood. The bots did demonstrably slow down the site, and eBay maintained that this resulted in actual damage, since its internal research found that users spent a fixed amount of time on the site, and when the bidding was slow, they placed fewer total bids. Bidder's Edge countered that its trespasses were minimal, equivalent to a few footsteps on another person's land, which the law generally forgives.

In February 2000, Bidder's Edge took the offensive, filing an antitrust claim against eBay, charging that it was the one being victimized. Bidder's Edge presented evidence that eBay dominated online auctions—with an 88 percent market share, and as much as 95 percent of daily gross merchandise sales. It was fighting, it said, for all of the Davids battling this Internet Goliath. "We never thought eBay had the right to be the largest auction site for the rest of history," a Bidder's Edge executive said. But Bidder's Edge had trouble showing it was harmed by eBay's alleged monopoly, since it did not directly compete in the online auction market. One of its key complaints was that *eBay Magazine,* a periodical eBay briefly published about happenings on the site, had refused a Bidder's Edge advertisement. In the wake of Bidder's Edge's lawsuit, the Justice Department opened an antitrust inquiry into eBay's practices.

Judge Whyte was not convinced by eBay's claim that it owned the intellectual property rights to its listings. If Bidder's Edge had simply copied them by hand and posted them on its site, he said, he might have ruled in its favor. But he did accept eBay's trespass claim, one of the first times a court had applied the doctrine to computer use. "Even if [Bidder's Edge] searches only a small amount of eBay's computer system capacity, [it] has nonetheless deprived eBay of the ability to use that portion of its personal property for its own purposes," Judge Whyte wrote. That appropriation, the court held, was classic trespass to chattel. "One crawler may currently use one percent of eBay's resources," the judge observed. "What if hundred[s] of users used similar crawlers?"

EBay hailed the ruling as a victory not only for itself, but for "all Internet entrepreneurs who hope to create businesses based on databases without fear that trespassers will come in and steal the fruits of their labor." All Bidder's Edge could do was vow to appeal. In the meantime, the judge's order had an immediate and dramatic impact on Bidder's Edge's service. A search for Czech glass beads that had turned up 825 auctions before the court order, one reporter found, produced just 190 after Bidder's Edge pulled the eBay auction listings from its site.

In its court documents, eBay emphasized the impact Bidder's Edge's bots had on its computer system. It was a winning legal argument, but eBay was at least as concerned about harm to something just as valuable: its network effects. By aggregating auction listings from eBay and other online auction sites, Bidder's Edge was creating a collection of auctions that was bigger than any one auction site alone—including eBay. At the time of the litigation, eBay had 4 million items listed, but Bidder's Edge had 7 million. EBay's success, as

Omidyar liked to point out, was due in large part to the fact that sellers went where all the buyers were, and buyers went where all the sellers were. But if aggregators like Bidder's Edge caught on, buyers would no longer go to eBay—they would go to an aggregator. Sellers could put their items up for sale on any site, including any of the free sites that were constantly appearing, because their listings could be seen by anyone who went to an aggregator.

Bidder's Edge appealed Judge Whyte's ruling, as it said it would. But in early 2001, before it could get a ruling from an appellate court, Bidder's Edge settled the lawsuit, agreeing to stop listing eBay auctions on its site, and to pay eBay an undisclosed sum. It also shut down its auction aggregation business, due, it said, "to market and financing conditions."

◆

On July 4, 2000, the eBay community had its first revolution. Rosalinda Baldwin was, of course, on the front lines. But this time, she had an unlikely comrade in arms. Bobby Beeman ran a small toy business out of a warehouse in an industrial neighborhood in northwest Dallas. Beeman, a sturdily built man with shoulder-length brown hair who had the look of an overgrown boy, was known to the eBay community by his eBay ID, Toyranch. He specialized in baby boomer toys: Hot Wheels cars, battery-operated toy robots, board games, and lunch boxes memorializing long-ago TV shows like *The Beverly Hillbillies* and *Family Affair.*

When Beeman first came across eBay, he had an antiques-and-collectibles store. Items that were not selling in his store went fast on eBay. He was able, he says, to sell "just about anything I could take a photo of." And the prices he got were better. "You could put a dollar bill on and it sold for two dollars, just because someone wanted to do the transaction." In March 1997, he closed his store and moved his business entirely online. As Toyranch, Beeman became a regular on eBay's message boards, which he describes as "like a party." It was, according to Beeman, eBay's golden age. "I told my friends to enjoy it, because it's not always going to be such a friendly place," he says.

Beeman's disenchantment with eBay began when it became a
public company. Like Baldwin, he was troubled that eBay did not
make pre-IPO stock available to people like him, who had spent
countless hours on the message boards tutoring new users. "We realized then that we had done all this to feather someone else's nest,"
he says. But for Beeman it wasn't only, or even mainly, about the
money. He claims that when eBay went public it underwent "a big
philosophical shift." Until the IPO, he says, eBay acted like it was in a
partnership with its users. Afterward, management's priorities
changed. "Their only objective used to be improving the marketplace, but after the IPO their objective was to increase the share
price," he says.

Beeman thought eBay had behaved badly during the gun ban
and the reserve-auction controversy, but it was the toaster ad that
turned him into an activist. EBay's rush to sell ads that competed
with its community was, for him, the clearest evidence that eBay was
abandoning small sellers. The company did not seem to realize, or
care about, the damage it was doing to people like him, who supported themselves and their families selling on eBay. "People can't
pay their bills, their rent or mortgage," Beeman posted on
AuctionWatch's eBay board. "They can't buy books for their kids'
school. Their mother gets booted out of the nursing home."

Even though Beeman's side won in the toaster-ad flap, he was
worried about the direction eBay's management was headed. Beeman
knew Baldwin from the message boards, and they exchanged regular
e-mails. He wrote to her now to say that he was becoming increasingly frustrated with eBay. He dreamed, he told her, of organizing a
boycott that would teach eBay not to take its users for granted.

It was the e-mail Baldwin had been waiting for. She agreed with
Beeman's diagnosis, but not with his prescription. Baldwin did not
support a boycott, she replied, because this was not about punishing
eBay, or trying to extract a list of demands for better treatment.
Online auctions would not improve, she argued, until eBay had a
strong competitor, and the way to introduce competition into a
sphere that had never had any was to encourage sellers to take more

of their auctions from eBay to other sites. Baldwin even had a name for the effort: the Million Auction March. That weekend, while Baldwin was off at Army Reserves, Beeman registered the domain name millionauctionmarch.com.

Beeman and Baldwin recruited twenty march organizers, mainly from AuctionWatch, OTWA, and eBay's own message boards. They were geographically dispersed, but they were able to convene in cyberspace. Beeman handed out assignments. Some volunteers created the MAM website, others designed a logo, and still more were dispatched to the message boards—both online auction boards and those that catered to collectors of various kinds—to educate and proselytize. Beeman and Baldwin agreed on July 4 as a fitting day to launch their campaign for independence from eBay. In keeping with the movement's name, they vowed to move one million auctions from eBay to what they called VOTES, Venues Other Than eBay, by September 1.

The Million Auction March, which was protesting what it regarded as eBay's overly corporate orientation, had the feel of a 1960s activist organization. Membership in the movement was based on participation, and there was no hierarchy or formal decision-making mechanism. MAM was also, in the tradition of the sixties, noncommercial and nonprofit. As the movement gained momentum, commercial auction sites began to approach Beeman about underwriting the effort. But he insisted on paying the expenses himself so no one could question MAM's motives.

The Million Auction March's mission statement was pragmatic, emphasizing what the group saw as the continuing degradation of eBay's small sellers. It objected to eBay's handling of the eBay Motors launch and the toaster ad and it raised concerns about the purchase of Half.com, which it argued could hurt eBay sellers who specialized in books, music, and movies. But the movement also had a more philosophical inspiration, the Cluetrain Manifesto, an online call to arms that set out a vision for how businesses and community should work in cyberspace. The Cluetrain movement, begun by a group of Internet theoreticians and entrepreneurs, took its name from the idea that Internet businesses needed to get a clue—or, as a veteran of a corporation that was falling from the Fortune 500 put it: "The clue train stopped there four times a day for ten years and they never took delivery."

Cluetrain was, at its core, an appeal for honesty and humanity in Internet commerce. The group's website, cluetrain.com, included its own *95 Theses*, a variation on Martin Luther's original, the first of which stated that "markets are conversations." The website explained that people generally communicate in language that is "natural, open, honest, direct, funny, and often shocking." Most corporations, however, "only know how to talk in the soothing, humorless monotone of the mission statement, marketing brochure, and your-call-is-important-to-us busy signal." When Beeman first read the Cluetrain materials, he could not help thinking of what eBay was becoming.

In August, eBay invited Beeman out to Campbell for a day. EBay told him it wanted to hear his ideas, but Baldwin was convinced it was trying to co-opt Beeman the way it had co-opted Pinkham. When Beeman arrived in Campbell, Whitman cleared her schedule to meet with him personally. Whitman was aware of the Million Auction March—Beeman noticed some of the MAM materials on the table in front of her—but the subject did not come up directly. "We were not worried about that event per se," Whitman said later. "We were worried about the disease that this was a symptom of." Beeman used his time to talk about all the ways he saw eBay becoming more corporate, and to explain the damage that was being done to small sellers.

If eBay's goal was co-optation, it was largely successful. When Beeman returned to Texas, he still did not agree with all of eBay management's decisions, but he was impressed with their sincerity. In an interview on AuctionWatch, and in a series of message board posts, he briefed the community about what he had learned. He had come away, he said, with a greater understanding of the challenges eBay faced in trying to create a business unlike any that had ever existed. "They've done it right more than they've done it wrong," he wrote in an August 12 posting. "All of them are at ebaY because of the challenge it presents and they are passionate about addressing that challenge."

The Million Auction March had an impact. EBay's listings were almost flat from March 1 to September 2000, a period during which Yahoo! added almost 1 million new auctions. Yahoo! credits the Million Auction March with generating many of those new listings. Still, the movement failed in its primary goal: creating a strong competitor to eBay.

The biggest hurdle was the usual one, the size of eBay's network. Even at the height of the Million Auction March, eBay remained the place for sellers to go if they wanted to find buyers. "It took Herculean efforts to get people to try other sites," Baldwin recalls. "Then they would say, 'I listed one item on Yahoo! and it didn't sell.'" The same message boards that had erupted in anti-eBay rebellion were now filled with grumbling from sellers whose auctions on competing sites had ended in failure. "I tried several times to list at Gold's," a seller named goldie999 wrote in an AuctionWatch post. "Semiexpensive items ($200 to $500) with absolutely no luck at all. Seven-day auctions with maybe five or six hits total and zero bids. . . . The same items on eBay received close to two hundred hits and all sold. There is nothing wrong with Gold's site except no one bids there. Too bad."

There was another factor working against the Million Auction March—the more users learned about other sites, the better eBay looked. Beeman sat down with Yahoo!'s auction managers around the same time he visited eBay. He explained to them that they had the potential to be a more community-minded alternative to eBay. But it seemed to him that Yahoo! was even more focused on the bottom line than eBay, and it lacked eBay's long tradition of involving the community in its decision making. Million Auction March organizers investigated other eBay rivals and came away similarly unimpressed. "I still think competition is good," Beeman said later. "But I'd hate to see any of the other auction sites be in the dominant position eBay is in." It was hardly the rallying cry of an anti-eBay movement.

chapter ten

Jerry Marcus, a tall, soft-spoken accountant from Queens, New York, already had fifteen hundred clothing irons, but he was hunched over his computer at home, bidding on one more.

Marcus had beat-up five-dollar castaways, rummaged from boxes at flea markets, and an early-twentieth-century horse-shaped iron, worth about five thousand dollars at auction. He had a 150-pound iron, an Iron Rite mangle board from the 1940s, used to press bedsheets. And he owned more than two hundred laundry sprinkler bottles, used to dampen clothing before the invention of the steam iron, the most valuable of which he could have sold for a thousand dollars. Marcus also dabbled in the third part of the iron-collector's trinity, memorabilia associated with New York's Flatiron Building. Among his favorites was a rare bank shaped like the Manhattan landmark. "I'm a fanatic," Marcus says. "Unfortunately." Marcus's wife, Jeannie, like many iron-collector wives, had a collection of children's irons, including one that was less than an inch long, worth five hundred dollars.

But Marcus did not have a "swan-on-swan." An ornate swan-shaped clothing iron with a smaller swan perched on top, the swan-on-swan was for iron collectors what the "inverted Jenny" airplane was for stamp collectors, or a signed copy of the Declaration of Independence was for document collectors. Manufactured in New York in 1877, only fifteen swan-on-swans were known to exist, and most were in the hands of collectors who would not part with them. But Marcus had found one up for auction on eBay, listed by a non–iron collector from upstate New York, who apparently had no idea what a valuable commodity he had. The seller had listed the swan-on-swan with only a $700 reserve, a small fraction of what it was worth.

Marcus resolved to win the iron at any cost. He was hoping he would be the only collector to find it, but he knew that was unlikely. So he went into battle with a plan. He would be at his computer in the final minutes of the auction, with four browser windows open at once. He would then start bidding wildly with all of them. The key to winning a hard-fought auction, he knew, was the well-timed snipe, and he was prepared to place his last bid in the final five or ten seconds. As the auction wound down, Marcus was in good shape—he was winning, with a bid of $13,000.

That was when it happened. Another bidder appeared out of nowhere, a Florida iron collector Marcus recognized from his ID, and placed his own last-second bid—for $13,500. Marcus tried desperately to place one last bid. "I wanted to get in, but my hands were shaking too much," he says. The clock ran out, and Marcus's swan-on-swan had flown away.

Marcus was reminiscing about the swan-on-swan while leaning against a wall in Ballroom B of the Kansas City Airport Hilton on a hot July morning. With table after table piled high with irons of every shape and description, a stranger walking into the room might have thought he had stumbled into the hotel's housekeeping department.

In fact, it was the seventeenth annual meeting of the Midwest Sad Iron Collectors Club, and the more than one hundred people crowded into the ballroom had come from as far away as Australia to talk about their shared passion for clothing irons.*

There is no easy answer to why someone decides to collect clothing irons. In Europe, where iron collecting is more widespread, irons have more cachet—centuries ago, only wealthy people owned them. But in America most clothing-iron collectors stumble on the hobby almost by accident. Marcus bought his first old iron to use as a doorstop when the hinges on a door in his Pennsylvania summerhouse stopped working. Iron collecting appealed to his practical side. If he collected something more common, like stamps or coins, he could never afford a leading collection. But irons were relatively cheap, and after years of work he was able to amass one of the best collections in American. "It certainly wasn't about ironing," says Jeannie Marcus. "To this day I send everything to the Chinese laundry."

The 2000 Midwest Sad Iron Collectors convention stuck to the usual script. After the welcoming remarks, attendees broke into discussion groups—iron cleaning against one wall, iron figurine collectors across the room. Saturday afternoon was display time, when club members took out their most prized irons for their fellow members to admire. Later came show-and-tell, with club members stepping up to the podium to talk about a rare Chinese ceramic iron, or a gas iron from the 1933 World's Fair. The keynote address, after the formal banquet Saturday night, was delivered by a British collector who, along with her husband, had the world's leading collection of mangle boards.

But in one respect, this year's convention differed from past years: the iron collectors could not stop talking about eBay. The best-attended panel of the week was one about online auctions, and the summer 2000 issue of *Iron Talk*, a bible with the clothing-iron

---

*Sad, in the club's name, was used in its archaic sense, "heavy," to denote old-fashioned metal clothing irons. The word *Midwest* was a misnomer: members came from throughout the United States and several foreign countries.

crowd, had a much discussed article on bidding strategy. The eBay effect came to the Midwest Sad Iron Collectors later than it did to many other collector communities, because irons attract an older, not particularly computer-savvy following. But by now, even the iron collectors had a website, irons.com, and at the convention everyone agreed that eBay had changed their little world forever.

Collecting communities like the iron collectors had been eBay's most loyal users, going back to the AuctionWeb days, and the driving force behind eBay's early growth. Hearing the Midwest Sad Iron Collectors talk about eBay, it was obvious why. EBay had completely transformed iron collecting, primarily by making it far easier to do. Before eBay, a collector like Marcus spent much of his spare time chasing down rare irons. He attended clothing-iron auctions around the country and made pilgrimages to Europe, where the oldest and best irons were still to be found. On one recent trip to Holland, Marcus had hauled back forty, buying another suitcase to carry them home. He had developed relationships with iron dealers, who would offer him their best irons when they came in. Then eBay came along, and suddenly his computer provided him with access to an endless supply of old irons—classic "Mrs. Potts" irons, children's irons, hand-painted folk-art irons, irons with matching trivets, even a swan-on-swan.

No one in the iron-collecting community disputed that eBay's impact had been revolutionary. The only debate was whether it was a force for good. Most collectors insisted it was, arguing that eBay had given them access to irons they would never have found off-line, and allowed them to cut back on travel to auctions and flea markets. Club president Jay Raymond had bought a good part of his collection of "streamlined" irons—art deco–influenced electric irons from the 1930s and 1940s—on eBay. His eBay haul included his most prized streamlined iron, a Knapp-Monarch from the 1940s that looked like a flying saucer. Marcus had bought many of his favorite irons and iron-related memorabilia on eBay, including a spoon with a picture of the Flatiron Building that he got from a seller in Oregon. "We weren't going to Oregon for a spoon," says Jeannie Marcus.

Still, some of the club members, especially the older ones without computers, complained that eBay had taken the fun out of the hobby. "I don't want to spend ten hours on a computer looking at irons," says Buck Carson, editor of *Pressing News*. "I'd rather go to an auction, or talk to dealers." Others said it removed the challenge and sense of accomplishment. All it took now to have a leading iron collection, one older woman complained after show-and-tell, was a computer and a checkbook.

But even on eBay shopping for irons could be a bit of a hunt. Unlike many collectibles, irons did not have their own eBay category. To find them, collectors had to be resourceful. Typing *iron* into the eBay search engine brought up an unmanageable number of auctions, few of which were for clothing irons. Marcus always did "smart" searches, starting with the word *iron*, and then subtracting words like *golf, wrought*, and *cross*, which would bring up non–clothing iron irons. But his most effective technique was searching for the user IDs of his fellow Midwest Sad Iron Collectors members. If they were bidding in a current auction, there was a good chance it would be one he would want to bid in. Marcus's fellow members knew what he was up to. "I should get a finder's fee!" one said about a recent auction Marcus won out from under him.

Critics of the Internet might have suspected that eBay would ultimately do harm to an organization like the Midwest Sad Iron Collectors. Conventional wisdom about the Internet was that it tore down the bonds of community. The social energy people would have put into interacting with friends and neighbors was being redirected to talking with strangers in chat groups, or reading endless web pages.* But some Internet theorists, notably Cornell computer science professor Dan Huttenlocher, were beginning to suggest a more nuanced theory: that where an off-line community already existed,

---

*In 1998, a well-publicized Carnegie Mellon study, *Internet Paradox: A Social Technology That Reduces Social Involvement and Psychological Well-Being?*, found that Internet use was associated with a decline in social interaction, and an increase in depression and loneliness. But three years later, the Carnegie Mellon team published a new study, *The Internet Paradox Revisited*, disavowing many of their initial conclusions.

the Internet could actually serve to strengthen the social bonds within it.

That appeared to be true of eBay and the iron collectors. The Midwest Sad Iron Collectors' membership ranks were growing, in part because it was recruiting new members on eBay. Marcus, the point man on eBay recruitment, tracked the iron auctions, and when he saw bidders who were not already club members, he e-mailed them, inviting them to join. EBay also strengthened the ties between individual club members. Most of the leading iron collectors had known one another for years, crossing paths at iron auctions and club meetings. But because they were geographically dispersed, with no state having more than a dozen club members, it was hard for them to be in regular contact. EBay gave them a shared activity, following the auctions listed on the site, and a reason to communicate more regularly. Club members were now spending hours every night on eBay, e-mailing one another about irons the whole time.

EBay gave the Midwest Sad Iron Collectors one more shared activity—online bidding wars, which they engaged in regularly. Raymond won his Knapp-Monarch iron by outbidding another club member. Marcus lost his swan-on-swan to someone who was also at the convention in Kansas City. When a hotly contested iron auction ended on eBay, there was invariably a round of e-mails discussing who won it, who had been outbid, who sniped, and who had been sniped. When club members gathered at their annual conventions, they could rehash the same auctions in person. "Every time Jerry was sniped this year, he e-mailed the bidder," says Jeannie Marcus. " 'See you in Kansas City!' "

◆

The two main off-eBay message boards, AuctionWatch and OTWA, both grew rapidly in the summer of 2000. AuctionWatch could easily handle the traffic, since its boards were supported by a well-funded private company, but keeping the OTWA boards up and running was becoming a burden for Jim and Crystal. To meet their expenses, including the growing number of computer servers the message boards required, they realized they needed to either go out looking for investors or sell the site to someone who could afford to pay their bills.

They turned to Scott Samuel. Samuel was an old friend of Crystal's from the Q & A Board, the first person, in fact, to say hello to her when she posted there for the first time. A part-time history and English teacher from the suburbs of Chicago, Samuel had once run a company called Dr. Defunct, specializing in memorabilia from extinct sports teams like the Brooklyn Dodgers and the Seattle Pilots. He had a successful collectibles business on eBay, but Samuel became famous in the eBay community because of a small feature he included in all of his listings—a counter.

Samuel had installed a piece of software in his listings that kept a running tally of how many people looked at the page. The counters gave him useful marketing information. When items did not sell, he could see if buyers were coming to the listing and rejecting the item—perhaps because the reserve price was too high—or if, instead, there was no interest in the listing at all. When other eBay sellers saw Samuel's counters, they e-mailed him, asking how they could install counters on their own listings. Samuel created a free counter, which he named Honesty, and began giving it away on his website, Honesty.com.

Word of the free counters spread rapidly. Samuel looked on in amazement as the number of Honesty counters on eBay listings climbed, with no promotion at all, from hundreds, to thousands, to millions a week. With that kind of demand—even for something that was free—it seemed to him he had a potential business. Investors agreed, believing that the millions of visitors to Honesty.com could be monetized, by either selling ads or offering them fee-based services. Samuel raised $2.5 million from VCs and individual investors and created Honesty.com, a start-up tech company that he ran with seven friends out of a rented house next door to his Internet service provider in Grayslake, Illinois.

Jim and Crystal saw Samuel's company as a convenient way out of their bind. They sold OTWA to Honesty.com "rather than go corporate," Jim says. But not going corporate did not last long. Right after Jim and Crystal sold OTWA to Honesty.com, Samuel sold Honesty.com to Andale, a large auction management company with more than $60 million in VC money. Honesty was hardly lucrative—neither the counters nor the OTWA boards generated any revenue at all—but it attracted a flood of online auction users. Andale, which was going head-to-head with AuctionWatch, saw it as a way of marketing its money-making services, including image hosting, bulk listing, and auction consulting.

With corporate funding paying for their computer servers and small staffs, OTWA and AuctionWatch thrived. They were, now more than ever, the Greek chorus of the online auction world, commenting ceaselessly on every twist and turn in the eBay community. Each site had its own loyal following, but there was little difference between the two in content. OTWA was, consistent with its "no complaints" history, slightly more positive in outlook and less likely to carry attacks on eBay, but the distinction was subtle. EBay viewed both boards as barometers of community sentiment and—much as Rosalinda Baldwin suspected—had its staff prepare summaries of their posts. In times of controversy, like reserve auctions or the toaster ad, the opinions expressed on OTWA and AuctionWatch could literally change eBay policy. But the bulk of the posts were more practical, asking for or offering advice about specific aspects of eBay usage. Despite their corporate ownership, the AuctionWatch and OTWA boards remained highly informal, one of their charms. They were still places where a post headlined "PRIORITY MAIL TAPE WEIRD SMELL" could draw fifteen enthusiastic responses.

◆

In August 1999, Dr. Kimberly Young, an adjunct professor of psychology at the University of Pittsburgh, presented a paper to the American Psychological Association's annual convention in Boston entitled "Cyber-Disorders: The Mental Health Concern for the New Millennium." One of the fastest-growing mental illnesses in America, she warned her colleagues, was eBay addiction.

EBay addiction had long been a running joke at eBay and on the message boards. In March 1999 eBay held an "eBay addicts" contest, in which it invited users to e-mail Mary Lou Song their most pathetic tales of dependence. "Does it mean I am addicted if [I] am a little bit late for work because I am searching for that special something?" one entrant asked. "How about a lot late for work (like two hours)?" Another wrote, "I love when I hear my boyfriend snore, because that means he's deeply asleep and I can go downstairs and turn the computer back on." The contest winner was a woman who sold toys and who offered up a mildly disturbing account of how eBay had taken over her home in the past year. "My husband became concerned and kept saying I was addicted to EBAY! 'No way,' I would say, as I stepped over the neglected dead carcasses of our cats!"

But in the mental health field, eBay addiction was more than just a punch line. Internet addiction was becoming a recognized disorder. Dr. David Greenfield, who also presented at the 1999 American Psychological Association Convention, reported on a study of Internet addiction he had done with ABC that appeared on the network's website. The survey attracted over eighteen thousand responses in two weeks, more than nine hundred of which appeared to meet classic definitions of addiction. "Clearly, something is happening," Greenfield told his fellow mental health professionals. On the eBay message boards, posters were beginning to talk about their need for eBay in less than humorous terms. In August 1999, AuctionWatch hosted "Are You Hooked?" an online forum that was one of the first serious discussions anywhere of eBay addiction. The site spoke with three past and present addicts, including one woman whose boss put her on administrative leave and threatened to fire her because she could not stop checking her auctions from the office.

One of the experts interviewed in the AuctionWatch forum was Kimberly Young. Young came to the field by chance, when she was finishing up clinical psychology postdoc work at the University of

Rochester's Strong Memorial Hospital. The husband of a friend had begun meeting women in online chat rooms. He was eating every meal at the computer, had stopped having sex with his wife and— back when AOL was still charging by the hour—was running up hundreds of dollars a month in Internet connection fees. Young saw a fruitful area for research. She developed a survey, adapted from the *Diagnostic and Statistical Manual of Mental Disorders'* compulsive gambling criteria, and posted it on a few Usenet newsgroups. "I got forty responses the next day," Young says. "I knew I had hit a nerve."

After graduate school, Young settled in Bradford, Pennsylvania, where she founded the Center for Online and Internet Addiction and began studying the uncharted territory of what she believed to be a new mental ailment. In her paper on cyberdisorders, she wrote that thirty-five mental health practitioners who had come across various online surveys she had posted on the Internet reported an average of nine, and as many as fifty, patients suffering from Internet addiction in the past year. Young also identified and classified the five types of Internet addiction she had observed:

- *Cybersexual addiction*—compulsive use of adult sex and pornography websites
- *Cyberrelationship addiction*—excessive involvement in online relationships
- *Net compulsions*—obsessive online gambling, trading, and shopping
- *Information overload*—compulsive web surfing or database searches
- *Computer addiction*—obsessive playing of computer games such as Doom, Myst, and Solitaire

Cybersexual addiction was, Young had found, the most common form of Internet addiction. But online auction addiction, which fell under her rubric of net compulsions, made up 15 percent of all cases.

In her own practice, Young had treated several hard-core eBay addicts. One, a wife and stay-at-home mother, had called her for the first time in April 2000. The woman told Young she had been raised in a well-to-do suburb, expecting a life of material comfort and intellectual stimulation. But she had ended up in rural Ohio, married to the manager of an auto-parts plant, with two daughters, ages twelve and ten.* The woman's family was well provided for, but certainly not wealthy, and her husband's life revolved around the blue-collar world of the factory. Young's patient had become disenchanted with her life and some of her choices, including the decision to abandon her career as a registered nurse to stay home with her children. Her fights with her husband, which were growing more frequent, invariably included her screaming at him, "All I am is your maid!" Depressed and dissatisfied, the woman discovered eBay. She bought tens of thousands of dollars' worth of stuff—pottery, knickknacks, household items—and found she could not stop herself from buying more. Her husband was angry about losing his wife's attention, and about the money. They fought more and seemed to be headed toward a divorce.

Young took the woman on as a telephone patient. The first step, she advised, was acknowledging her addictive behavior and trying to stop. On Young's recommendation, the woman installed screening software, the kind Young prescribed for her online pornography clients, to block her computer's ability to access eBay. Young's patient also moved the computer from her den to the family room, where it would be harder for her to stay on it for hours uninterrupted.

In weekly one-hour sessions, over a three-month period, doctor and patient explored the issues underlying the addiction. Many compulsive behaviors are rooted in low self-esteem, Young says, and eBay addiction fits this model particularly well. Like other forms of compulsive shopping, eBay addiction allows buyers to feel better about themselves by virtue of the things they have managed to acquire. And because many items on eBay are unique, buyers can feel special for having identified and purchased them. The auction format can

---

*Some identifying facts of the woman's story have been changed.

also give an eBay addict the adrenaline rush that comes from triumphing in head-to-head competition. "EBay was the one place she felt good about herself," Young concluded about her patient. "She was bidding and she was winning."

In this case, the treatment went well. Taking Young's advice that "you have to find a way to fill the void the computer was filling," the woman took a part-time job in a local library and entered marriage counseling.

But outcomes were not always so positive. Young treated another client, a government official from a large city, for eBay addiction. The government official, a divorced mother suffering from depression, was buying jewelry wholesale and reselling it on eBay from her office computer. She knew her employer had a policy against employees' using computers for personal projects, and that it monitored their usage. But she could not resist the money, or the positive comments buyers were leaving in her feedback ratings—some of the only positive reinforcement she received in any part of her life. The government agency fired the woman for misuse of her office computer. "It was humiliating," says Young. "And she knew it was so stupid." The woman intended to support herself by selling jewelry full-time on eBay, but as she became more depressed from the isolation of working alone, she started drinking and cut off therapy.

Young wants eBay to be more active about addressing Internet addiction. Just as many casinos post notices about how to get help for gambling addiction, eBay should post a checklist of warning signs for when eBay use has become an addiction, she says. Young does not blame eBay for the problem. When lonely, depressed people want to fill the emptiness in their lives, she says, they will find a way. But she says eBay addiction can be particularly insidious because it is available to people in their homes at any hour of the day or night, and it is socially acceptable. "If you drink all the time people say you're an alcoholic," Young says. "If you sell on eBay all the time people say, 'Oh, you like eBay!'"

◆

Karin Stahl was sitting on the top deck of a hulking metal ferry as it motored its way across Lake Atitlán, a vast mountain pool in southwest Guatemala. British author Aldous Huxley, who traveled the region in the 1930s, once pronounced Lake Atitlán more beautiful than Italy's Lake Como, and from Stahl's current vantage point it would be hard to disagree. The view from the top of the ferry was striking: an expanse of cobalt-blue water ringed by towering volcanoes. The sun was exploding overhead, a Goya painting in orange and red, and a stiff breeze was wafting across the lake—the late afternoon wind that, according to local legend, sweeps away sin.

Stahl, head of the eBay Foundation since shortly after the IPO, had flown into Guatemala City one morning in August with a small band of volunteers from Silicon Valley. After handing the machine-gun-toting soldiers at the airport a letter from the U.S. ambassador and saying a few reassuring words in Spanish, she had maneuvered her group, and a cache of new computers, onto a waiting bus. Undeterred by the bad roads that sent buses on fatal plunges on a regular basis, and recent incidents of Westerners being robbed, kidnapped, lynched, and stoned to death in the area, Stahl and her group settled in for the four-hour drive into the mountains.

In the village of Panajachel, the group caught the ferry across the lake. When the ferry docked in San Pedro La Laguna, the eBay contingent was met by the Battzes—the husband-and-wife principals of the Bethel School, whom Stahl had promised to help back in 1997. As Stahl's group walked through the dusty streets of San Pedro La Laguna, many for the first time, they could see how much work there was to do. San Pedrans were still living in hovels, without electricity or running water. Food was scarce, and there was no medical care. Since Stahl had started coming to San Pedro, three baby girls in the village had been named after her. One Karina had already died, and after she got off the boat Stahl was taken to see a second Karina, who had developed a life-threatening illness no one in the village could identify.

San Pedro's troubles were rooted in economics. Most of the men worked the fields, eking out a living farming coffee and corn on their own small plots, or selling their labor to large landowners for a few dollars a day. The women spent long hours crouched over wooden looms, turning out multicolored belts, clothes, and textiles in the traditional Mayan style. But when they finished, there was no one in the village to buy them. There was a market for them among tourists in Guatemala City, but tied down with children, and unable to afford the bus fare, the women could not make the trip. Instead, they sold what they produced to hard-driving middlemen—known locally as coyotes—who resold them at markups of up to 400 percent. A handwoven belt, bearing the bright patterns weavers in the region have used for centuries, could take a craftswoman five days to make, but she received less than three dollars for it from a coyote.

Stahl hoped to change that. In the three years since she had promised the Battzes she would do something to help the Bethel School, Stahl had been coming to San Pedro La Laguna regularly, bringing money, medicine, schoolbooks, and volunteers. But on this trip, Stahl was working on a bolder plan. Her experience with eBay Powersellers had shown her firsthand the Internet's ability to empower people financially—Omidyar's original inspiration when he created AuctionWeb—and it had given her an idea. "I was watching people who were quitting their jobs to sell on eBay full-time," she says. "I starting thinking, if these people can do it, why can't the Mayan people in Guatemala who have all those great crafts do the same thing?"

In August 1998, Stahl had begun bringing San Pedro into the computer age. EBay had donated three computers and two printers, and Stahl brought a team down to install them in a second-floor classroom at Bethel. It was San Pedro's first computer lab, and Emilio Battz, the school's principal, had recently named Juan Cruz Gonzalez, a twenty-three-year-old teacher who had studied computers in Guatemala City, the school's first computer teacher. Stahl's group showed Cruz Gonzalez, who had been taught on a simple DOS machine, how to use Windows. To the Bethel students who filed into the new computer lab for lessons, the machines Stahl had brought seemed magical. "A lot of the students had never even seen a typewriter before," says Cruz Gonzalez.

The following summer, Stahl led a second group of eBay employees, tech workers from other Silicon Valley companies, and medical professionals. She also brought more computers, including fifteen laptops, that eBay had donated to the cause. As the project began consuming more of Stahl's time, eBay created a new position for her, working half-time on the eBay Foundation and half-time coordinating eBay's charity auctions. As money began to pour in from donors, including eBay employees, Stahl put together an administrative structure for the San Pedro La Laguna effort, and took care of organizational details, like getting 501(c)(3) status for the project.

There were still many logistical matters to work out before anyone in San Pedro could use eBay directly. The village had only one phone line and five telephones—four public phones and another in the mayor's house. The Bethel School had been on a waiting list for a telephone for eleven years. On a previous trip, Stahl's group had brought an e-mail server, but the only way Ron Sackman, a networking specialist from Lucent Technologies, had been able to install it was by connecting a wireless cellular hookup through the Battzes' home, which was on the school grounds. The service was erratic, and Sackman frequently had to trudge through their house to troubleshoot. Still, the day e-mail arrived was even more remarkable, Cruz Gonzalez says, than the day the computers came. Cruz Gonzalez sent his first e-mail to a friend in Alaska, one of the American volunteers who had come to San Pedro La Laguna to help with construction of the Bethel School building. "When I sent postcards, it was two months between when I mailed them and when I got a response," Cruz Gonzalez says. "When I sent that e-mail, I got a response the next day."

Stahl had begun testing the waters on eBay. She bought woven materials, beaded jewelry, and paintings from the village's craftspeople, paying them about five or six times what a coyote would, and then put them up for auction. In her listings, Stahl told the story of

San Pedro La Laguna, explaining that 100 percent of the profits would go to the Bethel School. The crafts generally sold for more than Stahl paid. A three- or four-dollar piece of handwoven cloth might bring ten dollars from an American buyer.

In time, Stahl wanted San Pedrans to do the selling themselves. Her plan was to set up an office at the Bethel School, where crafts-people from around San Pedro could come to list their items. To get around the country's often unreliable mail system, she was considering establishing a fulfillment office in the United States, which could be staffed by student interns from San Pedro La Laguna, and having the goods shipped to America in bulk. Selling over eBay would not just bring in money, Stahl believed; it would bring the villagers directly into the world economy. They would learn which items sold and which did not, and adjust their businesses accordingly. They would learn marketing and customer service. And they would become self-sufficient. If her plan worked, before long the San Pedrans would not need her at all.

Members of Stahl's group had occasional qualms about their project, which they talked about over dinners at Max's, a simple local restaurant run by a Mayan couple. San Pedro La Laguna was part of a region that had struggled for centuries to hold on to its culture and traditions in the face of imperialist onslaughts. There was a danger, the Silicon Valley group realized, that the Internet and e-commerce might accomplish what Pedro de Alvarado and the Spanish conquistadors had failed to do. "If you're going to set up the Internet in a place like San Pedro, the first question is 'Can you do it?'" says Lucent's Sackman. "But the next question is '*Should* you do it?'"

They brought the question to Emilio Battz, who himself had grown up in a poor Mayan family in San Pedro La Laguna. To Battz, the answer was easy. Young San Pedrans should have the same opportunities as young people in the developed world. The Internet could turn the Bethel School library, which was now a single wall of books, into a place of limitless information. The money from e-commerce could build new homes and pay for better nutrition and health care, literally saving lives. Battz urged the visitors to continue with their project. "My dream," he told them, "is for every one of my students to have a computer."

◆

In August 2000, Meg Whitman asked Brian Burke to make a presentation to the management team about how to handle pornography on eBay. EBay had long taken a see-no-evil approach, restricting porn to the Adults Only category, which was separated from the main site and required a credit card to access. But the category had been growing bigger and racier every year. Its auction listings were now filled with photographs of topless women and scantily clad men that were not only being used to sell pornography—they were arguably pornographic themselves. EBay's adult site was, in fact, getting a reputation as one of the best free porn sites on the Internet. Making matters worse, more adult items were being improperly listed on the main site, and eBay was getting complaints. Whitman was particularly troubled by an e-mail from a grandmother who complained that she had been looking for dolls with her granddaughter, and the search had brought up a doll of an unexpected kind.

Burke, an in-house advocate for buyers and sellers, believed it would be a mistake to ban adult items. It would have marked a departure from eBay's libertarian roots as a venue for trading almost anything. Guns, alcohol, and tobacco all exposed eBay to legal liability. But if pornography were banned, it would have been purely a matter of eBay's imposing its morality on the community. A ban on adult items also struck Burke as counterproductive. As he saw it, eBay was a city, and the adult category was its red-light district. As long as there was an adult category, sellers had a place to put items that other users may not have wanted to see on the main site. But if the adult category were eliminated, that was exactly where most of them would end up.

When Burke briefed the management team, he brought along a pamphlet with about a dozen images taken from actual eBay listings. As the group discussed them, they realized how difficult it was to lay down a principle for identifying pornography more profound than

Supreme Court Justice Potter Stewart's much ridiculed formulation, "I know it when I see it." One of Burke's images was a naked woman resting on a rock in a provocative pose. Several of the eBay managers immediately said it belonged in the adult section. But when they looked at the picture more closely, they realized that the woman's fingers were unusually long, and that in fact it was a sculpture. The group could not agree whether that automatically made it less objectionable than if it had been a photograph of an actual woman.

Whitman had come to the meeting hoping to draw a clear line between X items, which eBay would allow to be listed on the site, and XXX items, which it would not. The management team talked about trying to create a "Spice Channel" level of pornography. But Burke explained that those standards had no actual content. There were no films rated XXX; it was just a marketing device used by the adult-movie industry to attract audiences. (The only official adult category recognized by the film industry, he told them, was NC-17.) The group also talked about barring "excessive profanity" from the site, but the discussion broke down over attempts to define "excessive" and "profanity."

EBay ended its reconsideration by taking a middle course. It renamed the Adults Only category Mature Audiences, and took some steps to clean up the listings. Users were barred from including sexually explicit items and terms. Among the prohibitions: references to bodily fluids; film taken with a hidden camera; and items with necrophilia, incest, or rape themes. At the same time, eBay made a concession to users of the category, adding the search engine they had long sought. Its absence had frustrated both sellers—who were convinced it hurt sales—and buyers. "The hell I am going to go through 200-plus pages searching for a video, or 300 pages trying to find an old vintage magazine," one AuctionWatch poster complained before the search engine was added. The new search function made eBay a better place to buy adult items; a key reason eBay added it was to reinforce the category's usefulness as a red-light district. If Mature Audiences was inadequate, Burke convinced management, sellers would simply list on the main site.

◆

In the fall of 1999, eBay celebrated its second anniversary as a public company. On Friday, September 15, work let out early and the staff filed into the San Jose Hilton for a combined company meeting and birthday party. As a thousand eBay employees settled into long rows of overstuffed hotel chairs, it was possible to pick out a few of the old-timers: Mary Lou Song and Maria Lee gossiping near the door, Jeff Skoll sitting in the front row, and Meg Whitman talking animatedly with a staff member about whether the audiovisual system was working. But these battle-hardened veterans—who had pulled off the migration from AuctionWeb to eBay, fended off the Onsale and Amazon launches, and survived the June 1999 outage—were lost in the sea of newly arrived marketers, technicians, and lawyers. EBay was growing so quickly, Whitman was about to tell the crowd, almost half of its staff had been hired in the last six months.

The crowd roared at an in-joke-filled video presentation, a riff on the then red-hot television show *Survivor.* Song and Uncle Griff, two stalwarts of the community, were voted off the island, and, perhaps revealingly, an eBay lawyer was the last one standing. Then Whitman took the stage to deliver a business report that Omidyar could not have dreamed of five years earlier, when he was trying desperately to drive traffic to his unloved auction website. As the screen behind her filled with a growth chart that climbed steeply along its x-axis, Whitman announced that eBay now had 1,500 employees and was hosting $5 billion in auctions a year. Another chart showed that it had taken Cisco Systems twelve years and 10,000 employees, Microsoft nineteen years and 16,000 employees, and Intel twenty-three years and 25,000 employees to generate the same level of economic activity.* If eBay's recent past felt like "an incredible rocket ship," she told the crowd, the chart behind her showed why. Before the assembly broke for birthday cake, Whitman delivered a final re-

---

*In comparing a retailer to manufacturers, Whitman overstated eBay's undeniably impressive accomplishments. Manufacturing and selling $1 million in goods, as Cisco and Microsoft do, is a more substantial economic contribution than simply selling $1 million in goods.

flection. "For those of you who haven't been in the business as long as I have," she said, "opportunities like eBay never come along."

It was, for eBay, a rare moment of looking back. Six days later, Whitman would be on more familiar ground, talking about where the company was headed, and delivering a bombshell. She was speaking at the Silicon Valley Conference Center to a large hall filled with Wall Street analysts who followed eBay. Flanked by the entire management team—including, in a rare appearance, senior scientist Mike Wilson—Whitman declared that eBay intended to reach $3 billion in revenue by 2005, which meant it would grow at an annual rate of 50 percent in each of the next five years. That would have been an extraordinary growth rate for any company at any time in history. But it was a particularly audacious goal given the dot-com collapse, which had sent revenues and market caps of other major Internet companies into free fall.

Whitman told the analysts that eBay intended to grow by sticking to its core business, serving as the world's leading trading platform. It would not do what some of its rivals had, buy up other companies just to get big quickly. Amazon, most notably, had squandered hundreds of millions of dollars investing in companies like Pets.com and the luxury goods site Ashford.com, with little but mounting debt to show for it. But eBay would, whether by growth or acquisition, work aggressively to "extend beyond the core business of United States collectibles," into new categories, new trading formats, and new markets around the world.

Central to eBay's strategy was its continued drive to change the mix of items on the site. The company remained committed to the collectors' markets, and not only for sentimental reasons. Listings of coins, one of eBay's most venerable categories, had doubled in the past year. Still, the company's greatest energy was going into initiatives like eBay Motors, Great Collections, and eBay's Business Exchange, a marketplace for small businesses. All of these were designed to push up the average sales price of items sold and, given eBay's fee structure, to increase revenues.

High-ticket items were already becoming far more common on

eBay. In August, a Texas-based airplane dealer sold a Gulfstream II business jet to an African charter aircraft company for $4.9 million, which eBay believed to be a new record. EBay was particularly pleased with the trajectory of the computer category. Large companies were now selling on it, notably Sun Microsystems, which in September listed five of its new $10,000 Sun Blade workstations. Average sales prices in the computer category were up sharply, and the conversion rate—the percentage of listed items that sold—was among the highest of any eBay category. The increase in average sales price had actually begun to change the metrics used to measure eBay's performance. Investors had long charted eBay's growth by looking at a single number that eBay put on its home page—auctions listed at that moment. But in May, when eBay introduced a new home page, it removed the auction count. The increase in the average sales price, Whitman explained, meant that eBay had effectively "decoupled" the revenue generated from the number of items being auctioned. "A Beemer is not the same as a Beanie Baby," she said.

EBay was working hard to attract sellers to the site, including government agencies. The state of Oregon had, on its own initiative, begun to use eBay to dispose of goods it acquired through seizure or repossession. Oregon's program had brought in far more in revenue than an off-line property auction would have, and eBay used it as an example to recruit other units of government, including federal agencies such as the U.S. Postal Service. Other states were reporting similar success: Massachusetts informed eBay that it had listed an old, rusted ship it had not expected to sell and got more than $125,000 for it.

EBay was constantly on the lookout for new categories to add. The best way to do research, it turned out, was to look at what sellers were listing in the Miscellaneous category, the same place Rothman had found so many automobile listings. Recently, eBay staff had noticed that sellers were listing tickets to live events there. EBay assigned a team to study the feasibility of creating a ticket category, with special attention to legal issues involving scalping. EBay ended up forming a partnership with a company called Ultimate Bid, and the ticket category was now listing more than eight thousand tickets at a time.

Whitman told the analysts to expect tremendous growth in overseas markets. Steve Westly, who was heading up international, ticked off the company's recent successes, including eBay Germany, which was now the largest e-commerce site in Europe, and eBay Canada, which was fifty times larger than its closest competitor. EBay intended to be in ten international markets, representing 120 million Internet users, by the end of 2001 and twenty-five countries, representing 325 million users, by the end of 2005. EBay's strategy was to first win Europe—the biggest e-commerce market outside the United States—building on its strength in Germany and the United Kingdom, and then to dominate Asia as its Internet use ramped up later in the decade.

Finally, Whitman told the analysts that alternative sales formats, particularly fixed-price sales, would be critical to eBay's future. Josh Kopelman flew in from Philadelphia to deliver the Half gospel and demonstrate how the site worked. By now, Half.com was old news. But the analysts were intrigued by a few brief mentions of a new format eBay was rumored to be working on. Storefronts, which would enable sellers to list their goods in separate parts of the eBay site that remained under their own control, were thought to be the next big wave in e-commerce. Storefronts would allow sellers almost as much autonomy as they had on their own websites. But by tapping into eBay's millions of registered users, they could solve the problem that had doomed so many small e-commerce sites—finding customers. Storefronts could, some analysts were saying, one day be bigger than either eBay's auctions or Half's fixed-price sales.

Several other members of eBay's management team made cameo appearances. Maynard Webb spoke about improvements in the site's stability since the July 1999 crash. "The first thing I want to tell you," Webb said, "is that I'm really happy to be this late in the agenda this year." Mike Wilson spoke about eBay's Application Program interface, which the company would now be providing to third parties, making it easier for them to write software applications that worked with the eBay site. Gary Bengier ran through the financials and explained in more detail how eBay planned to reach the $3-billion revenue mark.

When it was over, Whitman took questions from the analysts, who were seated at long tables, buried behind laptops, cell phones, and sheafs of paperwork. The young Wall Street numbers crunchers were filled with skepticism. They wanted to know whether eBay's growth projections assumed too much good news, and whether the company's profits would be hurt by the lower margins at Half.com. One analyst wanted to know if Billpoint had been prevented from making a presentation because it had been struggling. The real indication of the mood in the room, however, came when the doors opened and the analysts rushed past the coffee and pastries in the hallway to whisper their buy and sell recommendations into their cell phones. When the markets closed for the day, Whitman's audience had pushed eBay stock up more than 16 percent.

chapter eleven

One of the sellers Whitman mentioned to the Wall Street analysts at the September meeting was eValueville, a Hattiesburg, Mississippi, company that sold excess merchandise over eBay. EValueville— "Where value is Mayor!"— was founded by Andrew Waites, who was on his way to becoming the Henry Ford of eBay. In a warehouse in a poor neighborhood of Hattiesburg, he had created one of the first assembly lines for selling items on eBay.

The eValueville story began in May 1999. Waites, who was running a land-based excess-inventory company in Mississippi, received a delivery of fifty Kenneth Cole designer leather jackets. With summer fast approaching, Waites had no idea whom he could possibly sell them to. His assistant suggested he try putting the jackets up on eBay. Waites was hoping to get what they would have sold for off-line, about thirty to thirty-five dollars each. But when the auctions ended, the jackets had sold for between $225 and $275 each. "I may be a little slow," Waites says, "but I thought, there has to be a business model here."

Waites was passionate about clothing salvage. He had received an MBA from Regent University in Virginia Beach, Virginia, and was working in the school's development office when Bill Hudson, president of Hudson Salvage, gave an on-campus lecture. Hudson had a colorful story to tell, about how his company had gotten its start when his country grocery store, H. C. Hudson's, in Palmer's Crossing, Mississippi, had a fire in 1957. After the insurance adjuster settled the claim, Hudson wondered what would be done with the smoke-damaged groceries the insurance company had reimbursed him for. Hudson bought them back at a deep discount, and sold them to his customers at a fire sale using the slogan "Smoky Groceries, fifty percent off." From those humble beginnings, three generations of Hudsons built one of the nation's leading distributorships for distressed and overstocked clothing. When a flood damages the inventory in a large warehouse, or a tornado rips the roof off a Wal-Mart, there is a good chance Hudson Salvage will be the company called to cart off the damaged goods.

Waites realized he had just seen his future. He talked to Bill Hudson, got an offer on the spot, and moved to Hattiesburg. As vice president for inventory and procurement at Hudson Salvage, it was Waites's job to find clothing for Hudson's Treasure Hunt and Dirt Cheap stores, so-called extreme value retailers spread out across Mississippi and Alabama. At first, Waites's main source of inventory was H. C. Hudson's original one—insurance companies—which acquired a good deal of damaged goods after they paid out on claims. But while he was out looking for new inventory, he came across a significant new source: customer returns at major department stores. Most of it was brand-name clothing that a buyer had taken home and removed from the packaging, but it was otherwise as good as new. The average department store was generating $1 million a month in customer returns, he discovered, and had no way of reselling it. "Every store manager just had a friend they would slough it off on," he says. Waites went to the department store chains and made a pitch for their returns. "I said 'We'll take it, we'll pull a truck up to your loading dock.'" In 1998, his last year at Hudson, Waites bought $250 million in customer-returned clothing.

It was at this point that Waites decided to go into business for himself. His new company, Inventory Procurement Services, bought up customer returns and overstock, items that a store had pulled from the racks because they were no longer in style or just were not selling. Instead of reselling them in its own retail stores, as Hudson Salvage did, IPS resold them to other retailers. It was a good business, with what Waites considered to be decent profit margins, but when the leather jackets sold on eBay he realized how much better he could be doing. Waites launched what he called his "Internet Initiative," a rather grand name for one employee listing four items an hour on eBay. But by the summer of 2000, "eValueville," as the Internet division was now called, had thirty-five workers running fifteen hundred eBay auctions at a time, and IPS moved from its eight-thousand-square-foot office into a new eighty-thousand-square-foot space.

Waites's operation was as regimented as Ford's Model-T plant. The clothing—all of which initially came from Bloomingdale's— arrived at the warehouse by truck. "It's like Christmas when the boxes arrive," Waites says. "I have no idea what I bought." Workers pulled the clothing out of the boxes, put them on a mannequin, and took photographs of them. The clothes then moved from the mannequin to the workstation of a computer operator, who typed the color, size, fabric, and brand in Bulk Lister auction-selling software. The item was then given an inventory number, wrapped, and prepared for shipping, even before it was listed on eBay. At the end of each day, all the auction listings were transmitted to Andale, the Mountain View, California, auction-management firm that had created Bulk Lister—and the parent of the OTWA message boards. Andale took care of posting the auctions on eBay, hosting the photos of the items, and reporting back to eValueville when an item was sold, paid for, and ready to be shipped.

Waites took an equally regimented approach to the auctions

themselves. Every eValueville auction ran for three days, and they all started at one dollar. He had experimented with longer auctions, but found they did not result in higher prices. About 80 percent of all bids took place in the last hour, no matter what the auction's duration. About 3 percent of eValueville's auctions ended in nonpaying bidders, but that, too, was just part of the process. EValueville, which still had the item in its possession, just had Andale list it again and request a refund of the listing fee from eBay.

The economics of selling on eBay remained as appealing as when Waites sold the first leather jackets. Listing and final-value fees ran to about 5 percent of eValueville's total sales, and Andale's fees were another 1 percent to 2½ percent. But for the money, eValueville got services that were the equivalent, in the off-line world, of renting a store in a mall, inventory control, marketing, and billing. EBay also enabled Waites to sell to a nationwide, even worldwide clientele from a low-cost base in Mississippi, where he paid less than $1.50 a square foot in rent, and where there were, Waites says, "more people willing to work for minimum wage than I can hire." IPS's profit margins on its eBay sales were roughly 50 percent, about ten times its off-line margins.

Waites knows that many small eBay sellers suspected he was getting special treatment. In fact, he insists, he pays the same fees for the same services as sellers who list a single item. The only special service eBay has provided eValueville is permitting it to submit its list of nonpaying bidders in bulk, rather than one at a time, since it has so many of them. But small sellers would have no need to do that, he notes. "They've always made clear to me that eBay is a level playing field," Waites says. "If I want unique things I don't even ask, because I know we're not going to get them."

◆

John Freyer, a twenty-something fine arts grad student at the University of Iowa, was lanky and pale, with geek-cool black-framed glasses and a laid-back but earnest take on life. In October 2000, Freyer opened his wrong-side-of-the-tracks Iowa City apartment to about thirty of his friends, and another twenty strangers who saw the posters he put up around town. He had recently decided to put everything he owned, or nearly everything, up for sale on eBay, and had registered the domain name allmylifeforsale.com as a base of operations. Now he was having an "inventory party" to choose which items in his home to auction. Freyer served homemade salsa and "as much Pabst Blue Ribbon as I could afford," and handed out a thousand tags to guests as they arrived. Their job was to look through his eight-hundred-square-foot apartment and decide which items best represented his life. "The party itself was a kind of sociological experiment to see if people would go through my drawers and closets," he says. They would and they did. One guest tagged the two false front teeth he used to wear but no longer needs. Another tagged his Calvin Klein boxers.

Freyer, who was pursuing an MFA in photography, saw the project as a work of performance art. The University of Iowa has long been a pioneer in arts education—back in the 1940s, it was one of the first fine arts programs to give studio work equal credit with written work. Freyer had been trying to keep his school on the cutting edge. He had already used the skills he picked up in a printmaking class to make a book of images taken from classic Atari video games like Pong and Pacman. Now he was using eBay for what he was calling an "interactive performance piece," for which he was hoping to get academic credit.

The inventory party went until 5:00 A.M., and when it was over, more than eight hundred of Freyer's possessions had been tagged. Freyer drew up an inventory list, took photos, and wrote up descriptions, and then he started putting the items—such as his Jesus night-light and a brewing company T-shirt—up on eBay. The write-ups Freyer prepared formed an elliptical autobiography. The entry on a box of Girl Scout cookies reported that it was a gift from his niece Avery, the oldest of his sister Marnie's three daughters, and that the girls called him "Scary Uncle Johnny." The entry for his old Hamilton College sweatshirt reported that he spent a "good chunk" of his time at Hamilton trying to eliminate discriminatory practices from the school's fraternity system. Other descriptions told of his stints as a busboy at a restaurant in Syracuse and as a snowboard instructor in Salt Lake City, and recalled drunken nights of debauchery and karaoke.

Freyer started with a "soft opening," putting about ten items on the site. Some didn't sell, and others went for as little as a dollar. Then he sent out an e-mail to everyone he knew, telling them about the project. A woman he met over the summer did a small piece about his project for *Time Out New York,* a weekly entertainment magazine. Other media followed, including the *New York Times,* MSNBC, and the *London Evening Standard.* "I have a digital answering machine, and suddenly it was all full," he says. The press attention brought better prices. A thermos that sold for $30 new went for $50. An "It's a Strike" bowling belt-buckle went for $48. A can of Chunky Soup sold for $2.75. Freyer's false teeth went for $27, bought by the curator of the University of Iowa Art Museum, who archived them in the permanent collection. ("It was kind of a validation," says Freyer.) His underwear went to a man in New York for $7.25. ("I'm not sure what he's going to do with it," Freyer says.) A few things didn't sell. No one bought his January 2001 energy bill of $433.66, which he listed at a minimum bid of $433.66. And no one bid on being his roommate at a conference he was attending in Savannah, Georgia, though a road trip with him sold for $11—to his girlfriend, who asked him to take her to the Omaha zoo when the weather got warmer. Freyer put his family's Christmas gifts up for auction, and made his stepmother pay $72.50 for the gift he had bought for his sister Sarah but put up on eBay instead. Freyer's stepmother got back at him on his birthday, when his own gift was the canceled invoice.

Freyer asked successful bidders to provide him with an update on the piece of his life they ended up with. In the summer of 2001, he started traveling around the country to visit his possessions and the people who bought them. Freyer insisted there was a serious point to his project: he meant it to be a critique of the consumer culture eBay was inextricably tied to. He said he was worried that when people emphasized their connections to things, they paid too little attention to connections with people. And he said people were allowing their possessions to define them. "Society tells us we are what we own," he says. "But I've sold all of these things of mine and I haven't changed that much." Freyer's lifestyle, however, had changed. "My girlfriend and I had breakfast on the floor this morning," he said. "I no longer have a kitchen table."

In late 2000, Freyer put his birthday up for sale. His friend Maya was throwing him a party in New York on December 28, at a bar in Tribeca, and the winning bidder would take his place as the guest of honor. The winner of the auction, which attracted two bids, was a young man named Brian Troyer, who paid $1.25. Freyer invited Troyer to Maya's house before the party to show him pictures of his friends, so Troyer would be able to greet them by name. As the guests arrived, Freyer told them the party was now for Troyer, and that he should receive their birthday congratulations.

Things did not go exactly as Freyer planned. Troyer, it turned out, had moved to New York recently from Indiana and knew almost no one. After the party he remained friends with some of Freyer's friends. Maya invited him, without charge, to attend her own birthday party. Freyer, who had resolved to teach the world a lesson about possessiveness, found himself becoming resentful of the inroads Troyer had made in his social circle. Troyer admitted in a letter Freyer posted on the allmylifeforsale.com website that the auction had expanded his social circle: "i . . . paid $1.25 and met people who've become some of the best friends I've ever known." But he objected to Freyer's characterization of the auction's ultimate outcome. "I disagree with the idea," he wrote, "[that] i purchased your friends from you."

◆

On October 16, 2000, eBay and Disney jointly launched a site called Disney Auctions. EBay.Disney.com, which a press release said was aimed at "anyone who wants to own a part of the Disney magic," offered auctions of the kind of authentic merchandise and experiences only Disney itself could provide. Among the first items listed were tickets to the premiere of *102 Dalmatians*, Bette Midler's costume from *Hocus Pocus*, and the original Disneyland marquee letters.

The Disney site was part of a deal, negotiated back in February, in which eBay agreed to pay Disney as much as $30 million over four years for traffic from its Go.com web portal. The deal did not work out as either side had planned. Disney's troubled portal was shut down in early 2001, and eBay had to ask to renegotiate the dollars-for-traffic part of the deal. But the more public problem with the deal had to do with the special terms eBay offered to Disney—and the uproar it created in the eBay community.

Disney was the first large company eBay had ever done a deal with for products to sell on the site. This deal was far different from the AOL pacts, which were only about banner ads and traffic. It gave Disney prerogatives that no seller on eBay had ever been given before. The Disney Auctions page included a search engine that looked for Disney-related items listed by Disney, but it did not search for items in the larger eBay site. Nor did Disney's web page even mention that buyers could find other Disney items on eBay's main site, which also would have meant more competition for Disney's own auction items. The Disney Auctions site was an island, set apart from eBay. It had its own terms of service, different from the terms that prevailed on eBay. Disney Auctions sales required a credit card, and there was a badly worded provision that made it appear that items bought on the site could never be resold again. Feedback on the Disney site was private, so users could not see if Disney was treating its customers badly.

EBay did not discuss the deal with the community in advance. Just before the launch it was presented to Voices 1, which protested that the deal marked a historic departure from eBay's principles. EBay scheduled a conference call between Voices 1 and Disney executives, so the Disney Auctions team could hear the community's objections firsthand. "We strongly encouraged them to go a certain way," says community-support manager Brian Burke. "But the choice was Disney's." In the end, Disney agreed to state more clearly that the terms of service on the site were different from eBay's usual rules, and to link to a page that described the differences. But Disney did not change its search engine, or create a link to the main eBay site.

The group that was most upset about the Disney site was eBay's existing Disney memorabilia sellers, who were convinced it would put them out of business. Jeff Taylor, vice president for product marketing, was a Disney collector himself, with one of the leading collections of *Who Framed Roger Rabbit?* memorabilia. Taylor was at a Disneyana convention just before the Disney site went up, and he was inundated with sellers who were concerned that Disney would compete too hard. EBay was hearing the same thing back at headquarters, in a flood of angry calls and e-mail. "There was a feeling the goal was to put Disneyana sellers out of business," Brian Burke recalls. The posts on OTWA and AuctionWatch were scathing. "EbaY wants to play with the big boys now," a poster named Waycoolman from Ohio wrote to OTWA. "The big boys won't want to tolerate sharing their venue with shoelace operation competition like us. EbaY was founded as a level playing field. The field is beginning to tilt." The reaction on eBay's own boards was just as impassioned. "Today Ebay Announcement Bd brags about another site which ruins the market for a lot of Disney sellers and throws the $$$ to the Big Bucks Companies once more," one seller wrote on eBay's Discuss New Features board. "I hope their is a Pierre clone waiting in the wings like the Pied Piper so a few million of us can follow him/her to a new site which will work."

The decision about how to proceed was Disney's, since it had a signed contract with eBay allowing it to run its site the way it was. Still, within a few months Disney had backed down and made many of the changes the community asked for. It modified the search engine so that it offered two possible searches: Disney Auctions only, which was the default, or a broader search of all of eBay. Disney also added a link on the site, though not an especially prominent one, that connected to the Disneyana category on the main site.

According to Burke, Disney eventually saw that being separate was not in its own best interest. "A stand-alone site sounds great," he says. "But they came to realize that they needed access to the eBay buyers."

The uproar soon died down. It helped that the anticipated reduction in Disney sales on the main site never happened. In fact, some sellers admitted eBay had been right when it predicted that Disney's presence would be good for all sellers because it would bring more Disney buyers to eBay. But the Disney deal changed eBay's thinking about the kinds of deals it would enter into with big sellers. Whitman concedes that Disney did get "special privileges" on the site. "It was because they were Disney," she says. But seeing how the arrangement worked in practice convinced eBay that extending "more and better attention" to selected sellers was not something it should try again. "We've concluded that eBay has to be a level playing field," she says. "That is a core part of our DNA, and it has to be part of it going forward."

◆

It was a bright October afternoon in Draper, Utah, and Jeffrey Totland, a clean-cut twenty-nine-year-old raised in the Mormon Church, was at his computer in a cubicle in eBay's Community Watch division reading e-mail from the community. Totland, a customer-support representative, worked in a group called List Practices, which handled complaints about listings on eBay. His job could be routine at times, like when the jewelry sellers charged each other with sneaking items into the wrong categories. But this afternoon, Totland was going through the "erotica" queue, acting on e-mails that raised concerns about eBay's adult listings.

The first few e-mails Totland read were of a single type, a seller of *Playboy* reporting listing violations by other *Playboy* sellers. Unscrupulous sellers often ignored eBay's rule requiring post-1980 adult magazines to be listed on the adult section, and honest sellers complained that the rule-breakers cut into their own sales. Totland recognized the e-mail address on these complaints as belonging to a longtime *Playboy* seller who regularly searched the main eBay site and turned in listing cheats. The e-mail mentioned specific auctions that the sender said were improper. Totland checked them, and found that they were for post-1980 *Playboys*, and were in fact in the wrong place.

Totland pulled down the errant auctions and did a search of the seller's eBay history. The seller, it turned out, had violated listing rules three times already, putting him over eBay's limit. With a few keystrokes, Totland brought up ninety-eight other auctions the same seller had going at the time, and ended them all. Totland then fired off two quick e-mails, one to the Suspensions Department, asking it to review the seller's record for possible termination of user privileges, and one to the complaining *Playboy* seller, telling him what action had been taken. Incorrectly listed adult magazines were one of the easier problems customer-service representatives had to deal with, according to Totland. "It's either in the right category or the wrong category," he says.

The next e-mail presented an issue Totland, and every other customer-service representative who worked the adult queue, dreaded: used underwear. EBay did not like to talk about it, but at any given time there were hundreds of listings for used underwear on the site, and they had caused the staff no end of headaches. At first, eBay treated used underwear sales like any other used clothing sale. But users began to complain that when they searched for ordinary used underwear to wear, they came across listings designed to appeal to fetishists. The ads featured attractive men and women selling their underwear, invariably with a representation that it had been worn and not washed.

EBay had imposed a rule it hoped would solve the problem. Used underwear could be sold, but the listing had to state clearly that it had been cleaned. But sellers just became more creative in how they wrote up their listings, sending subtly coded indications that the underwear would not be clean. Many listings put the phrase in quotes, "cleaned to eBay's specifications." Other sellers stated that their underwear was clean, but at the same time they offered to "customize" it or "take special requests." Confirming eBay's suspicions, these auctions inevitably ended at prices that no clean, used underwear would command. Code words about underwear were grounds for pulling an auction, but they could require some tough judgment calls. Sellers sometimes wrote "e-mail me with any questions or suggestions." It was hard to know if it was improper customization, or just good customer service.

The e-mail that landed in Totland's computer had been sent by a seller who objected that her used underwear auction had been pulled, while a similar auction was allowed to continue. Totland looked at the auction the e-mailer was complaining about. "You kind of learn what to look for and what not," he says. It featured a series of pictures of a busty woman selling workout clothing which, she promised, she had exercised in for a week. When she wore the clothing, she wrote, she never wore underwear, and she promised to keep wearing it until it was time to send it to the auction winner. ("Thats a lot of wear, hope you don't mind," the listing stated.)

Totland applied eBay's rules with legalistic precision. It was prohibited to list used clothing with "extraneous information" on the main site ("leggings worn by a college coed," or athletic socks "belonging to a college football player"), a way of keeping off prurient appeals. But this listing was in the adult section, where extraneous information was permissible. The description of the condition of the item was troubling, but the seller had saved herself by writing at the end, "of course my items are all sent fresh and clean as per eBay standards." Totland guessed that she had learned after having had a few auctions canceled. The photograph of the seller modeling the item was suggestive, but nothing in it broke a specific rule. Totland checked her "About Me" page, the personal web page eBay allows users to create about themselves. There was a sultry photo of the seller in fishnet stockings, and a *Playboy* centerfold–style list of salient facts about her: her hair was red, and her favorite things included roller coasters, Woody Allen, autobiographies, rainy days, and good friends. "There's nothing wrong with the auction," Totland concluded.

Next, Totland looked at the e-mailer's auction, to see if it had been properly ended. The auction in question was for a pair of Betty Boop boop-a-doop panties. He checked her "About Me" page, and found a picture of the seller wearing them. EBay had ended the auction, with the bidding at $20.50, for listing violations. That was, Totland determined, the correct decision. The seller had put in the obligatory statement that the underwear would be washed. But the listing also stated that they would "arrive at your home just the way you like them." That was an explicit offer to customize, and it violated the rules. Totland e-mailed the seller explaining that eBay had been correct in pulling her auction and allowing the workout-outfit auction to remain. But Totland would not need to draw these lines much longer. Before the year's end eBay tired of just this sort of endless line drawing and banned all used underwear from the site.

◆

Al Hoff's home, in a leafy, middle-class neighborhood of Pittsburgh, Pennsylvania, is a red-brick, tall-ceilinged shrine to low-priced kitsch. Walk into the sitting room and the first thing you see is a bulky hair dryer, found at an Oakland flea market, that had been rewired and turned into a reading lamp. The odd-looking chair off to the side turns out to be a 1950s "egg," made by Danish designer Arne Jacobson. Vintage egg chairs sell for thousands today, but Hoff picked hers up at a thrift store for $6.99. And against a wall is a display cabinet with her extensive collection of vintage alcohol memorabilia. It's joke stuff, and the joke is that even decades ago it was never funny. There's a replica of the famous little Belgian boy peeing, which pours drinks into a glass. There are jiggly go-go girl drink mixers, goofy miniature moonshine stills, shelves of pink elephants, and the ever popular drunk leaning on a lamppost. Worst of all: a set of shot glasses sporting miniature jockstraps and the inscription "for your highballs."

Hoff, a trimly attractive woman in her thirties, carries the theme of carefully cultivated schlock throughout the house. A small bedroom on the second floor is her Tiki Room, framed by two large tiki poles salvaged from a defunct Trader Vic's in Washington, D.C. A floor-to-ceiling bookshelf holds scores of tiki mugs of every size, shape, and color. "You used to see tiki mugs all the time when you went to thrift stores," Hoff says with a sigh. "Now you rarely do." In the basement, she has turned a small bathroom into a sportsman's cabin, its walls buried under cedar plaques bearing corny hunting and fishing slogans. "In case of rain," the Sportsman's Thermometer advises, "visit wife." And back on the first floor, Hoff is taking steps—elaborate steps—to convert her kitchen into a replica of a southwestern carnival.

Most of the paintings in the house are more eclectic. Hoff calls it "thrift store art," but she points out that if she wanted to get fancy she could refer to it as "vernacular art." When it comes to art, Hoff has a simple rule: she almost never pays more than ten dollars for a piece, and tries to keep it under three dollars. It's fortunate that she has a weakness for children's paintings—which their unsentimental parents at some point unloaded on a thrift store—particularly paint-by-numbers. And she's partial to pet pictures. "There's something about kids doing dogs that's great," she says breezily. One wall of her sitting room holds an array of bad dog paintings. She takes down a black spaniel on which the paint bears only a loose correlation to the spaces laid out on the paint-by-number canvas. She flips it over, and the inscription on the back reveals that it was painted in 1958 by "Elaine, Age 8." Hoff's taste also runs to portraits with ineptly drawn hands ("it almost looks like there's a sixth finger"), paintings on velvet, and prison art. One wall has a piece by a homeless man purported to be of John Wayne, but whether by chance or by act of the artist's subconscious turns out to be a dead-on likeness of Ronald Reagan. Another has a painting drawn for the old "Can You Draw Skippy?" contest that used to run in the back of comic books, done by an inmate in Joliet Prison (in this case, the answer was "not very well"). Like many homes, Hoff's boasts a collection of family photos. But hers are what she calls "found photos," of other people's families. "I don't think there's a single photo of a family member of ours," she says without a hint of regret.

One stairway in the house is filled with Sillisculpts, those gift-store scourges no one wants as a gift. The idiotically cheerful figurines all have their hands stretched wide, and the bases all proclaim, "I love you this much." But Hoff is proud to point out that no two of the twenty characters—a girl, a boy, a baby, a mouse—are the same. A corridor off an upstairs bathroom has been dubbed the "Hallway of Sorrows." Every available inch of the wall is covered with paintings of those big-eyed, sad-looking children, cats, and dogs that were the rage in the 1960s. Some are the work of Margaret Keane, the Bible Belt artist who originated the style, but Hoff likes the knockoffs just as much. She points happily to an oil painting of a saucer-eyed boy twirling a similarly pie-eyed girl. "They're dancing, but they're miserable," she says.

Hoff may be the world's leading authority on thrift-store shopping. She published a witty, highly readable 'zine about thrift shopping in the mid-1990s, and wrote the book *Thrift Score*. The daughter of a Linotype setter for the *San Francisco Examiner*, she attributes her aesthetic sensibility to growing up in San Francisco's Upper Mission neighborhood, near the Castro district. "A lot of gays in the neighborhood were into funky things," she explains. "I knew as a child that art deco was cool." Fortunately for her, her husband is just as avid an accumulator. "As the French say," says Hoff, "it's a folie à deux."

Hoff would seem like a natural for eBay. In fact, she hates it. In one of the last issues of her now defunct 'zine, in a story billed with the cover tag line "Are the Good Times OVER?" Hoff warned that eBay was ruining everything. "They're skimming the best stuff from the stores and auctioning it over the Internet," she wrote. "When you shop in a thrift store, you only have to pay more than anyone else they think is going to walk into the store," Hoff says. "When you shop on eBay, it goes to the person in the world who's willing to pay the most for it." Thrift shopping, Hoff believes, rewards the adventurous, the people willing to go to the most out-of-the-way neighborhoods and look the hardest, whereas eBay rewards the lazy, and people with a lot of money to spend.

EBay's impact can be seen, she notes, in the Pittsburgh-area thrift stores that she frequents. When she first started going to the Red, White & Blue thrift store in the South Hills neighborhood, before the collectibles craze and the advent of eBay, vintage lunch boxes went for sixty-five cents. Now they are marked as high as forty dollars. The offbeat records she likes were once six for a dollar. Now, they are as much as two dollars each. And time was, Hoff says, when you could walk into a thrift store and find a bin full of eight-track tapes in the corner, selling for a quarter each. A friend of hers recently tried to buy a Pink Floyd eight-track on eBay, and watched as it went for $227.

But Hoff's greatest objection to eBay is that it takes away the pleasure of shopping in the real world. Most of the things in her home come with stories, bizarre or sentimental, of how she came to possess them. Her husband found the enormous 3-D painting of Philippine village life that hangs in their Tiki Room at a thrift store in Colorado Springs. He paid three dollars for the painting, and then another thirty dollars at a hardware store for the shipping supplies to bring it home. Hoff and her husband found the steel bed they sleep on in an antique store in Wichita, Kansas. They paid a hundred dollars for it, put it in the back of a truck, and hauled it to D.C. Shopping, Hoff insists, should be a social activity—and unpredictable. "Thrifting is a contact sport, so you have to get in there with your hands. You have to be touching things. How can you tell if it's well made? Touch it. Look at it. Grab it. Throw it. Pull it." These are things you cannot do on the Internet, she says. "Online, you're at someone's mercy to tell you what shape it's in, does it fit, does it smell, is it missing a button?"

To hit a thrift store with Hoff is to see firsthand the kinds of experiences the Internet cannot offer. According to Hoff, thrift shopping is a skill, and she has honed her abilities for years. Arrive as early as possible on Saturday morning, when stores put out the newest stuff. Shop the whole store, not just the one area you are most interested in. Be aware that many stores sell items that have been out on the floor for over a week at half price, using a system of color-coded price tags to keep track. If you're desperate, you can hide things and come back to buy them a week later. And dress to shop, in old clothing you can crawl around on the floor in. "But most of my tips are about looking at things real closely," she adds.

Hoff pulls her car up to the Eastland Mall, a defunct Pittsburgh shopping mall that now hosts a weekend flea market. Regular distributors come every week to set up stalls, and the atmosphere is decidedly downscale. The aisles are filled with large families, for whom this is clearly the day's entertainment. Over the loudspeaker, an oldies station is playing a medley of 1950s hits, starting with "Teenager in Love." Hoff pounces on a table off to the side, where someone is handing out free slices of chocolate-iced sheet cake. "When they're passing out free food," says Hoff with determination, "I'm there." The stalls, since they are privately owned, turn out to be little worlds that reflect the interests and lifetime accumulation patterns of their sellers. Hoff likes scoping out what she calls the "guy booths," in which an older man, usually wearing a baseball cap or a fishing hat, presides over a display of sports-insignia items, knives and guns, hardware, or military collectibles. She talks to a few of the other sellers, focusing mainly on kitschy figurines and cooking items, but it doesn't take her long to decide there's nothing she needs. This was, it turns out, a warm-up.

The next stop is a Goodwill store off a major highway. Hoff walks in and makes a sharp left, veering toward the bins of used records. As she flips through the offbeat collection of dust jackets, it's clear that none of the records is the kind that anyone would knowingly type into an Internet search engine. Her flipping stops and she stares intently at an LP labeled *Banjo in the Bluegrass*. Banjo records, it turns out, are one of her things. She throws it in her cart. As Hoff moves methodically through the store, she furtively stops in front of a door that leads to a sorting area in the back. Lined up in front of the door are several shopping carts filled with fresh merchandise that the staff has not yet put out on the shelves. When you "shop the carts," you substantially increase your odds of finding something amazing. But it's also generally regarded as an infraction. "Sometimes they'll yell at you," Hoff says. This time it pays off. She has found a Pyrex cooking dish inscribed with red lettering that reads "Compliments of the Irwin Savings & Trust Co., Irwin, Pa." Amazed at her good luck, she heads to the checkout.

The final stop on Hoff's excursion is the large Red, White & Blue store that Hoff has been coming to for more than a decade. "It used to rock," she says. "We came here and just filled up the carts." As she walks in the door, Hoff immediately falls into an established route. First she hits the record bins. She tosses a ninety-five-cent copy of a polka record called "Beer Beer Beer" into her cart, along with one called "Ronnie and His Calypso Ramblers at the Nassau Beach Hotel." In the old days, Hoff explains, it was common to stay in resort hotels, hear a band, and then buy the record, which was often autographed by the band members.

From the record bin, Hoff moves along the front wall of the store, which contains long shelves of china and cookware. As Hoff shops, she keeps up a running commentary. At the moment, she is looking for three things: a tan-with-brown china pattern called Desert Tan; a line of Franciscan pottery from the 1950s; and dinnerware made of Melmac, the revolutionary plastic from the 1940s. "I started collecting Melmac three years ago, but now, poof! it's all gone," she complains. "It became collectible." Hoff finds none of the china she's looking for, but she does find a trivet made of Puka shells. It seems like a natural for the Tiki Room, she notes, but she passes on it. Hoff's hands expertly work their way through the merchandise to uncover the treasures that may lie behind and below. "A lot of what I find is a result of digging," she says. She's amused as she looks through plastic bins filled with old silverware that someone has handwritten "Not for Sale" on the bins themselves. "As if you'd want to," she scoffs.

Hoff moves deeper into the store, walking down the dingy white Formica floors under the harsh fluorescent lights. She stops next at a wall with hanging grab-bags of household items. The bags are clear, so shoppers can see in and decide if the contents are worth the three-dollar price. Hoff rifles through the bags, talking all the while. She notices that one of the bags contains a roll of Scotch tape from the

1950s. She should buy it, she thinks aloud, for her friend Paul Wilson. Wilson lives in a 1957 ranch house in Phoenix that he has furnished entirely with items from the 1950s. In the mid-1990s, he created a fictional 1950s family, the Kimbles—a mother, a father, and three children. Paul dresses as each of the family members, photographs himself in each getup, and then makes a collage. The result is a roomful of Pauls—dressed as men, women, and children—giving a cocktail party, having a Tupperware party, or gathering on Christmas morning. Paul is always on the lookout for small items, like old-fashioned pipe cleaners. "He would really love this roll of tape," Hoff says. "He likes to get all the little details just right."

As Hoff walks through the housewares section, she thinks back to better thrifting days, when there were shelves of old metal fans. Now, there are none. Fortunately, she has thirty or forty at home. The lamp and lampshade area has also been stripped of its best wares. "When I first came here, this whole shelf would be dancing-ballerina lamps and hula girls." These items are disappearing, Hoff says, in part simply because as "collectibles," they have become too expensive for the average thrift store to stock. She also attributes the shortage to eBay, which has affected both the supply and demand. Thrift stores have trouble getting these items because more people are selling them on eBay, where they can usually get a better price. At the same time, buyers are trolling the stores for items, and re-selling them on eBay. As Hoff explains, "The code of ethics used to be that you bought things for yourself." Now, when Hoff thrifts, she spends more time on offbeat items that are not yet big on eBay, like old towels. "People overlook towels, but they used to make some great ones. Twister dances, and reminders to take your birth control pills." But even Hoff has her limits. She sees a display of plastic watches and frowns. "Why can't we just agree as a culture that it's crap and move on?"

It is much harder to find bargains in thrift stores these days, but Hoff has a good enough eye that she can still do it. As she stands at the checkout counter, she scans the glass case under the cash register. She spots a bag filled with oddly shaped yellow pieces of plastic, and asks an employee to retrieve it for her. The plastic pieces turn out to be just what she thought: yellow-ribbon stickpins worn during the Gulf War as a symbol of solidarity with the troops. "These are a piece of history," Hoff observes as she locates the price tag. "And at a dollar fifty, boy are they cheap."

As Hoff sees it, there is no way to have a true thrifting experience over the Internet. "The serendipitous pleasure is very key for me. There's no real fun in just typing in what you want and getting it." When Hoff thrifts with friends, it is an extended social experience. "On a good day, we start early and hit as many as five thrifts. Then Taco Bell for lunch, and back home in the late afternoon to open some beers." When the shopping is done, Hoff and her friends dig through their bags to see what everyone found. "People try on clothes, and some of my friends, if we are at their house, just do instant decorating—run and hang the picture up." Hoff has tried to replicate the social aspect online by signing up for a Listserv with other thrifters. "They'll say, 'Oh, I got something really cool,'" she says. "But it's not the same, because I don't know these people."

Hoff is not an anti-eBay purist. She used eBay to buy an Arizona license plate for her southwestern carnival-kitchen design. She's also had some notable successes as a seller. She has resold Hermès ties that she picked up for $1.49 at Goodwill for $30 to $40 each. Among her biggest successes as a seller: a rare *Bewitched* coloring book she found for a quarter at a church tag sale that went for $130. "I was absolutely flabbergasted. I had people e-mailing me asking if I would ship it to Japan." But Hoff still does not like eBay. She has not made any friends, and the communication she has had with other eBayers has been minimal. "To me these are totally random people. Sometimes people would write me and ask a question like, 'Is there a stain on the tie?' And I would say, 'No.'" And while every thrift-shopping experience she has had was unique, every eBay transaction was depressingly the same. "There's something a little sad and soulless about sitting in your underwear at three in the morning shopping over your computer," she says.

chapter twelve

In the summer of 2000, the moment that Mary Lou Song had been dreading for years finally came. She walked past Omidyar's cubicle and saw that his belongings were gone. "It was a sad day," Song says. It was also a final recognition of what had been obvious now for more than a year: that Omidyar's day-to-day involvement with eBay had come to a close. Almost no one on the staff knew about the changeover when it happened, but with eBay adding employees as quickly as it was, its significance would have been lost on most of them. For the old guard, however, Omidyar's abandoned cubicle was a symbol that eBay's wild youth—the beach chairs, spontaneously dropping by Omidyar's office, Pongo, Pierregrams, Skippy, and Uncle Griff—was finally over. The symbolism was made complete when the next occupant of the cubicle moved in: a new hire in marketing.

Omidyar's withdrawal from eBay was hardly unexpected. He had been speaking for years about wanting to move back to Paris with Pam, to reacquaint himself with the city of his youth. In March

1999, a year after he handed the company over to Whitman, he had finally made the move. Omidyar had traveled around Europe in the beginning, stopping in at eBay's fledgling outposts in London and Berlin and giving them advice from his AuctionWeb days. "One of the nice things is that they're small teams, very entrepreneurial," he said at the time. "The new markets are in a lot of ways similar to what eBay was when I was still doing everything."

Increasingly, though, he was moving on to other things. Within a year he and Pam would have their first child, a girl. When they were not parenting, they were spending much of their free time on philanthropy. They were working to establish a foundation that would dedicate a large part of Omidyar's money to advancing the values he had always tried to keep at the core of eBay. "I believe in community, and bringing back community, because we've lost it a little bit in the modern world," he says. Later in the year, Skoll would also begin to disengage. After several years working as an in-house champion for eBay's community, he left to devote himself full-time to philanthropy and fiction writing. Skoll established a foundation to work on community-building projects, locally and around the world. Its main offices were next door to eBay, in the Greylands Business Park.

Omidyar and Skoll's disengagement left eBay's old guard taking stock. Even those who had the highest regard for Whitman looked back wistfully on how much the company had changed. In part, it was simply the wages of success: a community of 20 million users could not work the way it did when it was 200,000. AuctionWeb's simple website was now dizzying: endless categories and subcategories, sellers' tools like Mister Lister, buyers' tools like Billpoint, tutorials, galleries, an eBay store, and press releases. Internally, informality had yielded to rules and structure. "It used to be that Gloria Vanderbilt would just call us up and say, 'Hey would you do a little thing for me?' and we'd put it on the site that week," says Song. (In fact, Song did just that for the famous designer back in 1997, helping her to list jewelry from her own collection, which she sold with a personal note.) "Now I have to make the argument and write up the case," says Song. "We have to present it in front of executives and get it prioritized."

The old guard was also concerned that the site had become too corporate. "Pierre always said, 'We never want to treat our users like an eyeball or a wallet,'" says Song. But inevitably, eBay's priorities had changed since the IPO. "We really lived in la-la land with our community for two wonderful years, and it was the time of my life," she says. "But once you go public the pressures are completely different. You've got investors and analysts looking at you, you've got the media looking at you, you've got to worry about shares and stock-holders and revenue." EBay's status as a publicly owned company had created a built-in tension between competing eBay interest groups. "When Whitman goes to meet with investors and analysts, they push her about what the company is doing to raise revenues in the next quarter," says Skoll. "Then it may get back to the commu-nity, which says, 'My God, they're going to raise prices on us.'" It was the pressure to produce profits that led to the Disney and toaster-ad blowups, Song observes. "Those were the ones that broke my heart," she says.

Another old-guard concern was that eBay's new generation of leaders had not grown up with the company. "Brian Swette, who spent twenty years at Pepsi, often thinks of our sellers as the bot-tlers," says Skoll. "Meg often thinks of our seller community like the florists because she was COO of FTD Florists. And they're both right. There are some similarities there, but they're missing something as well." Some of the biggest flaps at eBay—the eBay Motors launch, the toaster ad—came from eBay's more far-flung divisions, which Skoll says are too removed from the community and from eBay's traditions.

Whitman viewed Omidyar's departure as a challenge. "I've thought a lot about who is going to be the soul of the company," she says. Omidyar and Skoll could still help guide the company through their positions on the board of directors. But Whitman says that on a day-to-day basis, it falls to her and the management team to preserve and pass on eBay's founding culture, now that its founders are gone.

"They came at a unique point in time with a unique mind-set that you can't actually replicate," she says. "We have to figure out how to institutionalize their values and their view of the community, and try to imbue them in every single person in the company."

In her heart, Song remained what she called an "eBay purist," a believer in keeping the site the way it was in what she still regards as its golden age. She longed for the days of the "pure eBay experience"—only auctions, no fixed-price sales; only person-to-person trades—no corporate sellers; and a focus on collectibles. But she knew it was probably impossible to hold back the tides of change. The market has a will of its own. If large corporations wanted to sell by Internet auctions, and if buyers and sellers wanted more opportunities for fixed-price trading, these things would come, on eBay or somewhere else on the Internet. That was how Jeff Skoll, Song's fellow old-timer, saw it. "We can say to Disney and Wal-Mart, you guys build your own sites," he says. "And people will click away from eBay and go to them."

There was another reason the old guard was accepting of change: they realized it was part of life. They had all been around long enough to remember the dread-filled days when it seemed that rivals like Onsale and Yahoo! would put eBay out of business. In the back of their minds, they were convinced it could still happen, that if eBay remained too pure, if it failed to keep up with the times, it could still be overtaken. Any new site that defeated it, they believed, would inevitably be less concerned about the community than eBay was. Song's sadness at watching the site become more corporate and bottom line–focused—and watching Omidyar and Skoll cut their ties—was balanced by her feeling that it was, in a way, a testament to the success of the fledgling little website she had helped nurture. "It's like the first day of school," she says. "You're like, 'Oh man, where did the time go?'"

◆

In the days after the 2000 presidential election, as the wrangling over Florida's electoral votes raged on, two Palm Beach County men were arrested for putting a stolen voting machine—complete with the controversial butterfly ballot—up for sale on eBay. Florida undercover police contacted the men directly after the listing went up and negotiated to buy the machine for $4,000. They then arrested the men for unlawful possession of a voting machine—a felony—and dealing in stolen property.

The voting machine caper was only the latest example of a new role eBay had taken on: it had become the primary distribution channel for event-based consumerism. On the late-night talk shows, eBay was a fixture of Jay Leno's and David Letterman's monologues. (When the economy turned soft in early 2001, Leno joked that things had gotten so bad that eBay was for sale on eBay.) In more rarefied cultural circles, eBay was showing up regularly in *New Yorker* cartoon captions. Whenever major news stories broke, auctions on eBay inevitably followed. Earlier in the year, at the height of the battle over whether to return Elián Gonzalez to Cuba, a seller listed what he purported to be the raft Elián traveled to Florida on. He claimed to have purchased it from a government warehouse, and to have "all the necessary papers." At the same time, listings went up for dirt from Elián's yard, his crayons, and hair found in the garbage outside his home after his cousin gave him a haircut.

Murder and death were particularly likely to spin off related auctions. When celebrities died, especially under highly publicized circumstances—NASCAR driver Dale Earnheart, golfer Payne Stewart—collectibles associated with them appeared immediately on the site. After the Columbine massacre, controversial tapes released by the local sheriff's office turned up on eBay. A piece of the front door of the apartment building where Amadou Diallo, an African immigrant, was shot to death by New York police was auctioned with an opening bid of $41,000—$1,000 for each of the forty-one bullets shot at the unarmed Diallo. An inmate on Texas's death row tried to sell the five witnesses' seats he was legally entitled to at his own execution. The listing was pulled after the Texas Department of Criminal Justice said that the winning bidders would not have been permitted to attend the execution.

EBay was using some of the high-profile auctions appearing on the site to further refine its listing standards. In the fall of 2000, when a Florida man listed crime-scene and autopsy photographs of three eight-year-old children killed in Arkansas in 1993, eBay pulled the auction and toughened its policies on listing so-called murderabilia. At the same time, eBay's role in controversial auctions was gradually becoming more accepted. When the infamous kidney was listed for sale in 1999, the media's coverage of the story suggested that there was something slightly seedy about an Internet site that would auction such an item. A year later, the perception of eBay as a neutral venue was more accepted, and there was far less criticism directed its way.

◆

In January 2001, eBay won one of the most important legal cases in its history. A San Diego state court judge dismissed a $100 million class-action lawsuit filed on behalf of buyers of fake sports memorabilia. Since the days of AuctionWeb, eBay had insisted that it was "only a venue," and not responsible for items sold on the site. But the plaintiffs argued that eBay was actually a dealer, and that by creating a category like Sports: Autographs, it was certifying that the items listed in it were actual autographs.

The lawsuit, *Gentry* v. *eBay*, was filed shortly after the FBI released the results of Operation Bullpen, a three-year undercover investigation that led to the indictment of twenty-five people for sports-memorabilia fraud. The bureau's San Diego office uncovered a ring of forgers, led by a father-and-son team, that was allegedly responsible for tens of millions of dollars in forged collectibles. The ring members bought sporting goods and athletes' photographs at sporting goods stores and used them as the basis for a "black book" of forged signatures. With the black book as a guide, they forged signatures ranging from Babe Ruth and Lou Gehrig to Sammy Sosa and Michael Jordan. The investigation found that the ring included authenticators, who provided mass-produced certificates of authenticity that were used when the items were sold on eBay. Investigators seized more than ten thousand autographed baseballs, trading cards, and other pieces of sports memorabilia, including a baseball allegedly signed by Mother Teresa.

Under California's autographed sports memorabilia law, dealers and auctioneers may not represent autographed items as collectible unless they were actually "autographed by the sports personality in his or her own hand," and they must provide a certificate of authenticity. The plaintiffs charged that most of the autographed sports items on eBay were forged, and that despite complaints and warnings from consumers, dealers, and authenticators, eBay continued to list them. EBay's inaction, according to the plaintiffs, was "for the sole purpose of reaping millions of dollars in profits for itself." They also charged that eBay's Feedback Forum facilitated the crime, because two of the main offenders had hundreds of positive feedbacks — obtained before the transactional feedback rules — that they gave to themselves or obtained from shills.

EBay, for its part, insisted that under the law it was not an auctioneer or dealer. It was, eBay claimed in court, merely the "modern incarnation of the traditional newspaper classified advertisement, automated and accelerated for the twenty-first century." And eBay said it had neither the opportunity nor the resources to examine every item put up on the site and to determine whether it was genuine. Superior Court Judge Linda Quinn agreed with eBay and dismissed the action. The category labels were not intended to be descriptions of specific items, the court ruled, and it was the seller, not eBay, who described and decided what category to assign an item to. It was the second case in two years that ruled in favor of eBay on the issue.

Lawyers for Internet companies hailed the ruling as a victory for e-commerce generally. It was, however, a particularly crucial win for eBay. If the case had gone the other way, and eBay was stripped of its status as a venue, it would have been impossible for it to continue to operate as it did. The ruling's logic could well have extended beyond sports memorabilia to art forgery, knockoffs of designer goods, even items that were simply poorly described by the seller. EBay could not warranty items without examining them, and physically examining them would mean that eBay could no longer operate in the virtual way it always had.

In the wake of the FBI investigation and the lawsuit, eBay tightened its rules for sports memorabilia. EBay offered sellers an optional third-party authentication service, from the Professional Sports Authenticator (PSA), and allowed them to display the PSA logo if the item was found to be genuine. EBay also adopted new rules, requiring sellers who mentioned certificates of authenticity from any source to explain where they came from, and it banned the use of such certificates from several authenticators whose veracity had been called into question by the FBI. EBay also put a list of questions on the site for buyers to consider when evaluating certificates of authenticity, including who issued them, whether they were prepared when the item was actually autographed, and whether the seller was willing to provide a refund if the signature was found to be a forgery.

EBay has steadily increased the amount of money and staff it spends on deterring and investigating fraud. "I worry about it, I focus on it, I think about it a lot," Whitman says. "It's a critical issue for us because eBay is all about trust." When Whitman arrived at eBay, the entire antifraud operation was just three people in customer support. Now, eBay has a former assistant U.S. attorney on its legal staff working on fraud issues, and a sizeable antifraud division, headed up by a former investigator for the Immigration and Naturalization Service. Although well over 99 percent of eBay transactions are free of fraud, there will always be an element of caveat emptor for buyers in any online auction. Whitman advises buyers to be cautious, to look closely at feedback ratings, to ask a lot of questions of sellers, and to use escrow. But she also believes fraud will be less of an issue over time, as technology makes possible new ways of establishing authenticity and user identity.

◆

In thirty days in the spring of 2001, John Reznikoff sold on eBay a photo of the *Titanic,* signed by a survivor, for $86; the book *Peanuts*

Jubilee, autographed by Charles Schulz, for $799.99; a letter from Helen Keller to Henry Ford for $475; a copy of the equation $E=mc^2$, signed by Albert Einstein, for $4,050; and two strands of Ludwig van Beethoven's hair for $1,600.

It was an average month for Reznikoff, who may have been the most successful autograph dealer on eBay. Reznikoff's wares were often expensive, and usually presented significant authenticity issues. In other words, they were precisely the sort of items skeptics always said would never sell on eBay. Tall and youthful-looking for his four decades, Reznikoff had the bemused air of someone who has managed to turn his favorite childhood hobby into a multimillion-dollar business. He had come a long way since he dropped out of Fordham University in 1979 to sell stamps out of his briefcase. Leaving college at nineteen was not a popular decision with his family, least of all his father, who taught psychology at Fordham.

Within a decade, Reznikoff and a partner were running a $2-million-a-year stamp business. Reznikoff could have happily remained in stamps, but in 1990, on a trip to San Francisco, he was offered a chance to buy an autograph collection. The autographs, from the period 1870–1910, were not particularly valuable—one of the better ones belonged to Joseph Jefferson, a leading Shakespearean actor not much remembered today. Still, Reznikoff found that he liked autographs a lot more than stamps. "I was consumed," he says. He handed the stamps business over to his partner and began acquiring autographs and publishing catalogs that he sent out to prospective buyers. In a few years, he was doing $4 million to $5 million a year in autographs alone. His collection of hair—of Abraham Lincoln, Napoleon, the beheaded Charles I of England—came later.

Reznikoff got on the Internet in 1996, starting a website just because he figured that "some day the Internet would be important." He first came across eBay in 1998, and decided to try selling on it. He gave a client who understood online auctions some stamps to sell on eBay on consignment. They sold so well that Reznikoff set up an eBay sales operation, with three full-time employees listing autographs and stamps and managing the auctions. He found that on a good auction on eBay, he could get as much as five times the price he could when he sold to a catalog buyer. Within eighteen months of discovering eBay, Reznikoff stopped publishing autograph catalogs. "Someone said it, and it rang like a gong in my ear," he says. " 'The printed word is dead, but people don't know it yet.' "

Autographs are, in some ways, well-suited to eBay. Unlike stamps, which have recognized catalog values, an autograph's value is highly subjective. "A JFK letter saying 'I'll see you at the meeting at ten o'clock' is worth fifteen hundred dollars," says Reznikoff. "But if it has the line 'those missiles in Cuba are really pissing me off,' that's a hundred thousand dollars." Autograph sales take advantage of one of the things online auctions do best: set prices for items of indeterminate value. Autograph buyers are also particularly prone to the kind of auction fever eBay can stimulate. "What eBay does, what any auction does, is create urgency," Reznikoff says. "When someone comes into my office and looks at a Lincoln, whether it's true or not, they think it's going to be here in five days and they have time to think about it."

Reznikoff knew as much as anyone that autographs were prone to forgery. In the mid-1990s, he was in the papers a lot after he was taken in by Lawrence Cusack III, the son of a lawyer for the New York Archdiocese of the Catholic Church, who tried to sell 350 documents from what he claimed was a secret correspondence between John F. Kennedy and Marilyn Monroe. The documents, which Reznikoff initially vouched for, were later discovered to be forgeries. Cusack, it turned out, had made a few mistakes, like including zip codes on envelopes mailed before the zip code had been introduced. With Reznikoff testifying for the government, Cusack was eventually convicted of mail and wire fraud.

About half of the autographs Reznikoff listed on eBay ended up selling, the average conversion rate on the site. When an item did not sell, if the top bidders came within 25 percent of the price he was looking for, he generally e-mailed them, asking if they wanted to bargain. In nearly half the cases, Reznikoff sold the item in what he calls an "after eBay" sale. Even when the bidders did not buy that particular item, he contacted them with other autographs. It was the best and cheapest marketing Reznikoff had ever come across. A lease for Mount Vernon, George Washington's Virginia estate, attracted fourteen thousand hits—thousands of people who heard about University Archives, many of whom clicked through to Reznikoff's private website and looked at his other autographs.*

EBay contributed to Reznikoff's bottom line in other ways. Each catalog he does not publish saves him $20,000 to $30,000 a year. He is also cutting back on attending trade shows, which saves the company registration fees, travel costs, and employee time. Four years ago his company went to twenty-one shows in a year. The next year it was ten shows. Then it was three shows. "I prefer to press the flesh, to meet the person and see the interest in their eyes," he says. "But the time I save by not going to Brimfield, I can go to the school and kick the soccer ball with my son."

By 2001, Reznikoff was selling 25 percent of his autographs on eBay, and he expected it would be 40 percent in a year. He believed there would always be sales off-line—some people would never feel comfortable using computers, and there would always be buyers who wanted to hold the item in their hands before they handed over money for it. But he also anticipated that the day might not be far away when he made 90 percent of his sales on eBay. He realized he was ahead of many of his competitors in moving online, but that was fine with him. "If they don't go on eBay," he says, "they are going to be dinosaurs."

◆

Meg Whitman was sitting in "Sao Paolo," the conference room closest to her cubicle, dressed in jeans, a pink-and-white striped button-down shirt, and sneakers. It was mid-August 2001, nearly six years

---

*What Reznikoff saw as a marketing coup, eBay considers "fee avoidance." He paid no fees to eBay when he sold an item in the "after eBay" market. When he sold items by e-mailing an eBay customer, he also did not need to pay listing or final-value fees. When eBay learns of these activities, it warns, temporarily suspends, or permanently suspends the members involved; but eBay rarely learns of these deals.

after Omidyar launched AuctionWeb, and Whitman was pausing to reflect on how much had gone right.

In those years, the Internet revolution had gone through a boom, producing what was often called the fastest creation of riches in the history of the world. And then the dot-com bubble burst, wiping out billions of dollars in wealth, and throwing tens of thousands of onetime high-tech masters of the universe out of work. But through it all, eBay's growth had continued unabated. The company was actually ahead of schedule for the goal Whitman had announced a year earlier, 50 percent growth a year for five years. While Yahoo! and Amazon were struggling, eBay was widely acknowledged to be the most successful dot-com to emerge in the early years of the Internet.

EBay's success began, Whitman said, with Omidyar's model. "The headline," she says, "is that this was a totally new idea that could not have existed without the Internet." Because eBay was a virtual business, one that never touched its product, it could take advantage of all the efficiency that a wired world had to offer. That put it in a different league from Amazon, and all of the other shopping dot-coms that still had to engage in land-based activities, like storing inventory and shipping goods.

EBay outperformed its competitors, Whitman says, because it provided a better user experience. "The reason we were so successful against Yahoo! and Amazon was clearly focus," she says. "This was our only business." Whitman liked to say that every morning, she and her staff woke up thinking only about how to make online auctions better, something eBay's major rivals could not say. Of course, a large part of the user experience on eBay was the network effect that came with having so many buyers and sellers in a single place. Many users who tried switching to Amazon or Yahoo! complained not about the way auctions were run there, but of the relatively small number of buyers and sellers on the site.

From a business standpoint, Whitman credits eBay's success to conservative management. In Omidyar's time, the refrain was "spend it like it's your own money," with staff taking pay cuts to work at eBay, and assembling their own desks on their first day of work. Under Whitman, eBay pinched pennies on rent, salaries, and marketing at a time when start-ups were routinely blowing $250,000 on launch parties, and Pets.com, a notorious case, spent $2.6 million to put its sock-puppet mascot in a single Super Bowl commercial. "There was a mercenary underbelly to the whole dot-com explosion," Whitman says. "Many dot-coms were made to flip or be acquired," she says. But eBay's management never lost track of its goal: building a company that would last.

EBay also avoided investing wildly in other companies simply to grow larger. Amazon burned hundreds of millions of dollars on stakes in dot-coms like Living.com, Ashford.com, and, yes, Pets.com, which later went into meltdown. Yahoo! spent $5 billion to buy Broadcast.com, as part of a struggling effort to bring television on-line, and nearly $3 billion more on Geocities.com, essentially a huge collection of personal websites. But eBay always cast a critical eye on the business plans that arrived at its headquarters. "There was a theory that the laws of investment had been suspended," Whitman says. "With so many of the investment opportunities that came our way, our team said, 'There is no business model.'" EBay was much more interested in forming alliances with companies than acquiring them. Its few purchases — Half, Alando, iBazar — were carefully targeted to expanding eBay's core business.

Whitman says that eBay benefited from the experience and seasoning of its management team. In an era when billion-dollar companies were routinely being run by recent college graduates, Omidyar and Skoll readily stepped aside in favor of more experienced leaders. The average age of Whitman's team was mid-forties, and the senior managers had an average of twenty years of business experience before coming to eBay. What eBay sacrificed in hipness it made up for in business smarts. "So many times we said, 'We've seen this before,'" Whitman says.

There were mistakes. The June 1999 outage was the biggest, according to Whitman, and if she had invested more heavily in eBay's technology earlier, it could have been avoided. "Maynard Webb should have been here within a month of my arriving." she says. Reserve auctions and the gun ban were handled badly. But the key to managing the missteps was never losing sight of the biggest factor in eBay's success—the one element eBay could not survive without—its users. "The number one thing is to think about how an event affects the community," she says. "Community has always been central."

◆

There was another topic on Whitman's mind as she sat back in the Sao Paolo conference room to reflect, and this one made her think of eBay's future, not its past. She had recently taken a trip to San Pedro La Laguna with Karin Stahl and a small planeload of eBay staff. Whitman had read about Stahl's work, and had heard firsthand accounts from her older son, who had gone along on one of Stahl's previous visits. In the coming year, she wanted to put more of the company's resources into preparing the villagers to trade on eBay. Sometimes, she told Stahl, the head of an organization has to get directly involved in a project to be sure that it happens.

There were many reasons it made no sense for Meg Whitman to travel to Guatemala in June 2001. There were, of course, the never-ending demands on her time. Whitman already had a grueling tour through Europe scheduled for June, where she would stop in at the company's overseas operations and dedicate eBay's new centralized customer-service operations in Berlin. At home there were board of directors meetings, senior staff meetings, sit-downs with Wall Street analysts, and the usual round of industry conferences, public appearances, and media interviews necessary to keep up eBay's public profile. In a year with only 365 days in it, five days in San Pedro was a heavy commitment of time.

Then there was the matter of security. The Guatemalan countryside was rife with rumors about tourists: that they were coming to steal children or to harvest human organs for transplants. There had been scattered incidents in recent years of local vigilantes stoning foreigners to death or lynching them. And for the last decade,

Guatemala was developing a reputation as one of the world's centers for kidnapping of foreign business executives. A month before Whitman's visit, a German pharmaceutical executive was kidnapped in Guatemala City. Days before Whitman was scheduled to arrive, the executive was shot to death. Whitman's security adviser tried to persuade her to cancel the trip, or at least to postpone it until conditions stabilized. But Whitman would not be discouraged. "I decided a long time ago that you can't let fear run your life," she says. But she made one concession to security. She only told a few people who needed to know about the trip. During her time in Guatemala, she would not be identified as the CEO of eBay.

In early June, a small contingent flew down from San Jose: Whitman; Karin Stahl; Stahl's mother, Ingrid; eBay corporate communications chief Henry Gomez; a pediatrician who had been on previous visits; and Whitman's security adviser. They were loaded down with twelve boxes and eight duffel bags of medical supplies— some of which Whitman's husband and son had secured from a pharmacy that was going out of business—and another four boxes of computer monitors and software. The eBay group drove through the countryside and arrived at Panajachel at dusk, where a boat was waiting to ferry them across Lake Atitlán.

It was the last boat of the day, and hardly the pride of the ragtag fleet. The ferry had no roof to keep out the rain that had begun to drizzle and, the group noticed, no life preservers. As Whitman and the others began the half-hour voyage, they looked out at the soaring volcanoes that ringed the lake and talked about what they hoped to accomplish in the next few days. The ferry was almost precisely in the center of the enormous lake when its engine gave out. As the sky darkened and the ferry bobbed aimlessly on the water, Whitman's bodyguard kept up a running joke about how he could just barely make out the silhouettes of frogmen in wet suits who were swimming toward the boat to kidnap the gringos.

After furious efforts by the crew, the engine eventually came back to life. The ferry raced across the lake, getting the eBay group to shore just as night was falling. Whitman and the others headed to

Sak'hari Amanacer, the same six-dollar-a-night hotel on the lake-shore that Stahl always stayed at. The accommodations were modest. The water that came out of the taps was not drinkable, and Gomez kept finding scorpions on the wall of his room. Security at the hotel, as in much of rural Latin America, was provided by guard dogs that barked loudly throughout the night. "They sounded like they were in my bathroom last night," Whitman told Stahl cheerfully one morning.

Whitman and the rest of the group visited the homes of several of the craftswomen. No one knew who she was, but the villagers all knew Karin Stahl, and they doted on Ingrid Stahl. "I think Meg really enjoyed not being the center of attention," says Stahl. "For a few days, she didn't have to be CEO." In the home visits, Whitman and the others observed how the craftswomen did their weaving, and they learned how little the women knew about business. Most did not even know how much they spent on the raw materials that went into their products. And the difficulties of life in a poor village constantly intruded on their work. Two of the best craftswomen in the village had virtually stopped working in recent months. One had lost her daughter, who had been about to graduate from school in Guatemala City, in one of the frequent bus crashes that occurred on the winding roads around the village. Another had lost her husband and son in the same crash. To help the craftswomen in the short-term, Whitman decided on the spot that the company holiday gifts that year would be Mayan belts with the eBay insignia, and placed an order for nearly three thousand.

Whitman also toured the Internet café, which was also called a telecenter, that Stahl's group was in the process of setting up. EBay had recently announced a grant to Planet Outreach, a charitable group Stahl had organized to run the telecenter, and Stahl was using the money to rent the space, install computers, and secure high-speed satellite access to the Internet. The idea was for the villagers to learn about e-commerce in the telecenter, and eventually apply those skills to selling their goods on eBay. But that kind of direct selling by the locals was still a long way off. "Right now, they are still learning how to turn on a computer," says Stahl.

Over a meal of rice and beans and tortillas at Max's, the modest locally run restaurant Stahl's group always ate at, Whitman and the others talked about the necessary steps to get the San Pedrans selling on eBay. Whitman thought it would be a good idea for Planet Outreach to buy some sample goods and sell them first to test the market. Stahl and Whitman's son Griff, who had come down separately to join the group, offered to head up that effort. Stahl agreed to look into the possibility of securing microloans for the craftswomen, to help them buy fabrics and other supplies. The group also decided to work with Peoplink, a nonprofit organization with experience helping craftspeople from poor countries sell over the Internet. EBay wanted to end up with a project in San Pedro La Laguna that could be exported to other parts of Guatemala, and to the world.

Omidyar did not make the trip down to Guatemala. Even eBay's good works were part of a world he had decided to leave behind. But he had contributed money to the effort, and Stahl kept him informed of the group's progress. Bringing eBay to San Pedro La Laguna was Stahl's project, but it was Omidyar's dream, the one he had in the summer of 1995, when he decided to write the computer code for a single, global marketplace that everyone in the world could participate in on an equal basis. If his original thinking was right, he says, eBay could help transform San Pedro La Laguna—and the lives of the people who live there. "The financial empowerment you can bring people by giving them access to an efficient market is tremendous," Omidyar says. "That's what it was all about."

acknowledgments

This book arose out of a story I wrote for *Time* magazine, and my gratitude begins there. To Priscilla Painton, first of all, who knew before I did that I would be fascinated by eBay. Walter Isaacson could not have been more supportive, including sending me to Paris to interview Pierre Omidyar and making room for my eBay story in *Time*'s *1999 Man of the Year* issue. Jim Kelly, Walter's successor as managing editor, is both an inspiration and a friend to the journalists who work for him. Thanks, also, to colleagues who offered advice and support, and in many cases served as sounding boards for my thoughts about eBay long after, I'm sure, their own interest in the subject had waned: Josh Quittner, Dan Goodgame, Bill Saporito, Steve Koepp, Richard Zoglin, John Stacks, Eric Pooley, Chris Porterfield, Jan Simpson, Howard Chua-Eoan, Daniel Kadlec, Frank Gibney, Michael Krantz, Aisha Labi, Vicky Rainert, Elaine Rivera, Josh Cooper Ramo, Phil Elmer-DeWitt, David Van Biema, Chris Farley, Eric Roston, Bernie Baumohl, Kathleen Dowling, and Angela Thornton.

My appreciation, also, to Gail Collins and Phil Taubman for bringing me to the *New York Times* (with an assist from Howell Raines and Glenn Kramon) and to them and my other colleagues on the Editorial Board—Brent Staples, Ethan Bronner, Andres Martinez, Eleanor Randolph, Veryln Klinkenborg, Bob Semple, David Unger, Phil Boffey, Steve Weisman, and Dorothy Samuels—for making it such a stimulating place to work.

I'm particularly grateful to the folks at eBay for letting me move into their offices for two weeks with a reporter's notebook and a tape recorder. Opening up to a journalist is a leap of faith, and one that is not always rewarded in the end, but eBay's staff were generous with their time, and as forthcoming about their stumbles as their successes. My thanks to Pierre Omidyar, Jeff Skoll, Meg Whitman, Karin Stahl, Mary Lou Song, Steve Westly, Bob Kagle, Gary Bengier, Jim Griffith, Henry Gomez, Maynard Webb, Brian Burke, Maria Lee, Annette Goodwine, Simon Rothman, Patti Ruby, Tom Adams, Rick Rock, Shira Levine, Robin Rosaaen, Chris Agarpao, Sandra Gaeta, Keith Antognini, Brad Handler, Debbie Bailey, Jeff Taylor, Jeff Jordan, Kevin Pursglove, Jennifer Chu, Robert Chesnut, Jay Monahan, Kristie Reed, Jeff Totland, Sonny Wagner, Lesa Ward, Bob Hebeler, Chris Donlay, Walt Duflock, Charlie Carter, Josh Kopelman, Sunny Balijepalli, Mark Hughes, Kristin Keyes, Merle Okawara, Philipp Justus, Joerg Rheinboldt, Renate Maifarth—and, of course, to Kristin Seuell, who ably and amiably shepherded me through it all.

Members of the broader eBay community took the time to tell me their stories and talk to me about eBay. My thanks to Rosalinda Baldwin, Bobby Beeman, Al Hoff, David Lucking-Reiley, Karen Young, Stephanie Young, Jane Dee, Ron Sackman, Steven Williams, Mark Del Vecchio, Larry Schwartz, Johnny Wong, Karl Jacobs, John Reznikoff, Tom Derbyshire, David Eccles, Fred Krughoff, Jay Raymond, Jerry Marcus, Jeannie Marcus, Buck Carson, Suzanne White, David Irons, Faye Landes, John Freyer, Kembrew McLeod, Emilio Battz, Ester Battz, Juan Cruz Gonzalez, Christine Harmel, Kim Starkey, Jim Wells-Miller, Crystal Wells-Miller, Mark Dodd, Rodrigo Sales, Jerry Weissman, Bill Cleary, G. Patton Hughes, Myer Berlow,

Joe Spotts, Connie Bacon, Randy Pinkham, Rick Gagliano, Tom Bowen, Ross Wright, Mary Guibert, Justin Jorgensen, John Hannon, Scott Wellhausen, Carol Coleman, Andrew Waites, Munjal Shah, Jaron Lanier, Peter Thiel, and Max Levchin. The AuctionWatch and OTWA message boards, and their online archives, were an invaluable resource for learning the contemporaneous feelings of the eBay community.

At Little, Brown, Michael Pietsch, a fine editor and publisher and a committed member of the eBay community, was a champion of this book from the start. Geoff Shandler was good enough to take on the editing when the house tapped Pietsch to be publisher. Thanks, also, to Sarah Crichton, for believing in the book, Peggy Freudenthal and Rosemary Previte for a careful and thoughtful copyedit, and Elizabeth Nagle for making the editing process so smooth. William Sell did a masterful job with the interview transcripts. Kris Dahl is the best literary agent I know.

Friends and family were a source of encouragement, support, and enlightenment: Diane Faber, Paul Engelmayer, Caroline Arnold, Shan Sullivan, Eileen Hershenov, Dan Pool, Elisabeth Benjamin, Dan Caughlin, Olivia Turner, Amy Gutman, Laura Franco, Tina Smith, Michael Krantz, Carol Owens, Noam Cohen, Harlan Cohen, Beverly Cohen, Stuart Cohen, Harriett Shapiro, Seymour Shapiro, Carl Shapiro, and, of course, Liz Taylor, a great friend, who was as committed to this book as to the one we wrote together.

index